POSTCARD HISTORY SERIES

Blairstown and Its Neighbors

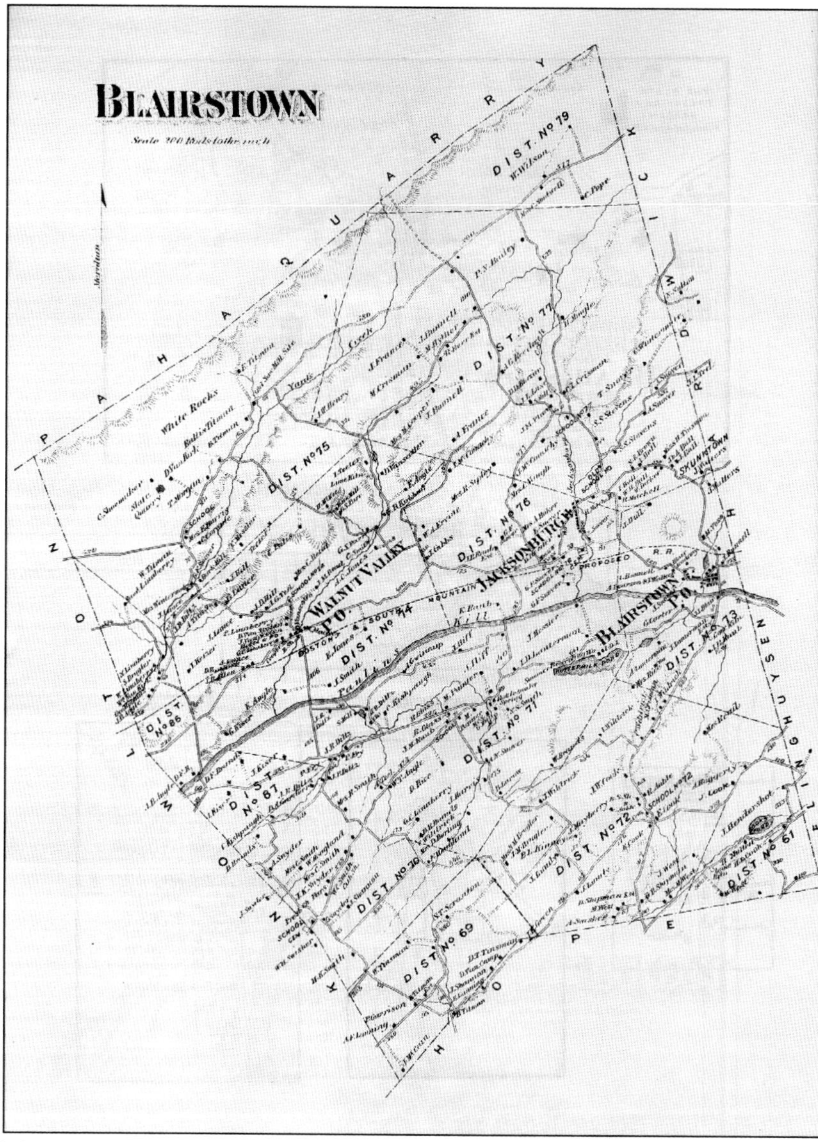

With slightly less than 1,400 residents spread over 32 square miles, Blairstown was a typical rural New Jersey community at the beginning of the 20th century. Bisected from northeast to southwest by the Paulinskill River, it consisted of a central borough and associated hamlets, including Jacksonburg, Walnut Valley, and Vail. The borough owes its existence to John Insley Blair, entrepreneur and railroad magnate, who settled there in 1821. (Courtesy authors.)

On the Front Cover: An eastbound New York, Susquehanna and Western Railroad train approaches the Blairstown depot about 1910. Construction of John Blair's Blairstown Railway began near this spot on July 4, 1876, and the station was erected in 1878 (additional information in caption on page 9). (Courtesy authors.)

On the Back Cover: When Blairstown's Main Street was part of the road linking Newton, New Jersey, with the Delaware Water Gap, the Blairstown House catered to weary travelers seeking food and lodging. (For additional information, see caption on page 24.) (Courtesy authors.)

POSTCARD HISTORY SERIES

Blairstown and Its Neighbors

Kenneth Bertholf Jr. and Don Dorflinger

ARCADIA PUBLISHING

ISBN 978-0-7385-7431-7

Published by Arcadia Publishing
Charleston, South Carolina

Printed in the United States of America

Library of Congress Control Number: 2010935099

For all general information contact Arcadia Publishing at:
Telephone 843-853-2070
Fax 843-853-0044
E-mail sales@arcadiapublishing.com
For customer service and orders:
Toll-Free 1-888-313-2665

Visit us on the Internet at www.arcadiapublishing.com

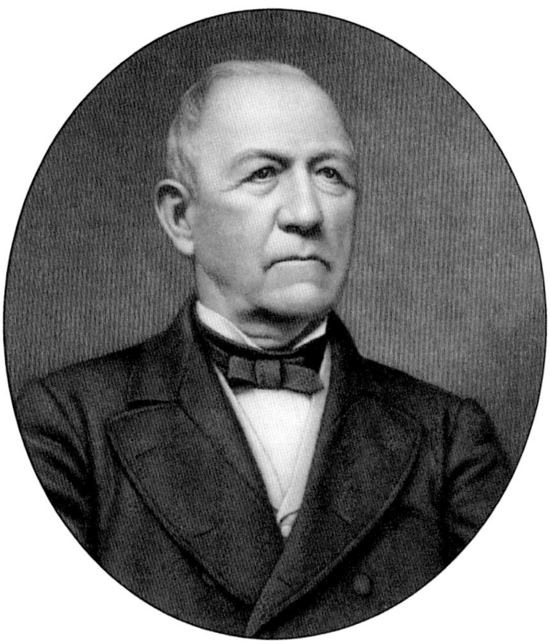

To John Insley Blair (1802–1899), entrepreneur, railroad builder, and philanthropist, who made this entire project possible.

And to our wives, Bonnie Bertholf and Marietta Dorflinger, who both understand what it means to be married to a historian.

Contents

Acknowledgments		6
Introduction		7
1.	Getting There: The Railroads	9
2.	Blairstown: John Blair's Village	21
3.	The Suburbs: Hidden Treasures	51
4.	Blair Academy: John I. Builds a School	65
5.	Hope: A Moravian "Experiment"	83
6.	Other Neighbors: Johnsonburg, Marksboro, and Hardwick	101
7.	Camping: King of the Summer	115
Bibliography		127

ACKNOWLEDGMENTS

The concept of a new postcard history of Blairstown and its neighbors actually began with two separate ideas that ultimately came together to bring the project to fruition. Village native Kenneth Bertholf Jr. had already written an Arcadia Images of America volume about Blairstown in 1998 and was considering doing an update using his extensive collection of local material, much of which was still untapped. Don Dorflinger, a retired high school administrator and amateur historian, moved to Blairstown in 1986 and, over the next 20 years, amassed a significant postcard collection of the area including early views of Hope and other nearby hamlets. Don, along with his wife, Marietta, had completed two previous postcard history books for Arcadia—*Orange, New Jersey* (1999) and *River Towns of the Delaware Water Gap* (2009)—and Don was considering a third on his adopted hometown. Although Ken and Don were acquainted, it took a local bookstore owner, Herman Shoemaker, to bring the two together to collaborate on this work.

As the project moved forward, others came forth to generously share material and information: most notably Ruth Hutchinson Gommoll, who provided additional local images; Fred Heilich, historian of the Blairstown Railway, who supplied rare views of the Lackawanna Cutoff; Hank Magnusen, who shared his collection of Hope material; and Mary Billow, of the Hope Historical Society, who spent time explaining some of the more obscure points of Hope's history. Special recognition must also go to Brian Rhodes, a local historian, who painstakingly preserved many of the views now in Don's collection, and Erin Rocha, editor at Arcadia Publishing, who kept the authors on task but always made the work easy.

Unless otherwise noted, all images appear courtesy of the authors.

Introduction

The northwest corner of New Jersey's Warren County has largely been a rural, agrarian region. Populated primarily by farmers and dairymen until the last half of the 20th century, its existence remained relatively unchanged from the docile days after the American Civil War. It was an area dotted by small hamlets, many of which, like Paulina, Ebenezer, Centerville, and Kalarama, have passed from the memories of all but local historians.

Of the incorporated villages that still remain, Blairstown is the largest and perhaps the best known, for it was the home of its namesake: the tycoon, railroad builder, and noted philanthropist John Insley Blair. Blair was a self-made man and a giant of his era, but he never forgot his New Jersey roots, living most of his life in the picturesque village that still bears his name. John I., as he was known locally, was born on August 22, 1802, in the town of Foul Rift, New Jersey, on the Delaware River two miles below the present county seat of Belvidere. He was the fourth of 10 children produced by the union of Scotch Presbyterian immigrants John Blair and Rachel Insley. At the age of 10, Blair entered the business world, trapping small game and selling their pelts at the rate of 16 for $1. Barely a year later, he began clerking at a store owned by his cousin, and by 1821, he was running his own store in the village of Butt's Bridge. Butt's Bridge became Gravel Hill on August 25, 1825, and Blair was appointed postmaster. By the time Gravel Hill was renamed Blairstown in his honor on January 24, 1839, the young entrepreneur owned five stores and was forming an association with the Scranton brothers of Slocum Hollow, Pennsylvania, that would begin his career as a railroad builder.

Blair's railroad ventures are legend and far too involved to discuss here, but suffice it to say that one of his local legacies was the mighty Delaware, Lackawanna and Western Railroad (DL&W). Blair built its New Jersey predecessor, the Warren Railroad, in anticipation of its acquisition by the DL&W as it extended its main line southeast from Scranton, Pennsylvania, to a connection with the Central Railroad Company of New Jersey at Hampton, New Jersey. Blairstown had no railroad of its own until 1876 when Blair constructed the Blairstown Railway, running 12 miles from its namesake village to a connection with the Lackawanna in the nearby hamlet of Delaware Station (later shortened to Delaware), a planned town built on property that Blair purchased decades earlier in anticipation of the Lackawanna's arrival. In 1872, Blair sold the short line at a handsome profit to the New York, Susquehanna and Western Railroad (NYS&W), which quickly assimilated the little rail line into the new main line it was building west to reach its coalfields in northeastern Pennsylvania. The NYS&W eventually extended all the way to Kingston, Pennsylvania, through a subsidiary called the Wilkes-Barre and Eastern Railroad and even operated passenger service from Kingston via Blairstown to the Erie Railroad Terminal in Jersey City, New Jersey, with ferry and later Hudson and Manhattan Railroad connections to New York City. Had John I. lived into the

20th century, he would have been overjoyed to see his beloved Lackawanna construct "the work of the age," its New Jersey Cutoff through Blairstown, which opened on Christmas Eve 1911.

Blair's nationwide philanthropic efforts were well appreciated and are best remembered in his hometown for the college preparatory school that bears his name. On April 6, 1848, Blair met with several prominent local businessmen and Presbyterian clergy, donating land, money, and a building to begin what is known as Blair Academy. Blair continued his generous gifts to the school for the next 50 years, and after his death on December 2, 1899, his legacy was continued by his son DeWitt Clinton Blair and other family members.

If Blairstown owes its existence and name to a rich entrepreneur, Hope's roots are quite the opposite, for Blairstown's neighbor to the south was founded in 1769 by Moravians from Pennsylvania as an experimental preplanned village named Greenland. The Moravians were a self-sufficient community governed by their church and did not limit their enterprises to farming. Their village, renamed Hope in 1775, eventually boasted a gristmill, stores, an inn (which once hosted George Washington as he traveled from Philadelphia to Newburgh, New York), a distillery, a tannery, and more. Unfortunately the experiment failed, largely due to poor economic times and the unscrupulous dealings of non-Moravian business competitors, and the small surviving band of Moravians returned to the commonwealth in 1808. Many of the buildings, constructed by the religious order with local cut stone over 200 years ago, still stand as a legacy to their enterprise.

Frelinghuysen Township, to the east of Blairstown, contains the villages of Marksboro and Johnsonburg. Marksboro was named in honor of its local hero, Col. Mark Thomson, a soldier in the American Revolution and member of the U.S. House of Representatives, who lived there and operated a large stone gristmill on his property along the banks of the Paulinskill River. An outbuilding behind Thomson's home still boasts the musket slits in the stone walls that were intended for use by local militia to fend off attacks by hostile Native Americans.

Johnsonburg, now a sleepy village in Warren County, was briefly the county seat of Sussex County and known by the moniker of "Logg Gaol" (Log Jail), denoting the primitive wooden lockup that was built there. Located on what was once the main highway from Philadelphia, Pennsylvania, to Kingston, New York, the Johnsonburg Hotel (or Lackawanna House, as it was called after the railroad arrived) hosted all manner of travelers from the "Pig Drover of Logg Gaol" to the "White Pilgrim" evangelist. The unkempt Pig Drover, who passed through the village periodically with his porcine herd close behind, was later found to be a down-on-his-luck herdsman from the Midwest and was returned to his appreciative family after a little detective work determined his true identity. The White Pilgrim evangelist, known far and wide for his white clothing, hat, boots, and horse, preached a sermon to hundreds of the faithful in Johnsonburg in April 1835, took sick later that afternoon, and died a few days later, probably of smallpox. He was buried in the nearby Dark Moon Cemetery and later reinterred in the Johnsonburg Cemetery, where he rests today under a large obelisk at the center of the graveyard.

Time has mostly been kind to the villages of the Paulinskill Valley and their neighbors. The Lackawanna and Susquehanna railroads, which threatened to citify the region, have long been abandoned, and manufacturing, which typically springs up along usable sources of waterpower, failed to materialize. Blairstown's Main Street became a detour off the main highway rather than a part of it and survives today with the appearance of a village forgotten in time. The postcards in this book provide a vivid look into the past, focusing primarily on the generation between 1907 and 1930, when bucolic locals lived out their daily existence, interrupted only briefly by outsiders who visited the region to enjoy the peace and tranquility offered by the rural lifestyle.

One

Getting There
The Railroads

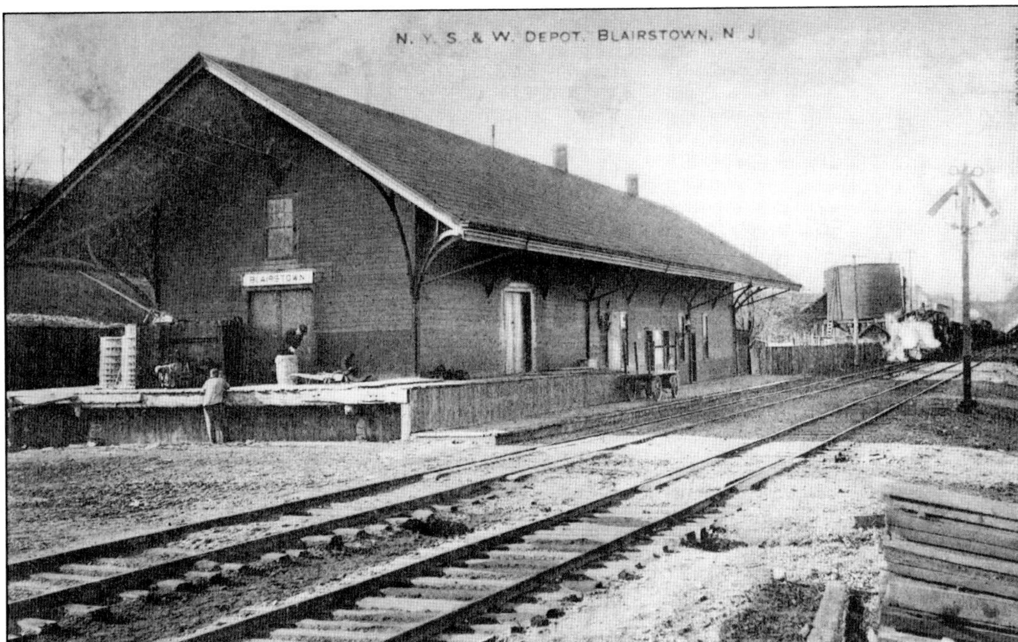

The first spade of earth for the Blairstown Railway was turned on July 4, 1876, near this spot. The 12-mile line was completed in a year, linking Blairstown with the Delaware, Lackawanna and Western Railroad at Delaware Station, New Jersey. In September 1882, the New York, Susquehanna and Western Railroad purchased the line to use as part of the new route it was building west to reach its Pennsylvania coal fields.

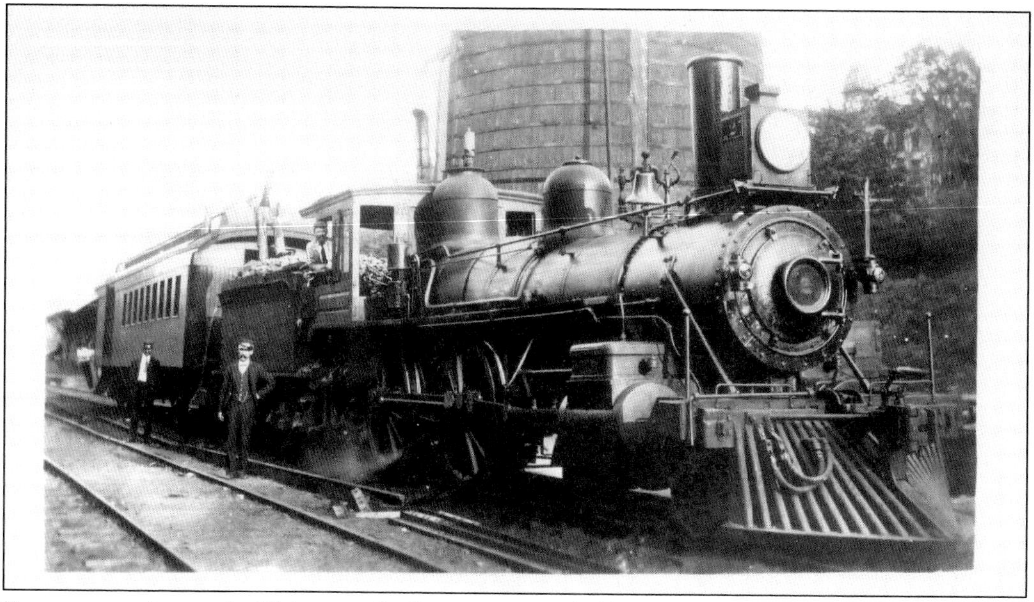

Passenger service on the Blairstown Railway was provided by a steam locomotive and combination coach running on a leisurely schedule over the 12 miles from Blairstown to Delaware Station. Turntables were provided at each terminal. Locals christened the train the "Dinkey." Engine No. 2, the former *John D. Vail*, sits with its combine and crew at Blairstown sometime after the Susquehanna acquisition, as the tender is now lettered for the NYS&W.

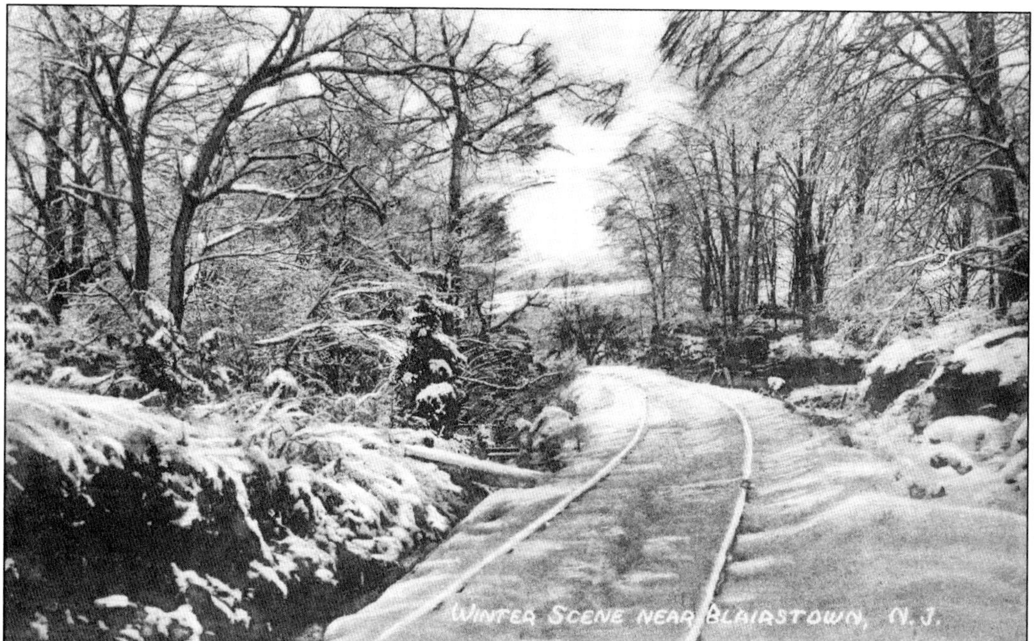

The rural territory of the Blairstown Railway is evident in this scene west of the depot. The Dinkey made its last run to Delaware on June 8, 1928, and passenger service between Blairstown and Jersey City ended in 1935. Later most revenue was generated by a trackage rights agreement with the Lehigh and New England Railroad (L&NE), and when the L&NE ceased operations October 31, 1961, the NYS&W filed for abandonment.

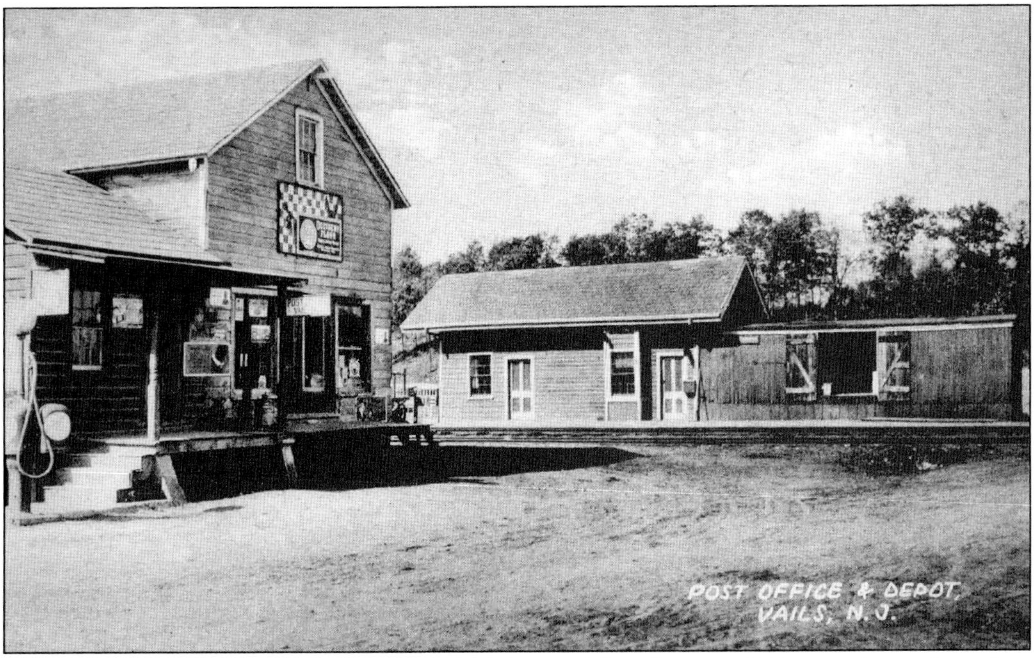

Vail was located four miles west of Blairstown and named for John Davis Vail, general superintendent of the Blairstown Railway and Blairstown postmaster. An unused boxcar served as the freight house in 1908 when 10 trains a day still stopped there, but the glory days were already waning. The feed store and creamery across the tracks were the primary customers for this station. Wells Fargo handled the express business.

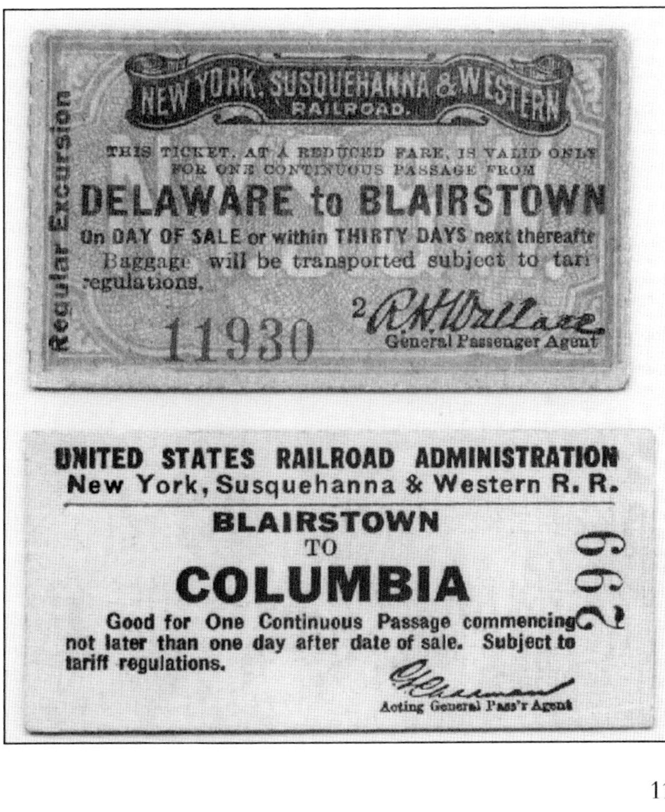

The ticket at right was good for a trip between Delaware and Blairstown. This one-way trip from Blairstown to Columbia (below) was issued during the United States Railway Administration's control of the NYS&W. When the Susquehanna absorbed the Blairstown Railway, trackage from Blairstown to Columbia Junction (now buried by I-80 near Columbia Lake) became part of the new mainline, and Blair's original road between the junction and Delaware was operated as a branch.

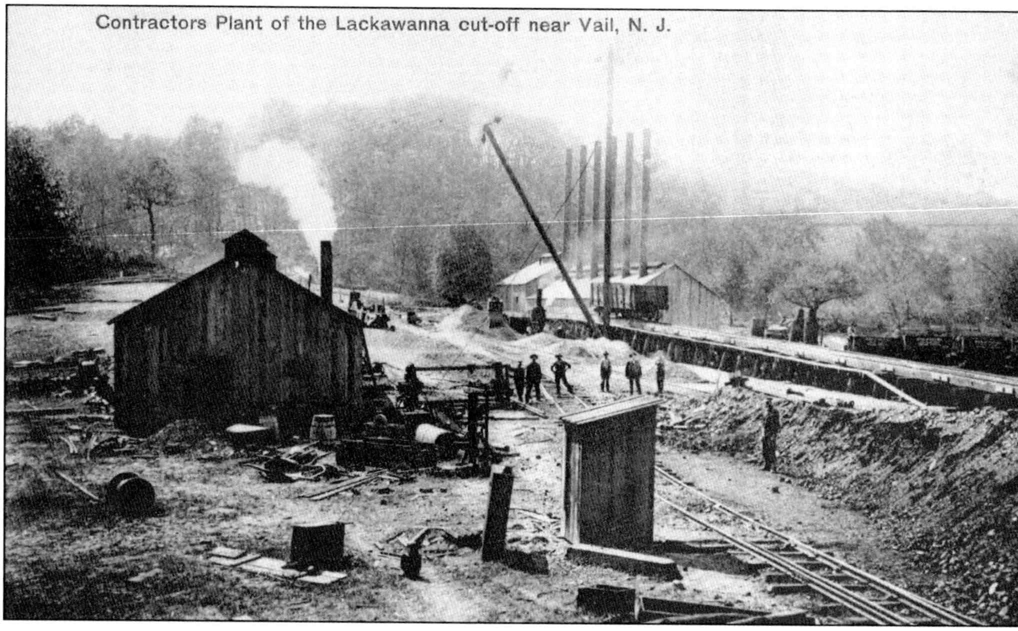

By 1900, the Lackawanna Railroad was faced with the choice of either making improvements on its main line between Port Morris, New Jersey, and Pennsylvania or building an entirely new route. The "Old Road," a legacy of the era when the DL&W connected with the Jersey Central at Hampton, was 39.57 miles of twists and turns with two tunnels, one of which was gantlet-tracked, creating bottlenecks that routinely snarled rail traffic.

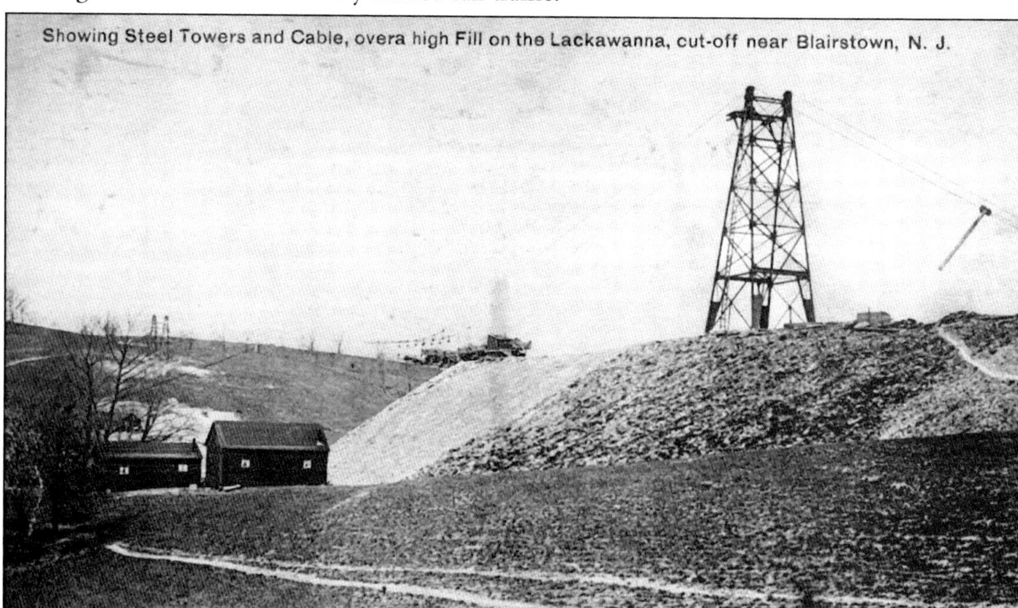

The railroad chose the "new route" option at a cost of just over $11 million. Striking out west from Port Morris, it would rejoin the old road at Slateford Junction, Pennsylvania, just across the Delaware River. It was a monumental engineering feat, requiring the excavation of over seven million cubic yards of earth and seven million yards of rock, most of which would be moved elsewhere to create giant fills.

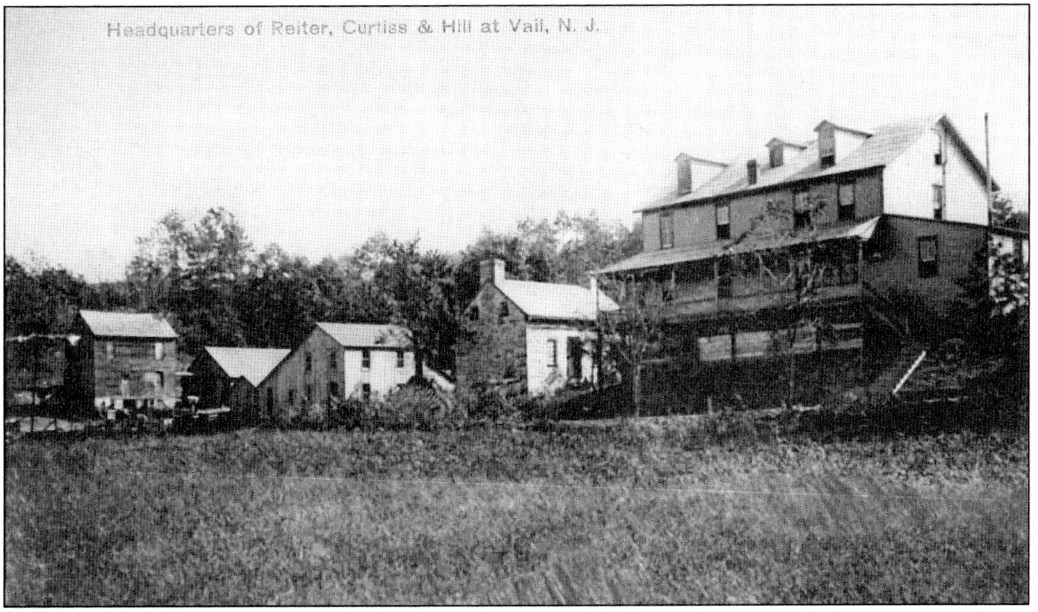

In 1910, Vail had a brief infusion of business as the Delaware, Lackawanna and Western Railroad was building its New Jersey Cutoff across Sussex and Warren Counties. Using new innovations in construction, the massive project was divided up and bid out in seven separate contracts, with the firm of Reiter, Curtis, and Hill winning number six. Their offices and construction crews were housed in these buildings at Vail.

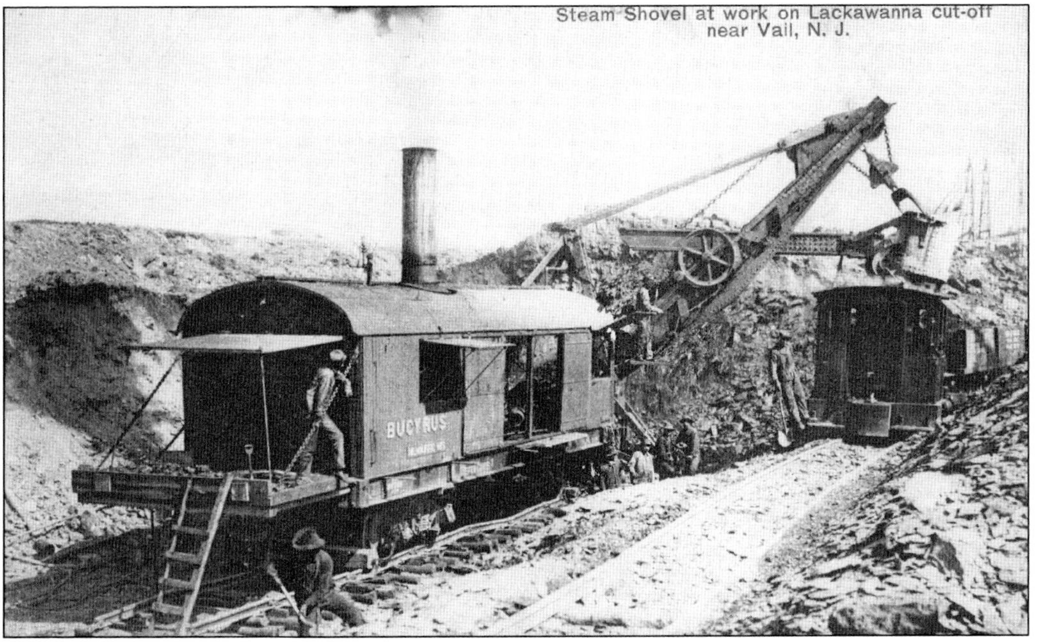

Use of the "cut and fill" construction technique on the New Jersey Cutoff is illustrated in this scene near Vail. The giant self-propelled steam shovel on a temporary track is excavating a cut. The earth and rock will be transferred to the cars of the contractor's train, which will transport them onto the spidery cableway (towers visible in the background), where the material will be dumped to create the fill.

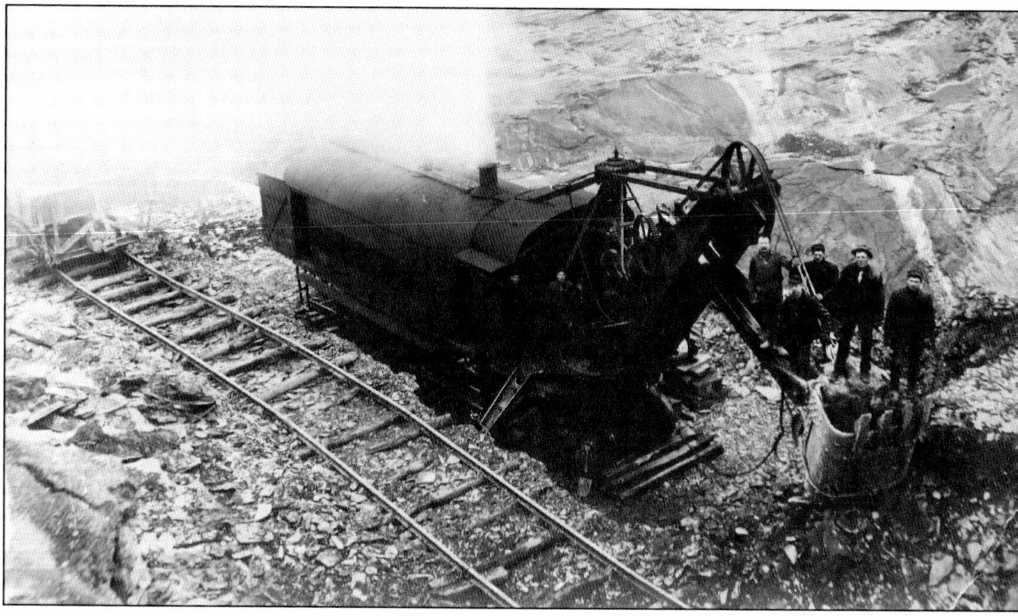

The crew takes time out to strike a vintage pose. Construction began on August 1, 1908, and was completed in just over 40 months. Five million pounds of dynamite was used to clear stubborn rock formations, which were then moved elsewhere where fills might be needed. In nearby Huntsville, the local school stood in the way of the railroad and was simply buried. The DL&W built a new one.

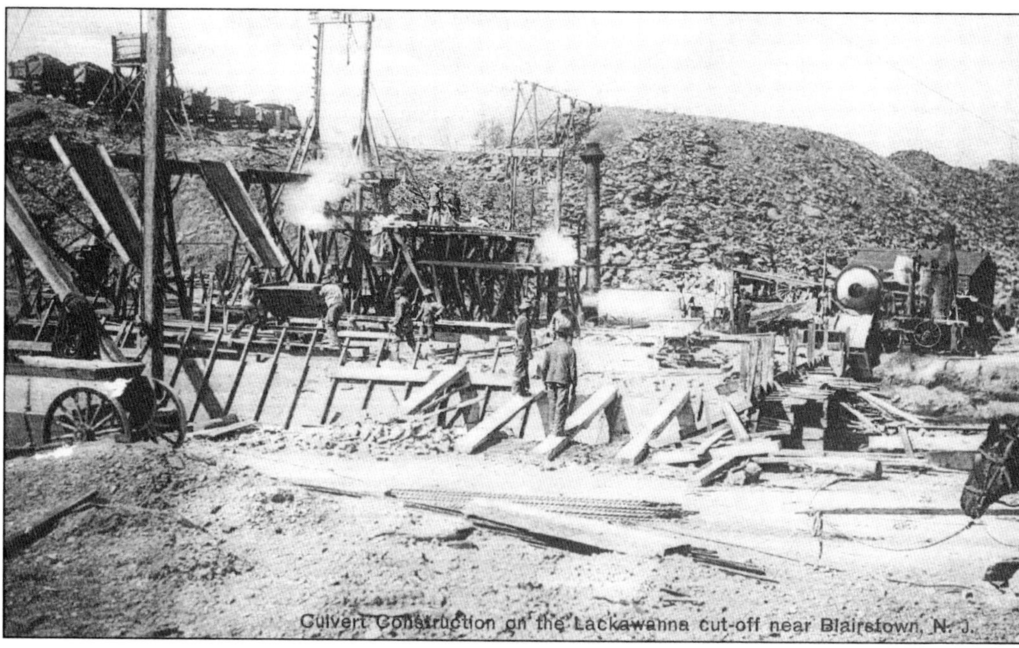

The Lackawanna was a pioneer in the use of reinforced poured concrete, with an ample supply available from plants located along its Bangor and Portland Branch. Nearly 267,000 cubic yards were utilized in the construction of bridges, culverts, stations, interlocking towers, and two major viaducts, one over the Paulinskill River and the other over the Delaware. Wooden falsework forms were built and the concrete poured and allowed to set.

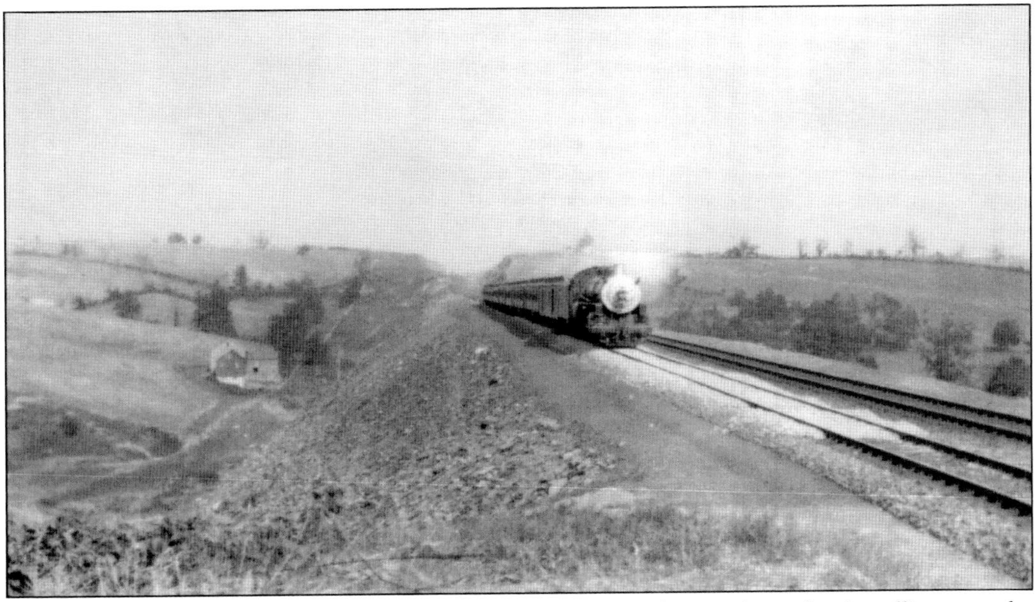

The completed railroad was magnificent, as demonstrated by this westbound train rolling over the Paulina Fill in early 1912. Recent ballasting to smooth out low spots is evident. Construction was completed, and the railroad conveyed to the DL&W's Operating Department on Christmas Eve 1911. It survived into the Conrail era but was removed from service in 1979, and the track was taken up in the summer of 1984. (Courtesy of Fred Heilich.)

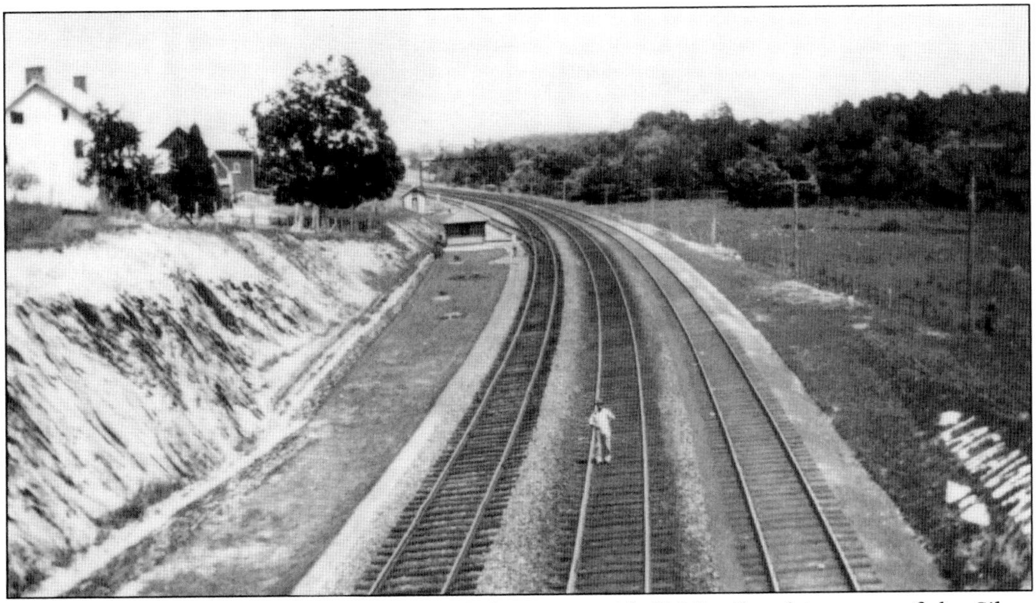

In halcyon days, section foreman Jacques Belet poses with "his" railroad just east of the Silver Lake–Marksboro Road overpass near Johnsonburg. No one can mistake the ownership of the line, as the word *Lackawanna* is proudly spelled out on the hillside to the right using white stones. The well-ballasted track allowed a speed limit of 75 miles per hour westbound and 70 eastbound. (Courtesy of Fred Heilich.)

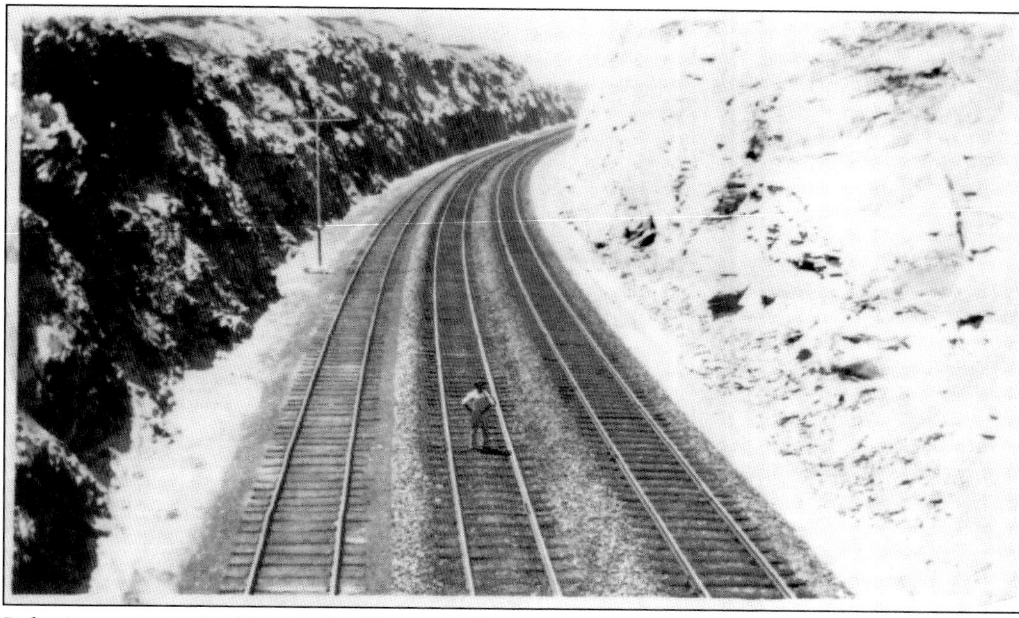

Belet is seen again in this view, looking west from the same overpass. The clean and immaculately trimmed ballast is a trademark of the Lackawanna men who took pride in the maintenance of their railroad. The same view today is obscured by large trees and brush growing up through the abandoned right-of-way. (Courtesy of Fred Heilich.)

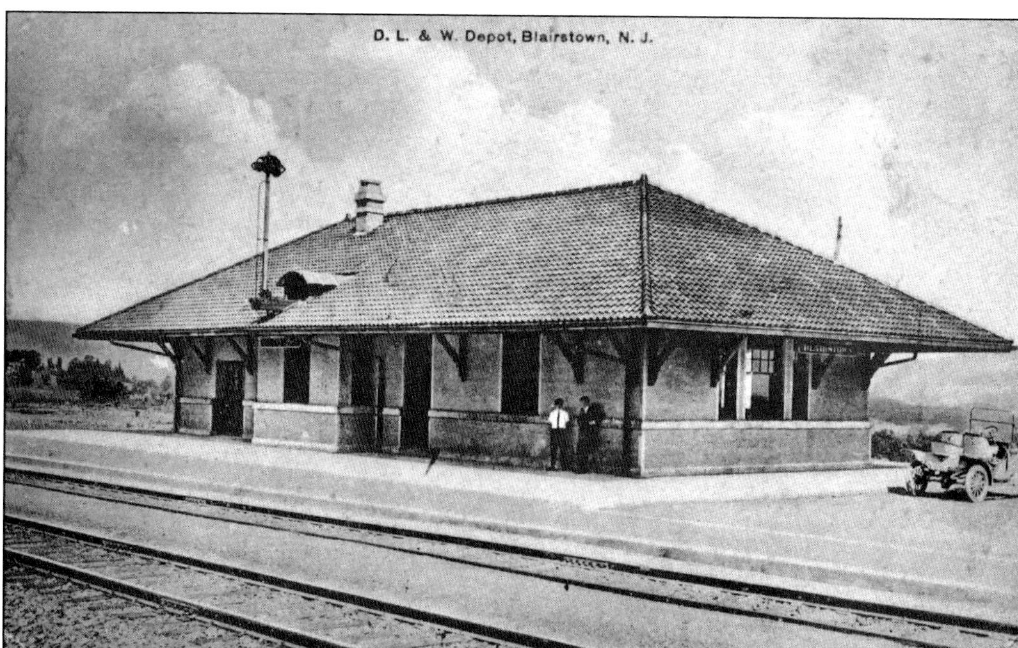

Blairstown received a handsome poured concrete passenger station and freight house with tile roofs as part of the cutoff project. Although located over a mile outside of town, it became the preferred depot for travelers, as the Lackawanna offered fast, frequent service to New York City and Buffalo, New York, as well as through cars to Chicago via the Nickel Plate Road. Despite its rural location, most named trains stopped here.

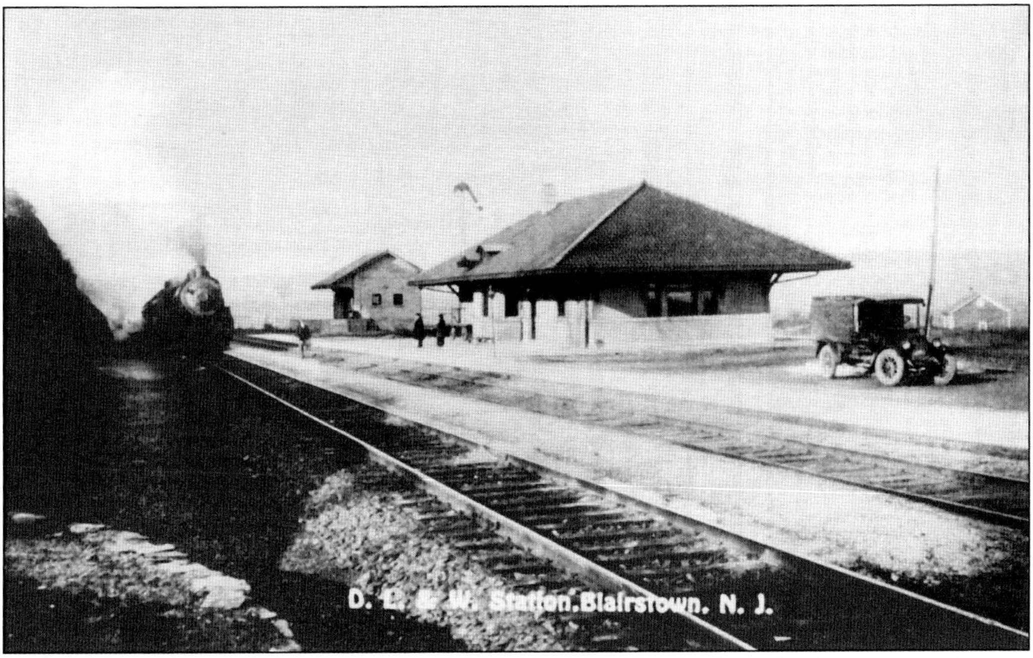

An eastbound Lackawanna train slows to a stop at Blairstown as a lone Railway Express Agency truck waits patiently for a delivery. Passenger service on the cutoff ended January 5, 1970, as the last Chicago–New York train, *The Lake Cities*, made its final stop. Although there have been several plans to restore trains on the former DL&W, nothing has come to pass as of 2010.

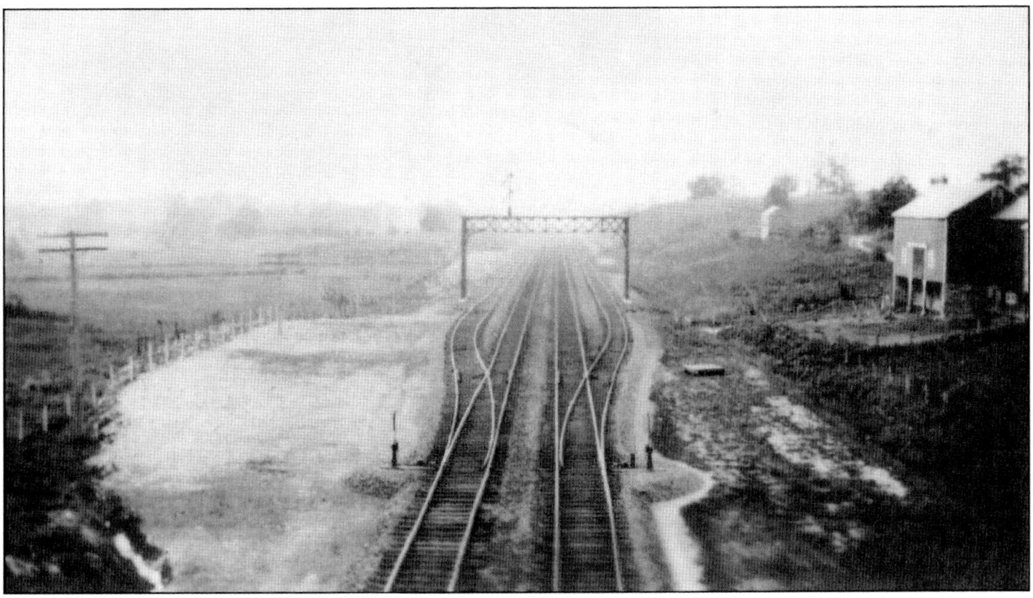

West of Blairstown, sidings were provided to permit crack passenger trains to overtake and pass slower freights. Fast expresses were permitted a maximum speed of 75 miles per hour over the entire cutoff, with only minor restrictions at several curves. In 1954, the Lackawanna's premier train, *The Phoebe Snow*, made the 28.45-mile run between Port Morris Junction and Slateford Junction in just 24 minutes. (Courtesy of Fred Heilich.)

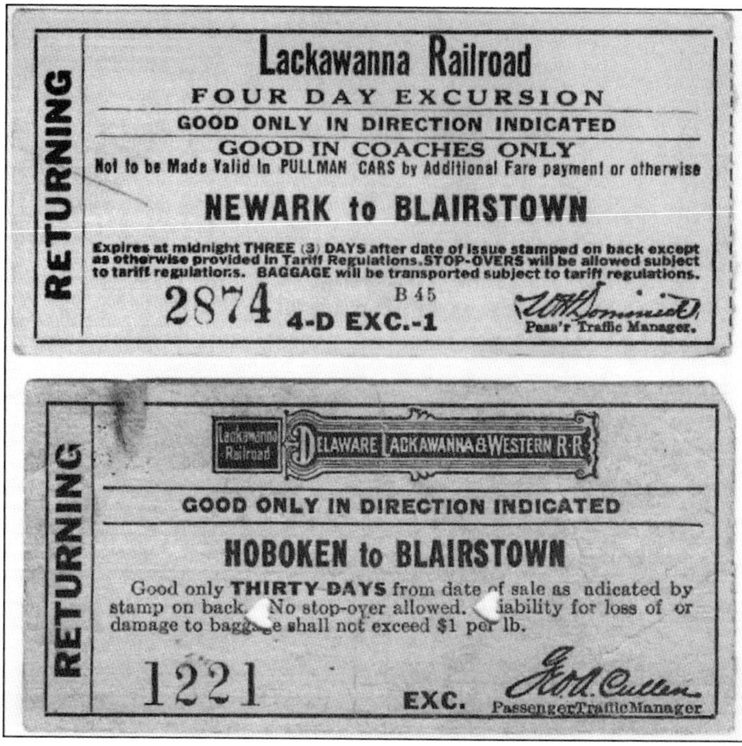

These two tickets were issued by the agent at Blairstown. In later years, after passenger service was discontinued, the depot initially became the studio for a local radio station and later the offices of a local contractor. A smaller poured concrete station located four miles east at Johnsonburg was demolished in 2007 after a trespasser was injured on the property.

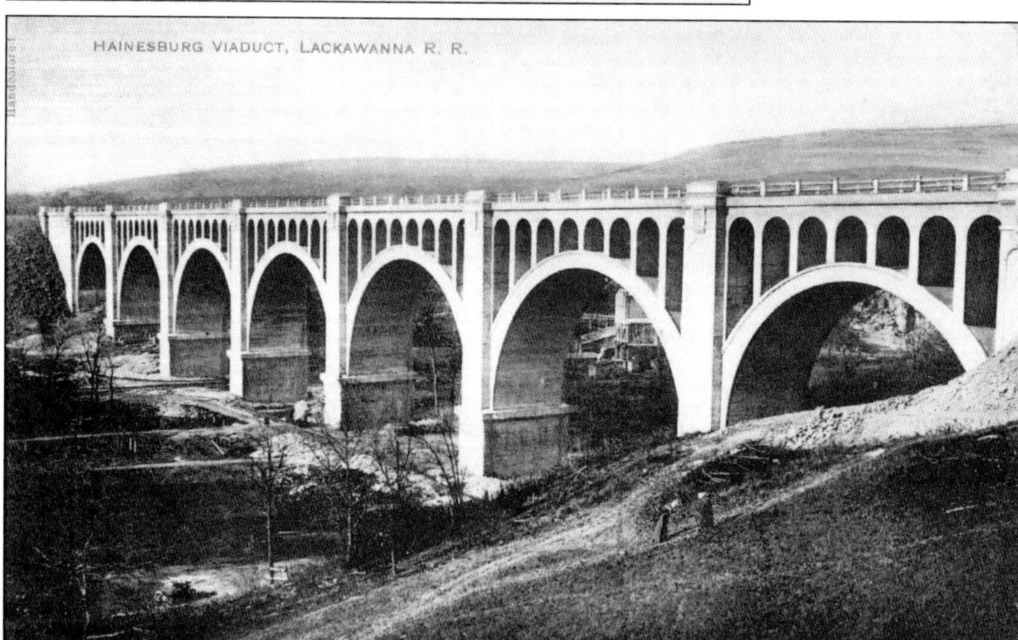

The jewel in the crown of the New Jersey Cutoff was the graceful Paulinskill River Viaduct, located some seven miles west of Blairstown in the village of Hainesburg. The seven concrete arches carried the Lackawanna main line over the Paulinskill River, Station Road, and the tracks of the New York, Susquehanna and Western Railroad, casting a giant shadow over the diminutive Susquehanna depot, which stood below it.

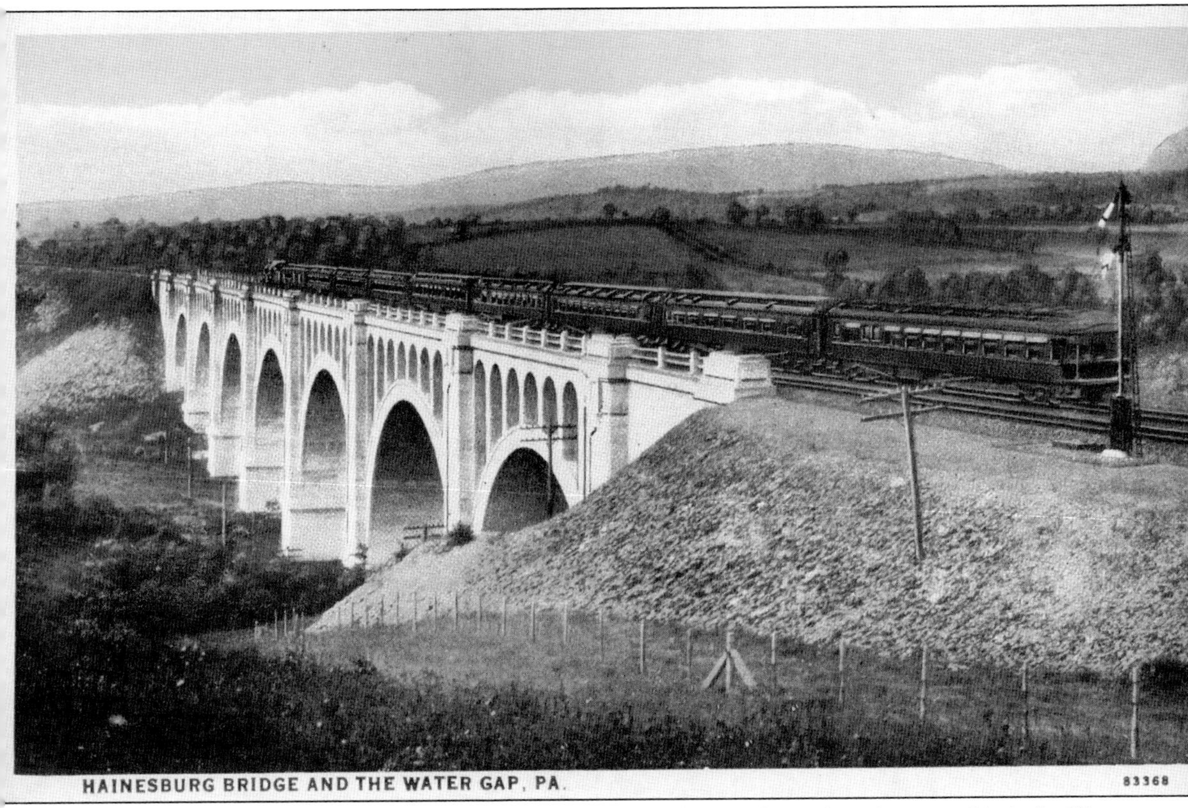

Another view of the Paulinskill River Viaduct depicts the westbound *Lackawanna Limited* rolling at speed toward the familiar profile of the Delaware Water Gap, which looms in the background. The viaduct was 115 feet high from the surface of the water to the base of the rail, 1,100 feet long, and was the largest reinforced concrete structure on the entire railroad until it was eclipsed by the Tunkhannock Creek Viaduct in Nicholson, Pennsylvania, in 1915. A passenger needed to be alert to catch a glimpse of the countryside from the top of the bridge since the train rolled over it at 75 miles per hour.

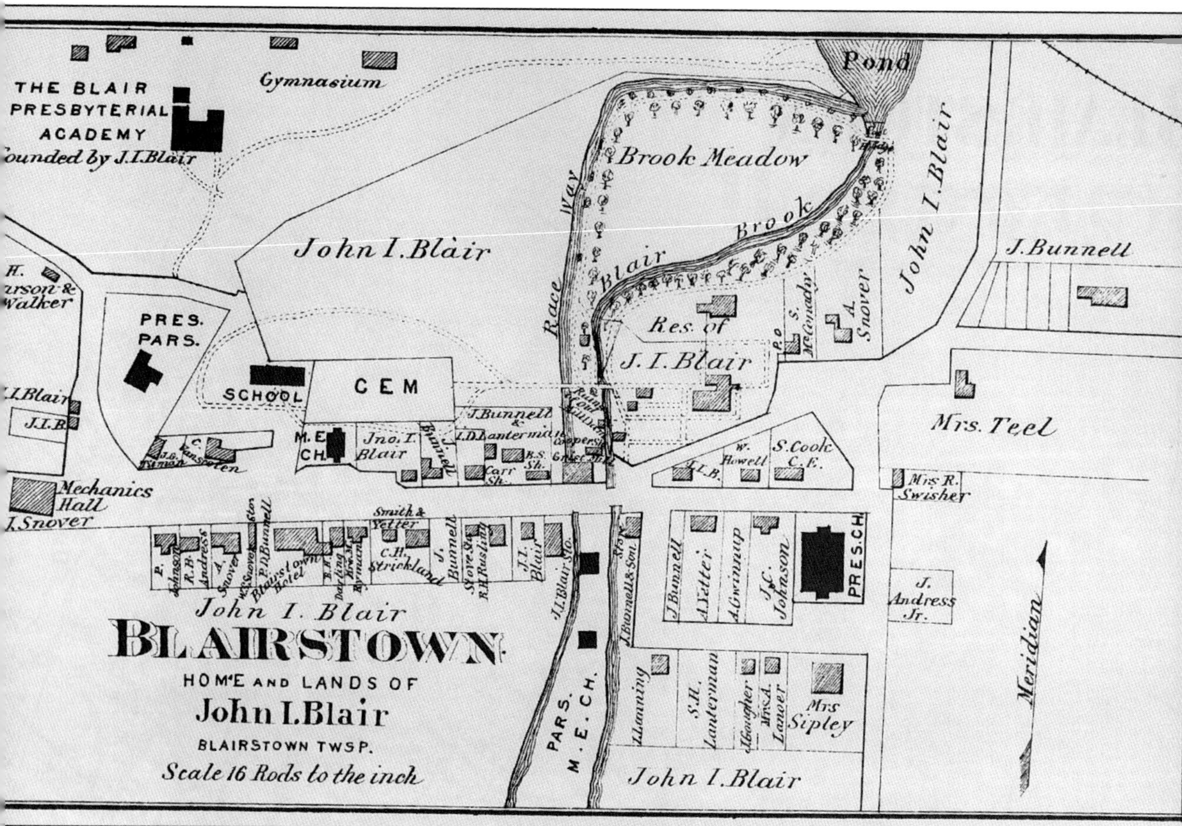

Much of downtown Blairstown was the property of John Insley Blair as evidenced on this plot map of the borough in 1881. The generosity of both Blair and his wife, Ann Locke Blair, was legendary, and many of the improvements made in the village in the 19th century, including piped water and electric lights, owe their existence to the Blairs.

Two

BLAIRSTOWN
JOHN BLAIR'S VILLAGE

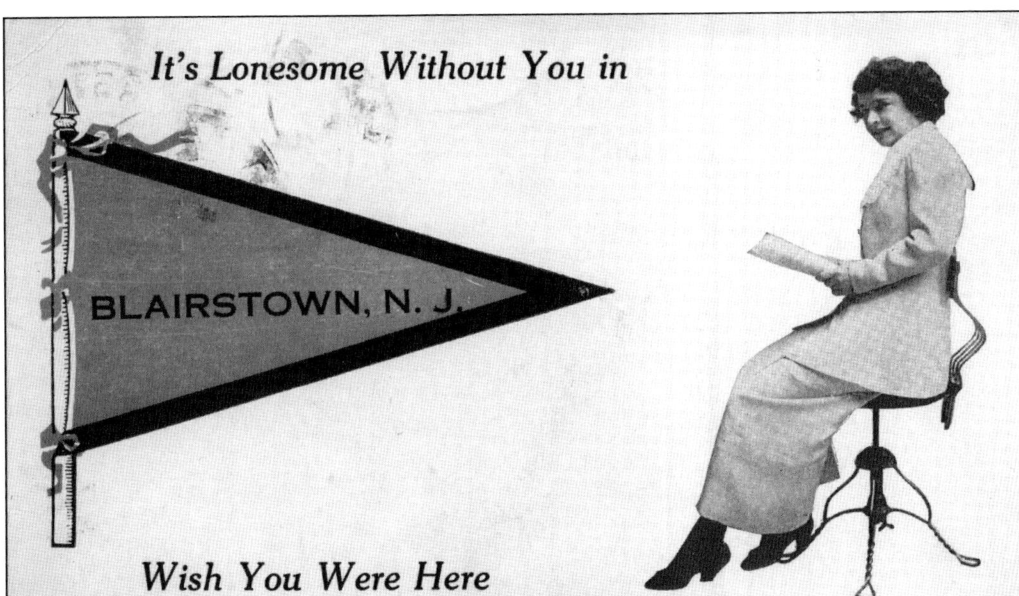

A winsome lass coyly beckons one to help cure her loneliness in Blairstown, which by 1910 boasted a population of less than 1,400 within its approximately 32 square miles. Although christened in 1839 for local industrialist and railroad magnate, John Insley Blair, Blairstown was not incorporated until April 14, 1845, when it was separated from Knowlton Township. Land tracts in the area were first surveyed by John Hyndshaw in 1729.

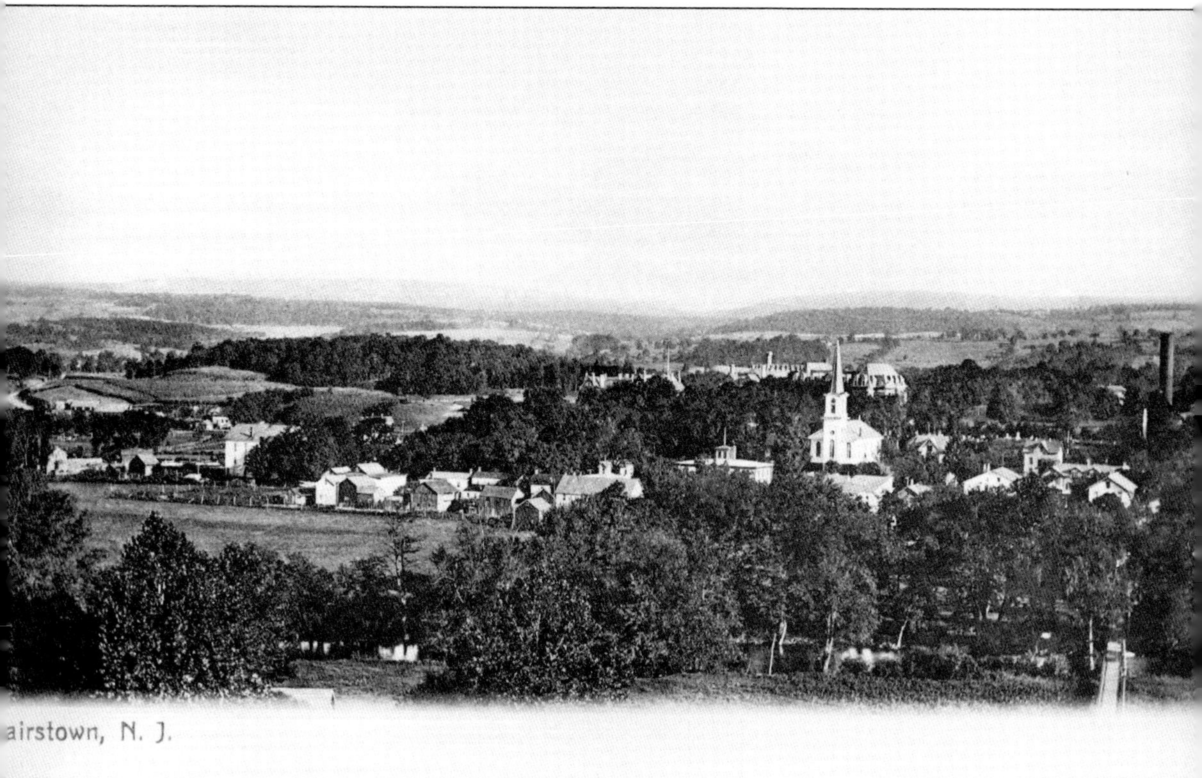

The photographer climbed Edge Hill above the Paulinskill at the south end of town to snap this impressive panorama of Blairstown about 1907. In the left panel, the white clapboard of the Methodist church on Academy Street dominates the scene, with the buildings of Blair Academy providing a backdrop. The cupola of the Blairstown House on Main Street is visible to the lower left of the church. In the right panel, the steeple of the First Presbyterian Church at the corner of

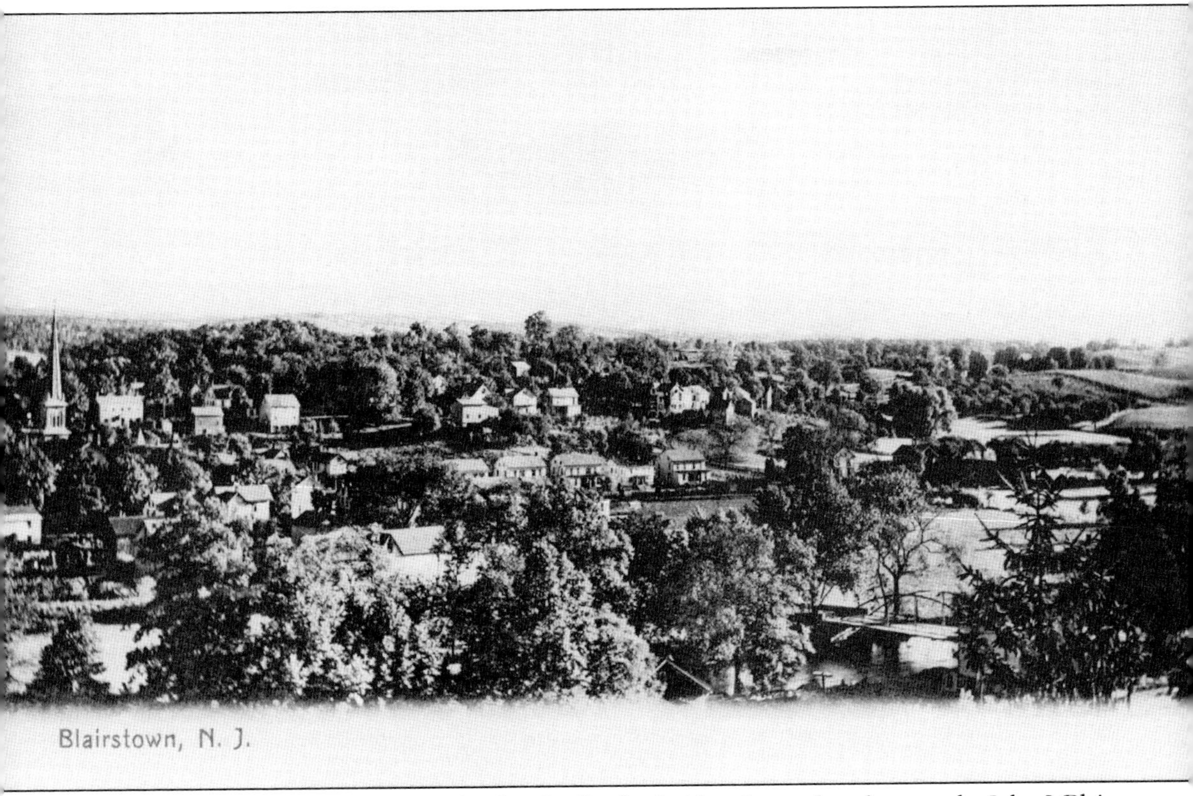

Main and Bridge Streets provides a landmark. The footbridge, donated to the town by John I. Blair, and leading from downtown to the New York, Susquehanna and Western Railroad depot comes toward the viewer at the lower left center of the image. The Methodist church was destroyed by fire on May 22, 1955, but the Presbyterian church survives today.

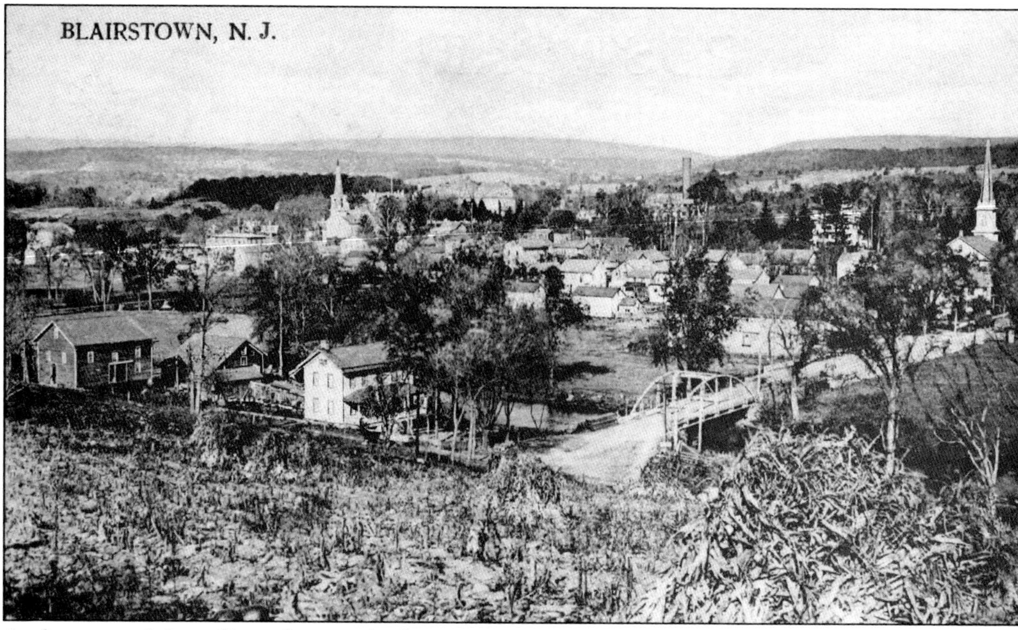

A close-up of the village from a similar vantage point again clearly shows the steeples of both churches. The iron bridge across the Paulinskill leading to the intersection of Edge Hill and Cedar Lake Roads replaced an earlier arched stone span that was built in 1840. The white farmhouse in the foreground and its two-story barn at the extreme left survive today at the entrance to Footbridge Park.

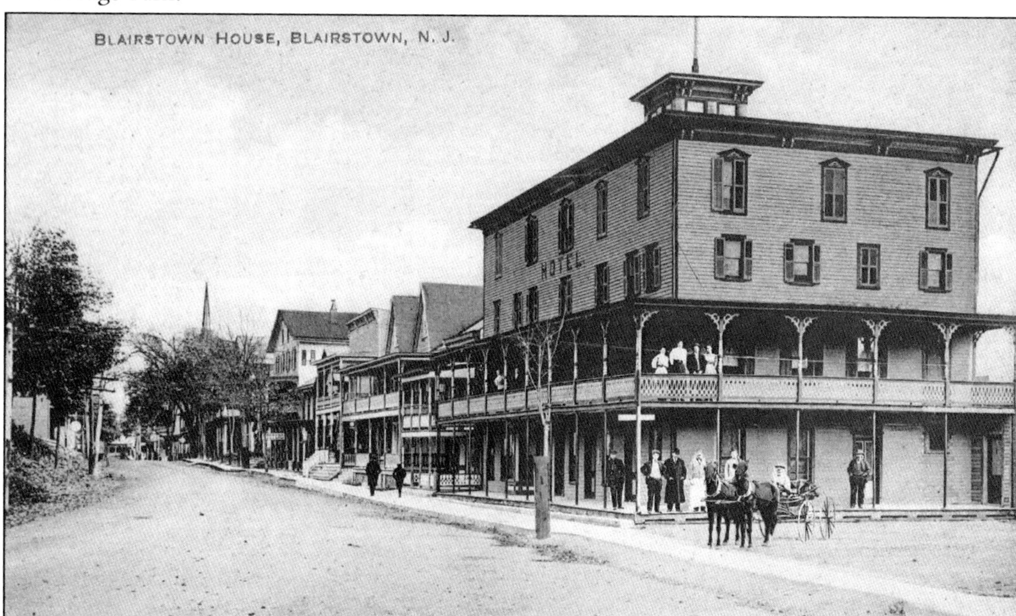

Since Blairstown was on the main highway between Newton and the Delaware Water Gap, the need developed by 1840 to provide a place of accommodation for hungry and weary travelers. In 1841, George Van Scoten built the Blairstown Inn on Main Street and the structure, expanded and altered several times over the years, provided this service until 1957, when it was destroyed by fire and not rebuilt.

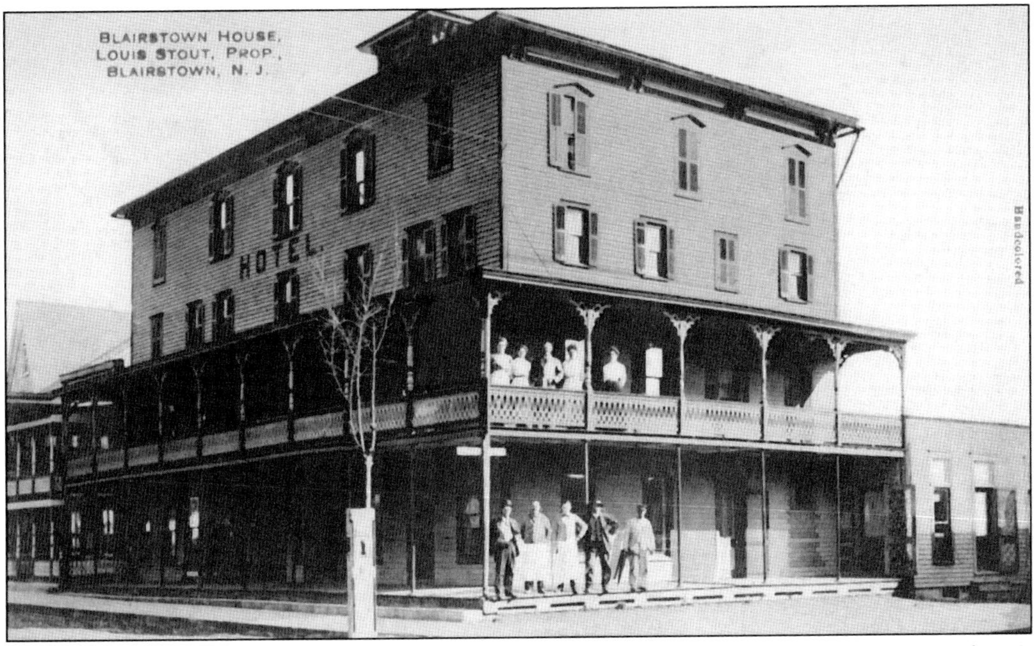

Two exterior views of the Blairstown Inn show how it evolved over the years. In 1913 (above), the proprietor was Louis Stoudt, who owned and operated it approximately between the years of 1890 and 1920. During the Roaring Twenties, the proprietor was Jack Quigley, a minor-league baseball umpire and close friend of the New York Yankee legend George Herman "Babe" Ruth. The Bambino was reportedly a frequent visitor, as he enjoyed hunting and fishing in the off-season as well as downing beers and steaks at Quigley's bar. By the 1940s (below), the inn had lost its cupola and second-floor porch, and Viola Williams was the proprietress. It now catered mostly to sportsmen who came west to the valley of the Paulinskill River for the great fishing and hunting.

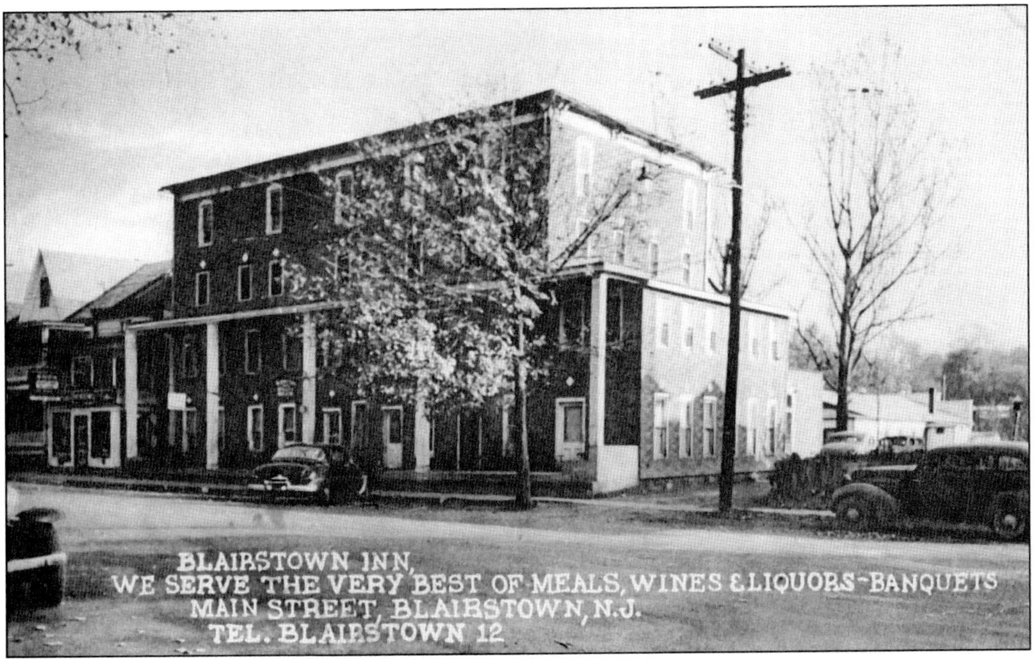

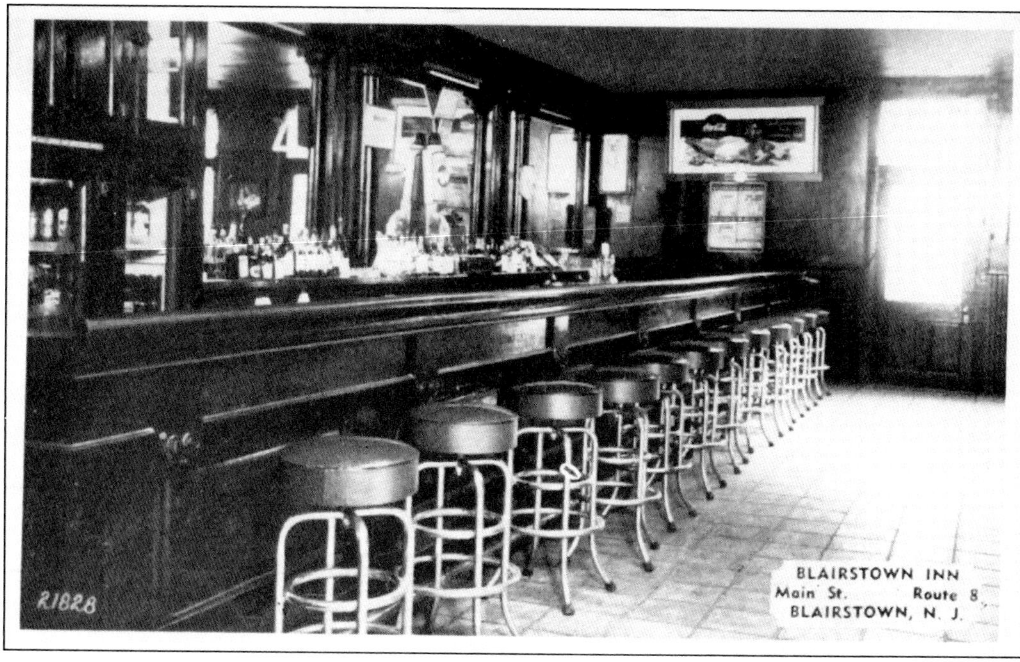

These period views of the interior of the Blairstown Inn date from the 1940s when Viola Williams tended bar and advertised "Restaurant, Good Eats, Comfortable Rooms, Tap Room, Cork and Bottle Lounge, and Shuffleboards." The bar itself was reported to be 35 feet long, and team shuffleboard was a popular sport among the locals. On March 1, 1957, the worst fire in Blairstown's history tore through a major portion of the block, destroying the inn and several adjacent buildings and leaving 35 people homeless. The structure was not rebuilt, and the business relocated to a new home on Route 94. The current Blairstown Post Office stands at its former location.

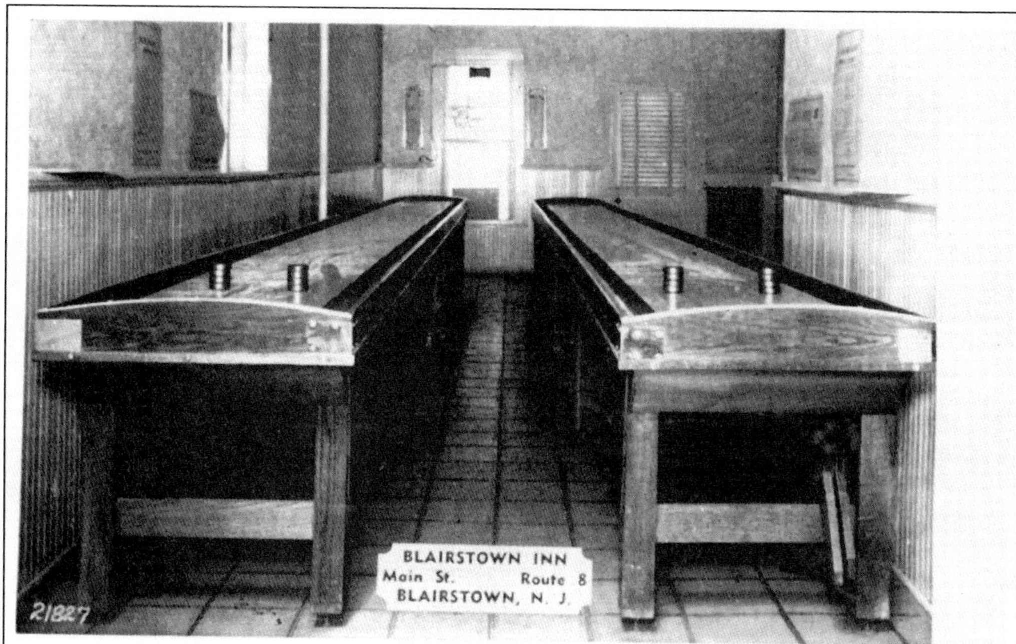

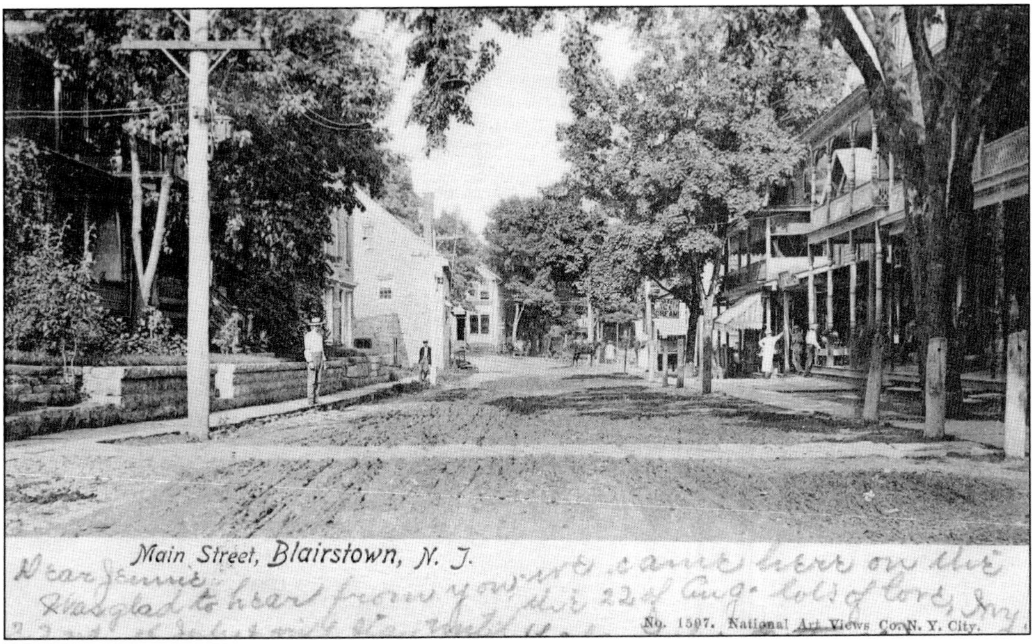

Looking east toward Bridge Street about 1910, Blairstown's Main Street has the ambiance of a frontier town. The stone gristmill dominates the center of the view, with the post office just beyond. An earlier mill, built before the American Revolution, gave the village its initial name, Smith's Mills, which later became Butts Bridge when the Butts family operated a span across the Paulinskill.

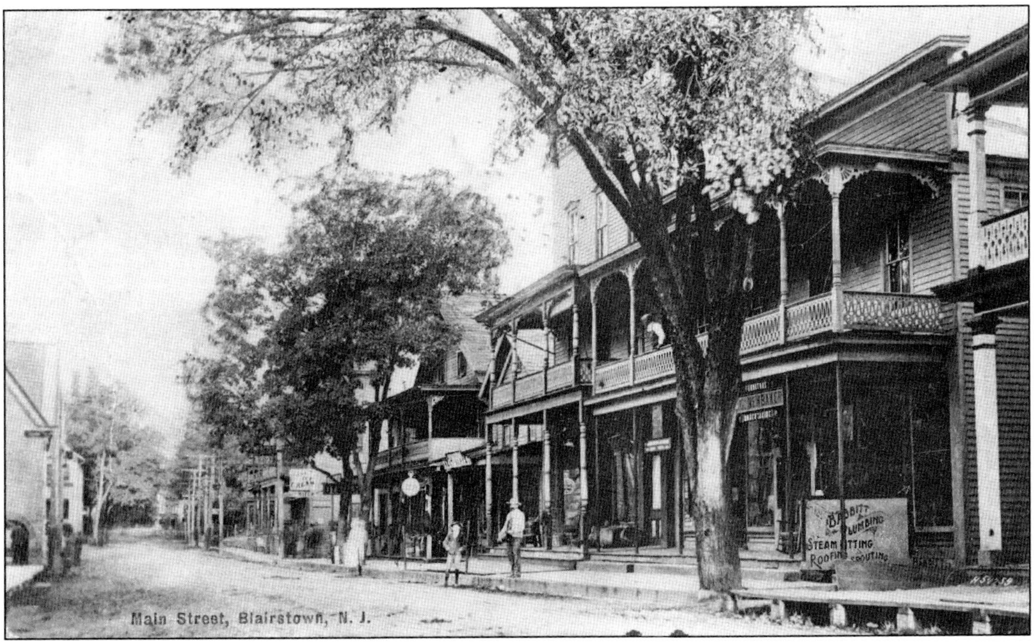

Although the sign on the porch of the first building reads "Babbitt Plumbing–Steam Fitting–Roofing–Spouting," the structure itself is the early home of Newbaker's Funeral Home. As a sideline to the sporadic undertaking business, it also sold furniture. Local residents find a man with a camera fascinating in 1910.

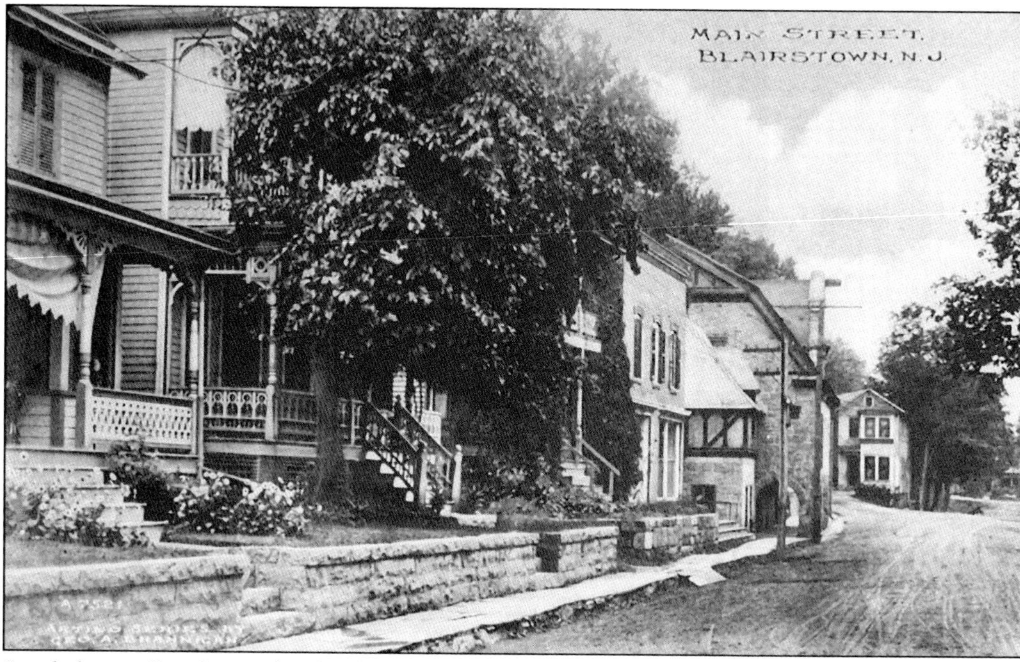

Stately homes line the north side of Main Street in the business district, which had wooden sidewalks. The smaller building adjacent to the mill is the original Blairstown Water Company, another local project of John I. Blair, who not only endowed the village with piped water but also with electricity generated from a power plant on the Paulinskill, just east of town in the suburb of Paulina.

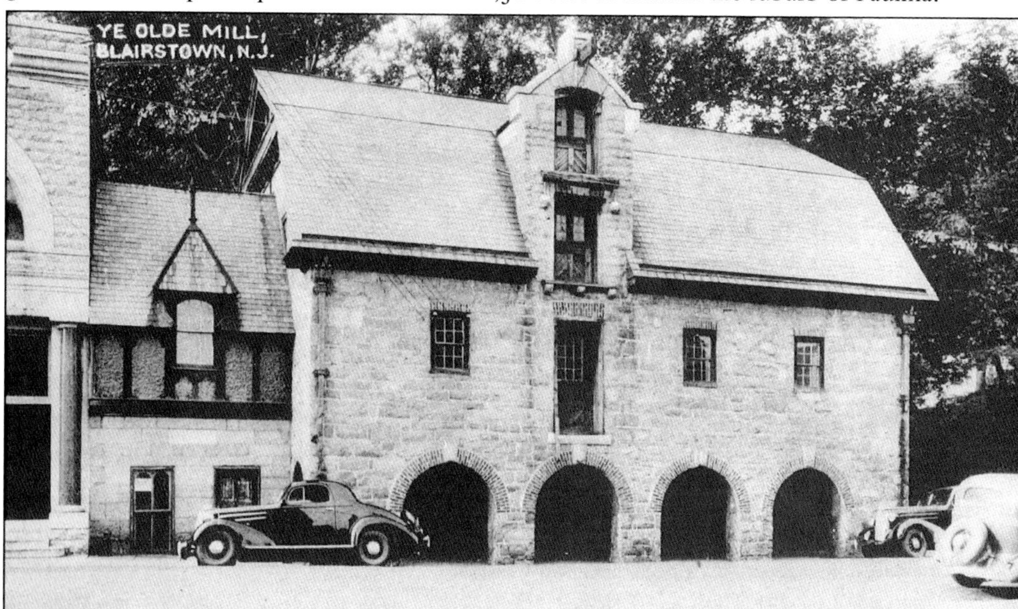

The gristmill, built with local limestone in 1825, overshadows the landscape on Main Street. A wooden addition extending east to Blair Creek was added about 1855 but had deteriorated so badly by 1900 that it was torn down after Blair Academy purchased the building in 1903. The academy added a third floor as well as the beautiful stonework arches that allowed the sidewalk to pass beneath the second floor.

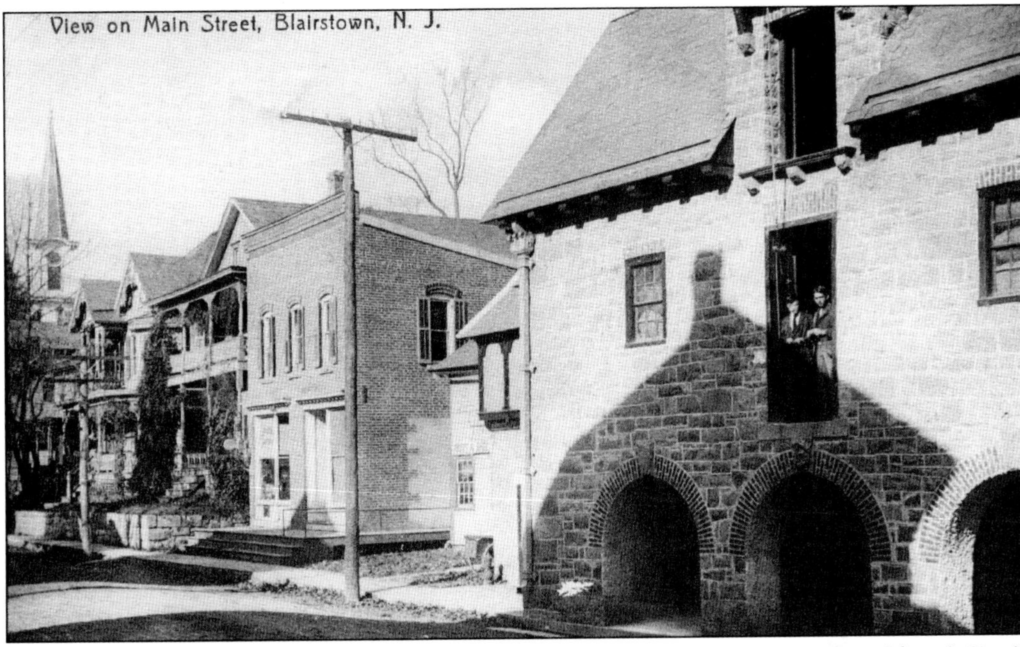

Here are two views of the mill looking west on Main Street. In a pre-1910 image (above), David Sliker's shoe store and newsstand peeks out from behind the corner of the water company building. Sliker was a collector, and his store was unofficially known as Blairstown's first museum. Two boys peer out the door where countless bags of feed and flour were delivered to local farmers. The First National Bank of Blairstown (below) replaced Sliker's in 1910, its architectural style fitting right in with that of its neighbors. Messler and Shannon were the last millers, grinding grain until the mill closed in 1932. In the 1950s, the building was leased to the Catherine Dickson Hofman Library, which remained there until 1995, when it moved into a brand new building on Lambert Road.

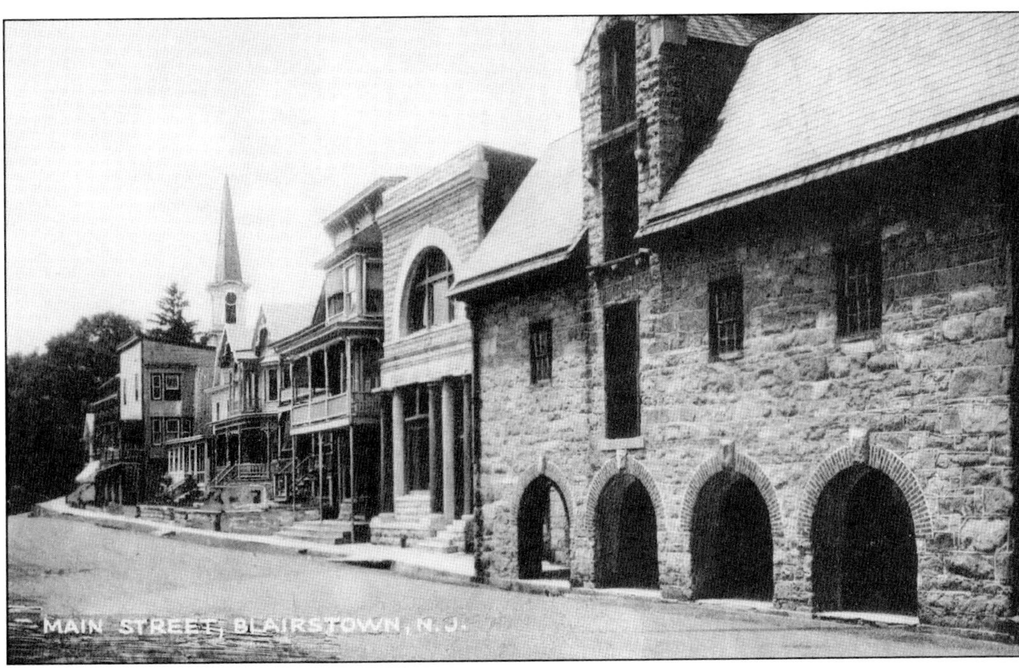

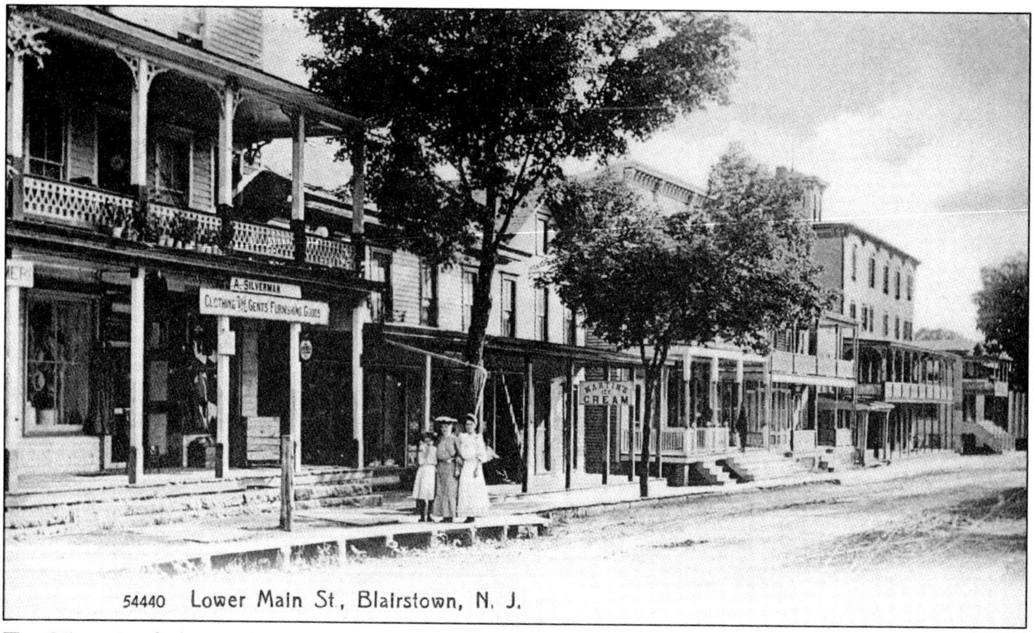

Two Victorian ladies and a young girl pose for the photographer in front of A. Silverman's Clothing store. As Silverman's sign advertises "Clothing and Gents Furnishing Goods," it is more likely the girls were headed for Martin's Ice Cream Parlor next door. Blairstown still had wooden sidewalks and shade trees in the business district in 1908.

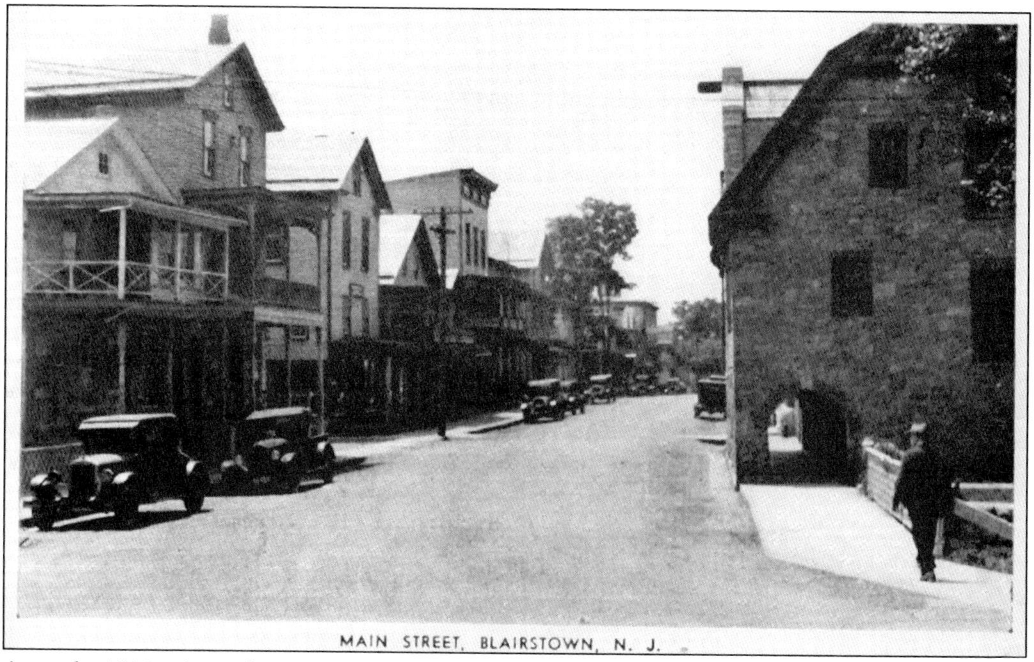

An early-1930s view of Main Street looking west from the mill near the intersection of Carhart Street shows an emerging "Small Town, U.S.A.," with paved roads and concrete sidewalks. Progress in the form of the Ford Model A has replaced the horse and buggy, but the well-dressed gentleman on the right still finds it desirable to eschew the horseless carriage for a pleasant Sunday stroll down the avenue.

Dressed in their Sunday best, members of the Cook family pose outside their restaurant on Main Street. This postcard was mailed on Tuesday, April 16, 1912, the day after the *Titanic* went down. Failure of the sender to mention the disaster could indicate that news of the sinking might not yet have reached most Blairstown residents in the era before mass media.

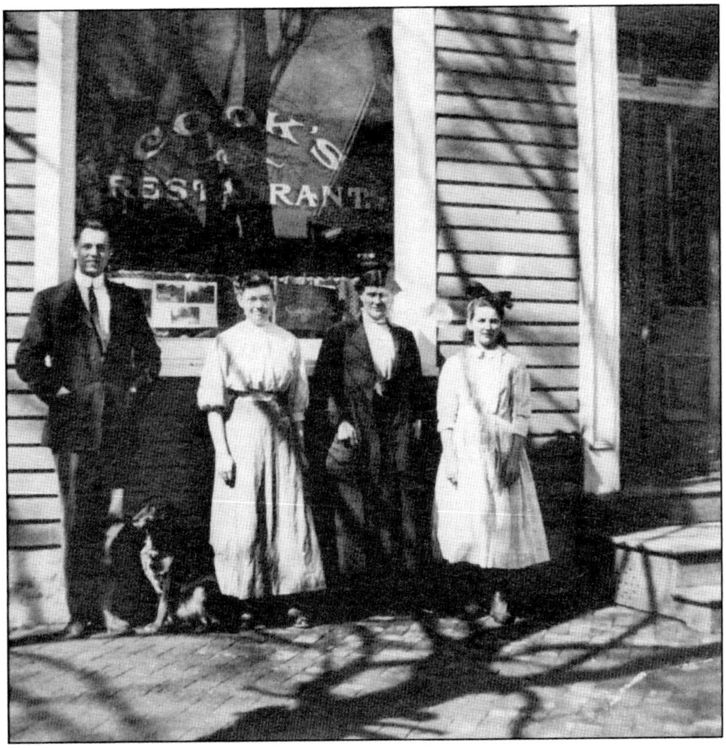

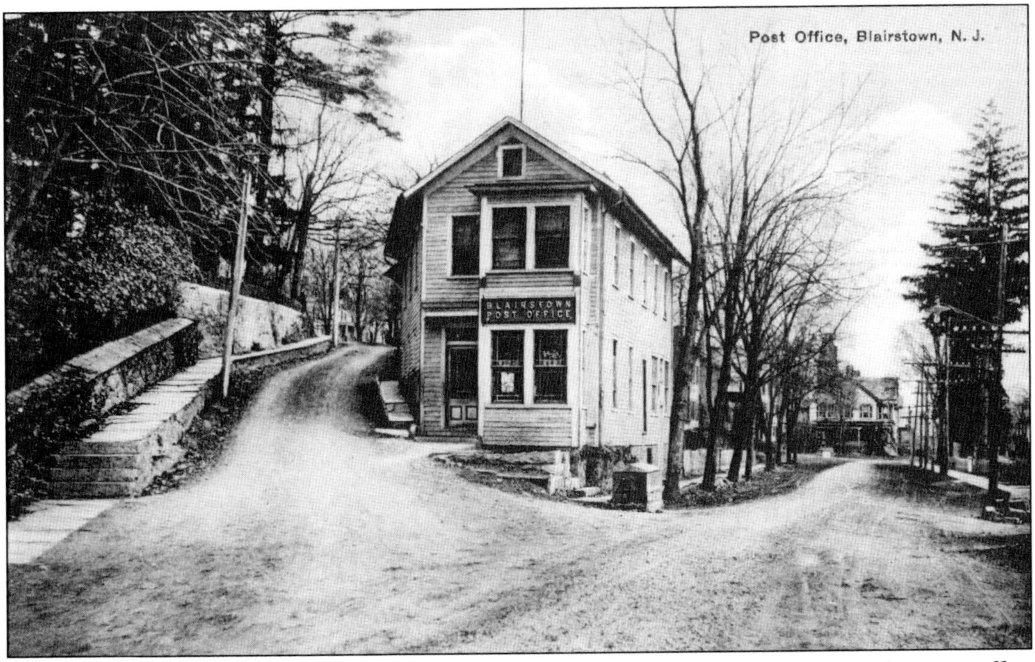

Smith's Mills' first postmaster was William Hankinson in 1818. Two years later, the post office name was changed to Butt's Bridge. When John I. Blair became postmaster in 1825, the name was changed again to Gravel Hill. At a public meeting on January 23, 1839, the town became Blairstown in his honor. In 1889, the post office was moved to the Flatiron Building, so called because of its somewhat triangular shape.

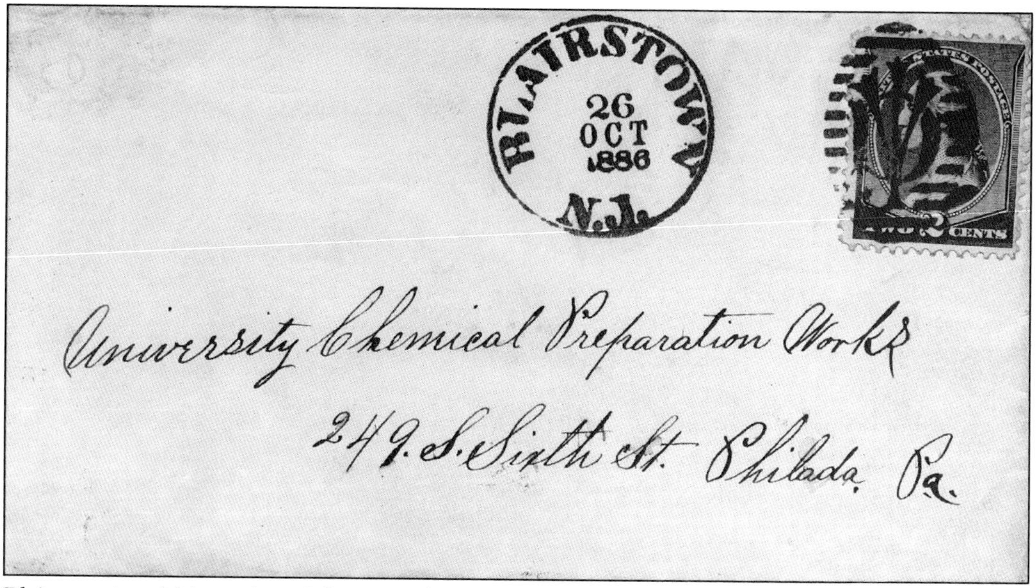

Blair appointed his nephew John D. Vail postmaster in 1875, and Vail served until 1901. He was also superintendent of the Blairstown Railway, leaving little time for his postal duties, so much of the work fell to his clerk, H. Hartman. Vail had his own special cancelation, JDV, shown on this letter postmarked October 26, 1886. On April 1, 1936, the post office moved to the corner of Water Street.

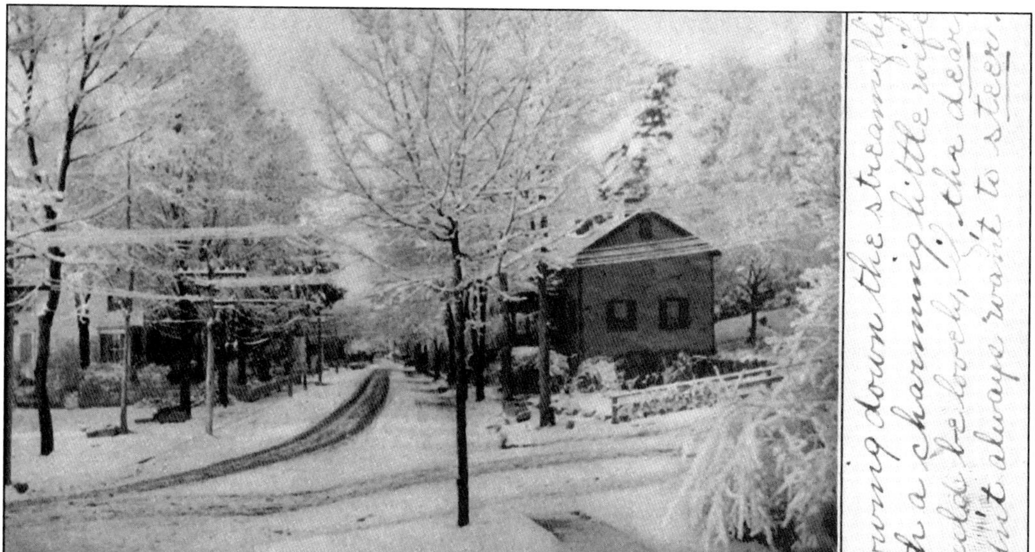

Not a car or horse is in sight as the fluffy snow of a long-forgotten winter blankets the east end of Main Street. Spring must be getting near, since the center of the road has been cleared, and heavy melting is underway. If one were to stand on the corner of Main and Bridge Streets during a snowstorm today, he would find this scene little changed.

Methodists were preaching at appointments in Blairstown as early as 1811 but the first church building, a 34-foot-by-45-foot stone structure, was not completed until 1838 on land donated by John Blair on Old Academy Street. By 1873, it became dilapidated and was demolished. A new 40-foot-by-60-foot frame church was erected on the same site for a cost of about $7,400 and dedicated on January 23, 1875.

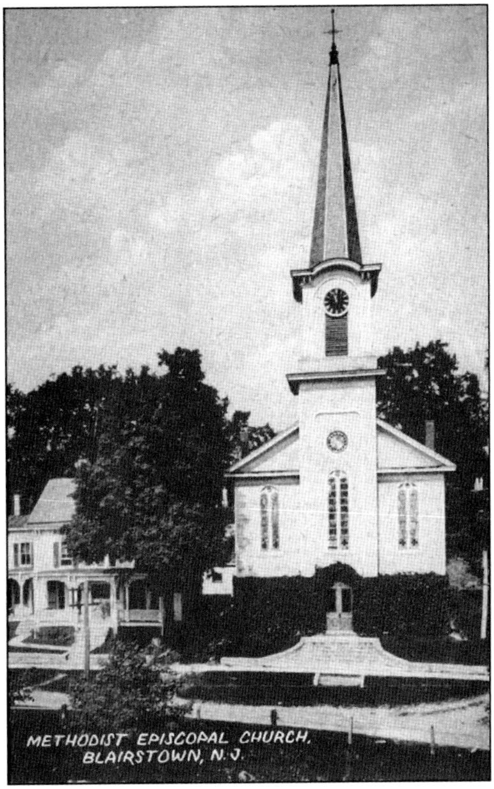

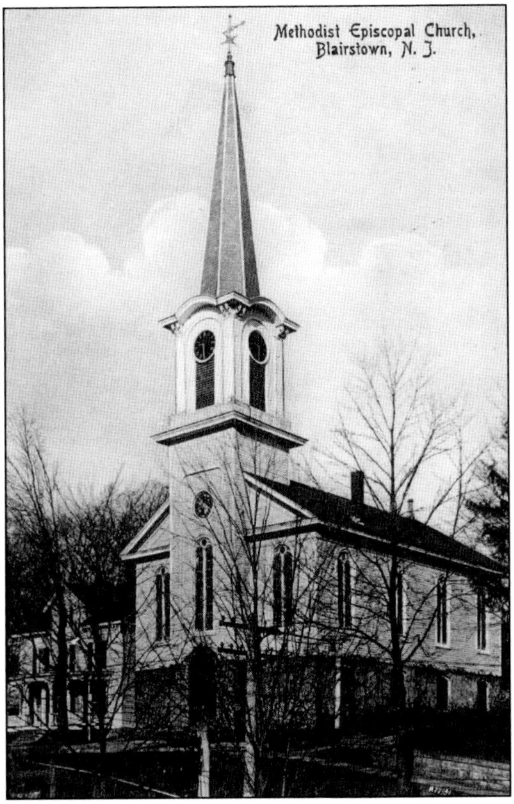

Rev. L. R. Dunn was pastor at the time of the dedication of this handsome building. The church was connected with the Harmony Circuit from 1838 until 1862, when it became a separate parish. A parsonage was erected off Water Street soon after. In 1902, a Jardine pipe organ was installed in the church. The building was destroyed in a fire on May 22, 1955, and not rebuilt on this site.

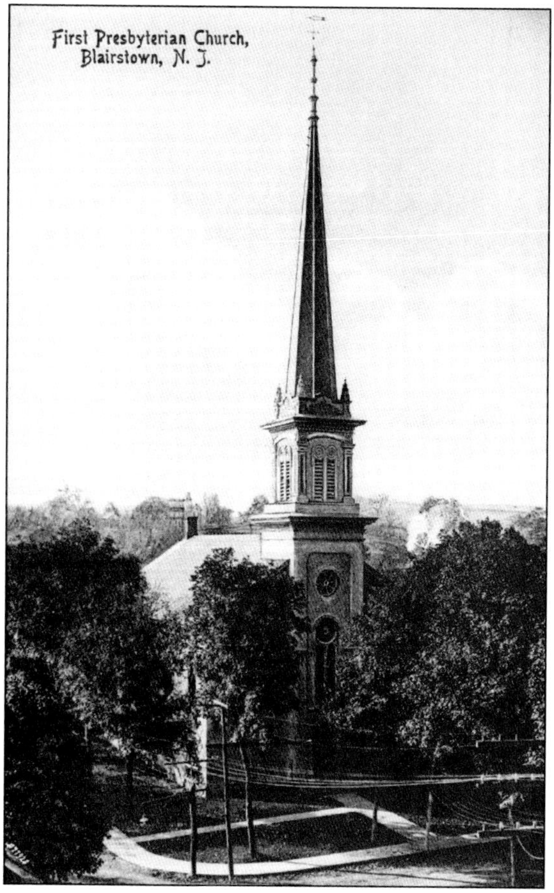

Early Blairstown Presbyterians attended services in Yellow Frame or Knowlton until their own stone church was erected in 1839–1840 at a cost of $2,865.98. While measuring only 49 feet by 50 feet, it still boasted a spire and belfry with a 218-pound bell. Reverend Condit dedicated it on December 10, 1840. By 1868, the parish had outgrown the facility, and it was demolished to make way for a new church.

The cornerstone of the new structure was laid on June 1, 1870, and the completed building was dedicated on February 15, 1872. Like its predecessor, it was constructed of limestone, but its increased size of 53 feet by 80 feet now accommodated 500 parishioners. The steeple was erected in eight sections, each measuring 72 feet long, and the one-ton bell was transported to the construction site by oxcart from Portland, Pennsylvania.

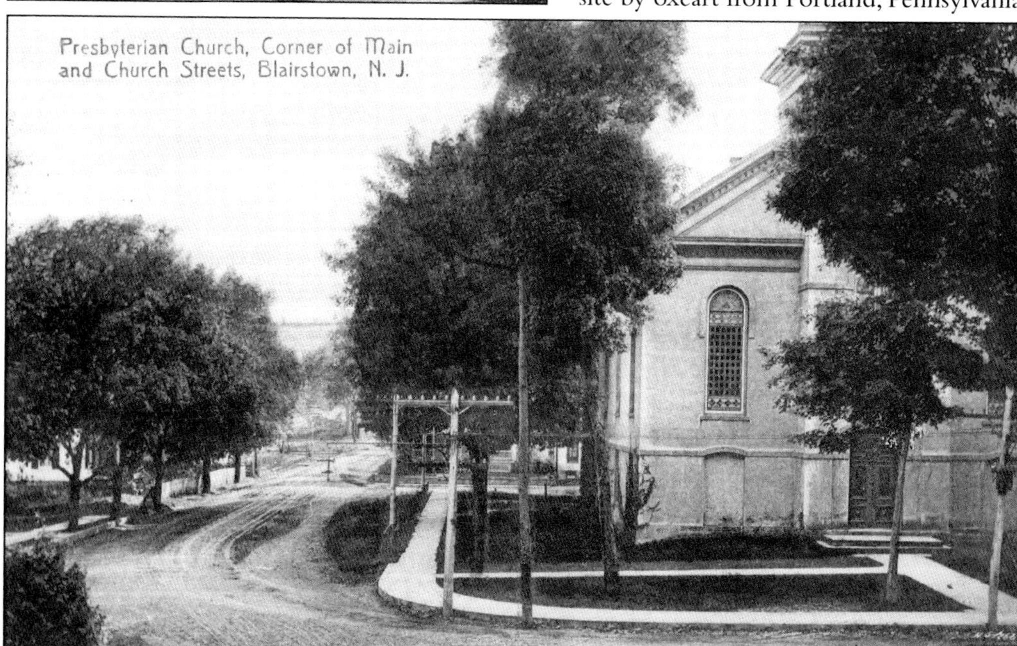

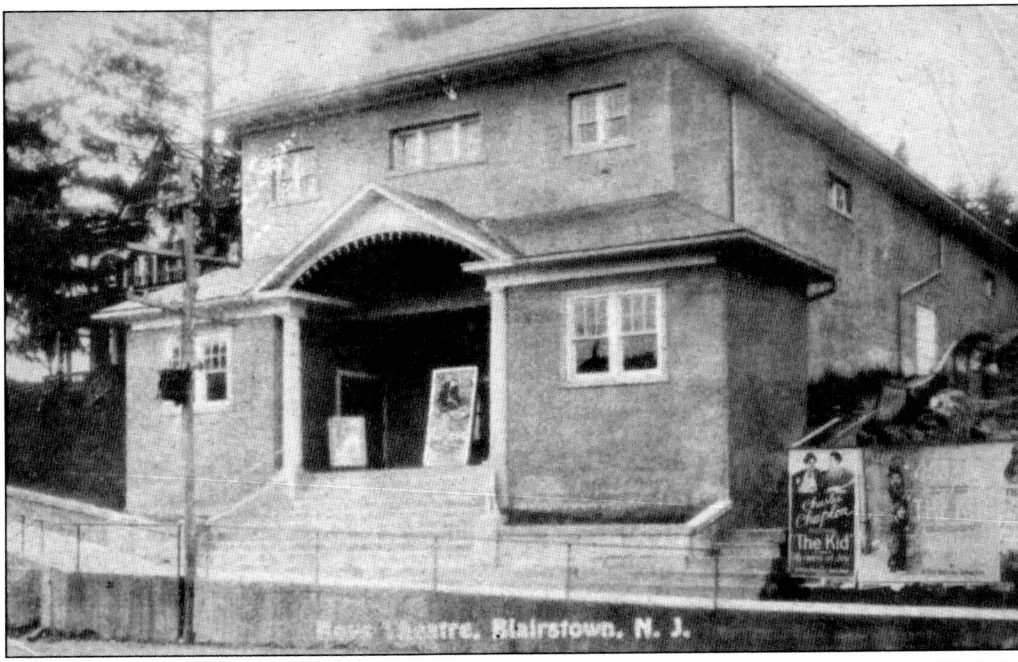

The Main Street Livery was remodeled into a movie theater by Robert Roy and Raymond Smith and opened as Roy's Hall on April 2, 1913. It was seriously damaged by fire on February 7, 1917, but was rebuilt and continued to serve Blairstown as a movie house until television silenced it on November 2, 1961. The photograph dates to 1921, as the feature film is *The Kid*, with Charlie Chaplin.

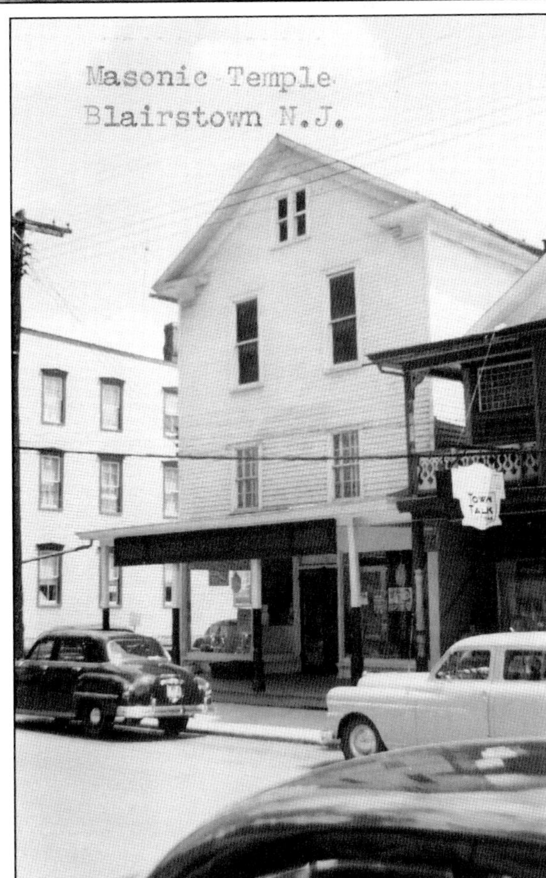

Local Freemasons met to organize their own lodge in February 1891, and on February 27, 1893, Blairstown Lodge No. 165 of the Free and Accepted Masons received its charter and held its inaugural meeting with John Fletcher Bunnell installed as worshipful master. John I. Blair had agreed to add a third floor to a building he owned on Main Street to house the lodge hall for a $48 annual rent.

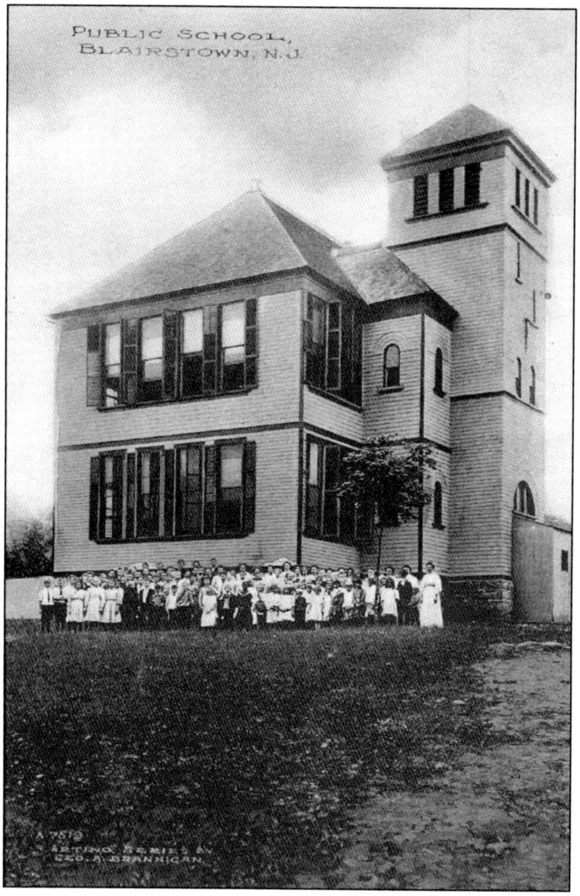

In 1867, the State Free School Law was passed, and Blairstown's first public school was organized, initially meeting in the Old Academy building at Blair. By 1896, when classes had outgrown the donated space and a new building was needed, the first united school was constructed at the end of East Avenue. Prior to this, Blairstown was the only district in the state without its own school building.

The school building originally had one floor, but as pupil numbers increased, it was jacked up and a "second" floor added underneath, effectively doubling its size. In 1912, after heated local debate, more additions were done to accommodate a high school program. The school burned to the ground in the summer of 1928, and classes were temporarily shifted to the Cedar Lake House while a new school was built.

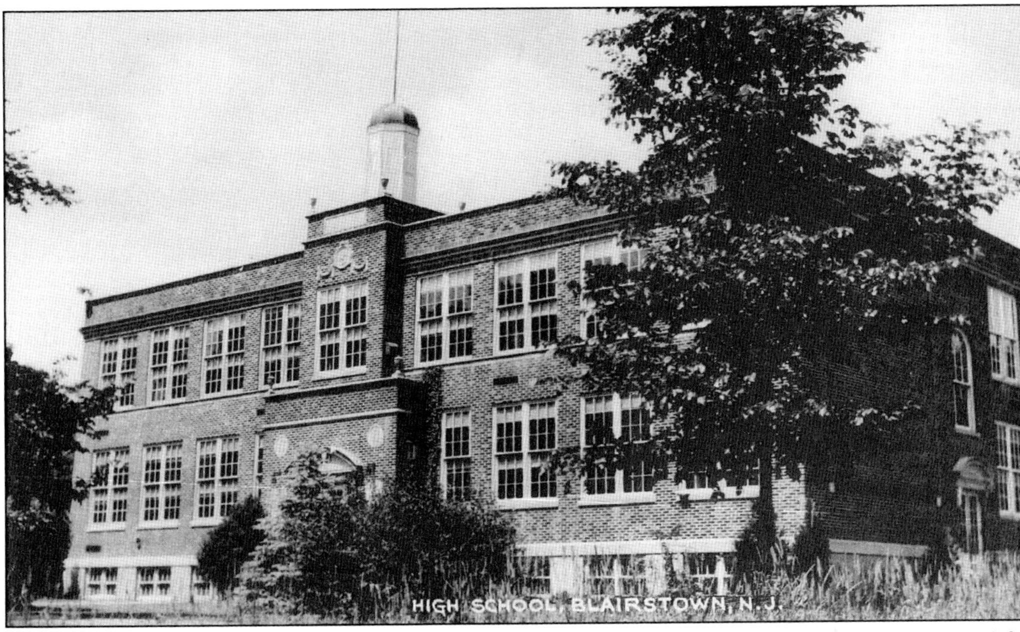

The new Blairstown School, educating students from kindergarten through 12th grade, opened for the fall term of 1930 and today serves as the center wing of the expanded Blairstown Elementary School complex. Additional athletic fields at the rear of the building were the gift of Melissa Gregory Vail, whose late husband, John, was the nephew of Ann Locke, wife of John I. Blair.

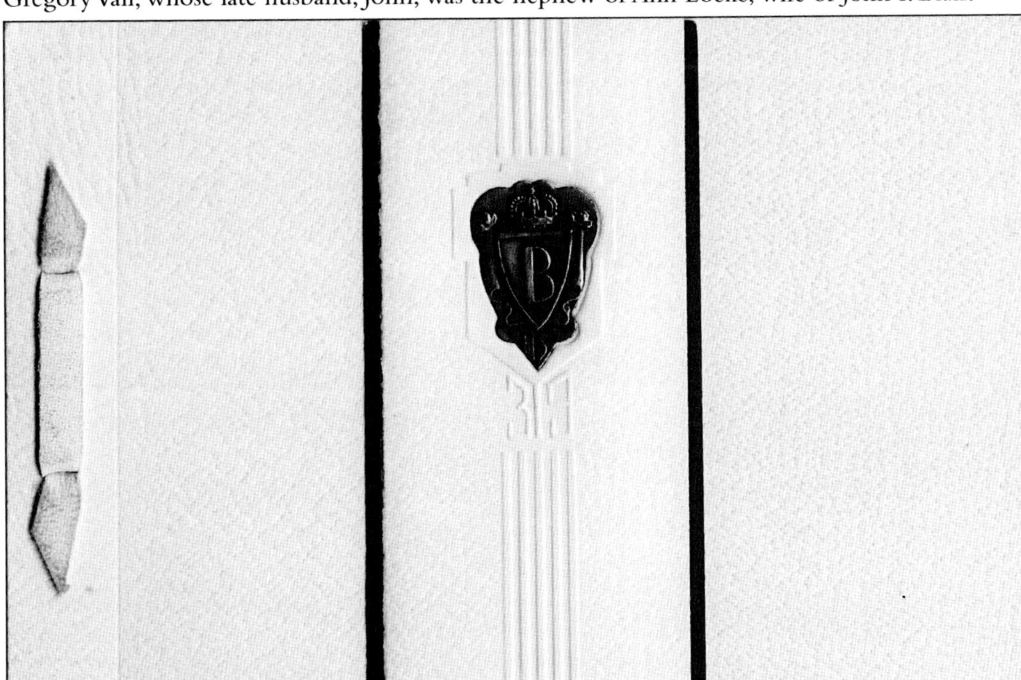

Guests at the graduation ceremonies for the Blairstown High School class of 1939 received this invitation and program. Blairstown enjoyed two centennial dates. While 1939 marked the 100th anniversary of Gravel Hill being renamed Blairstown in honor of its favorite son, 1845 is recognized as the year that the town was separated from Knowlton Township and legally incorporated.

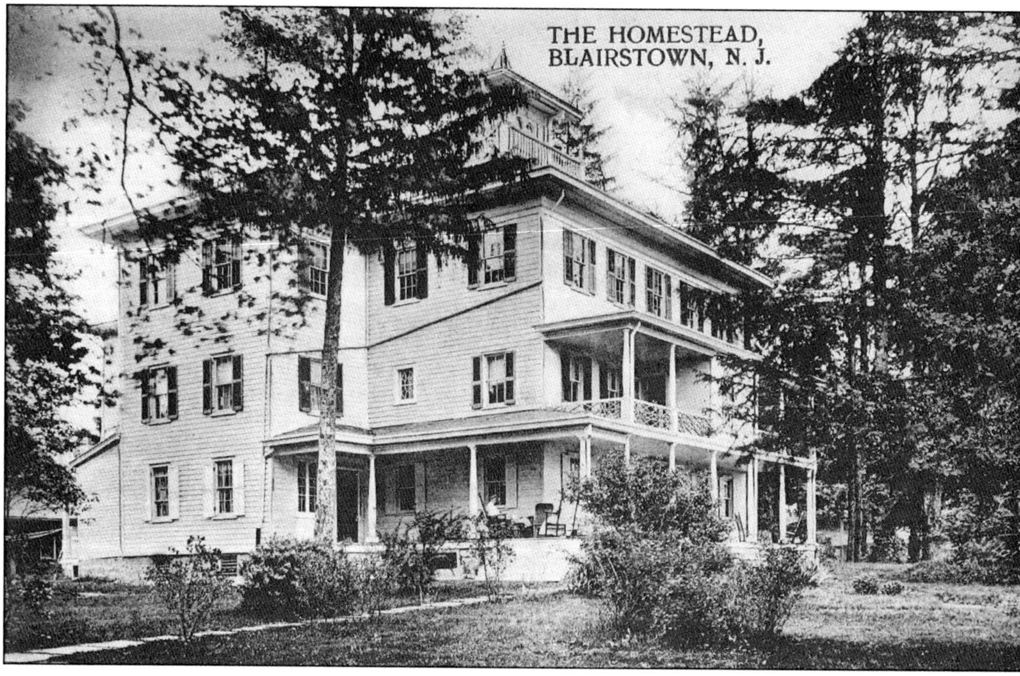

The Homestead was the residence of John I. Blair. Although he considered Blairstown his home, the millionaire financier and railroad builder was born into humble circumstances near Foul Rift, New Jersey, on August 22, 1802. He came to Blairstown about 1821, becoming postmaster in 1825 when the town was still known as Butts' Bridge. By 1839, his stature was so important the town was renamed in his honor. The house was built in 1833 when Blair was just 31 and modified over the years. Blair died there on December 2, 1899. The Homestead then came into the possession of Blair Academy but began to deteriorate and was finally torn down in the 1970s—a sad loss.

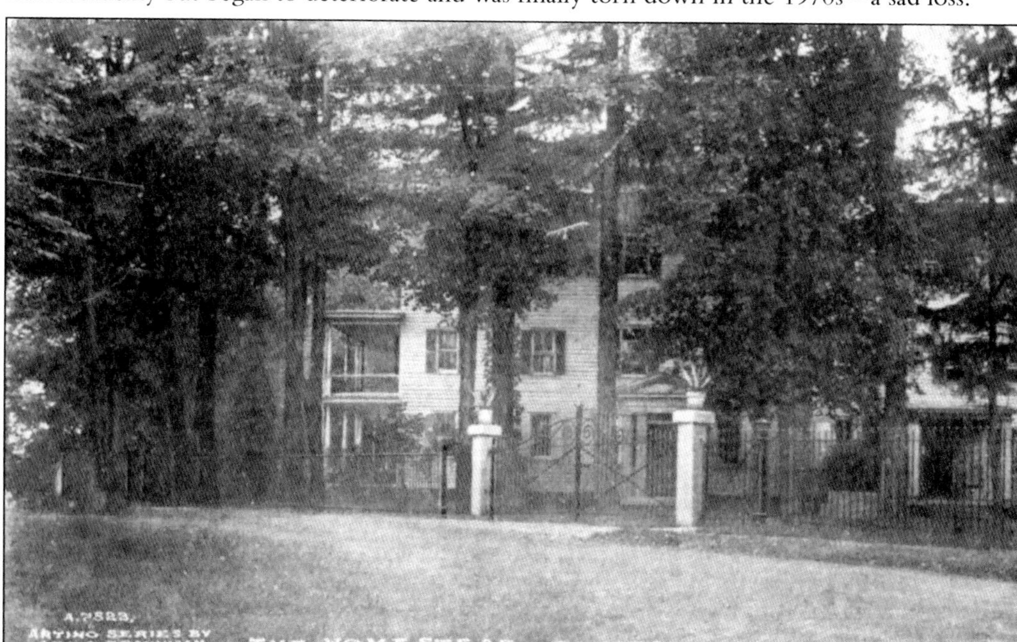

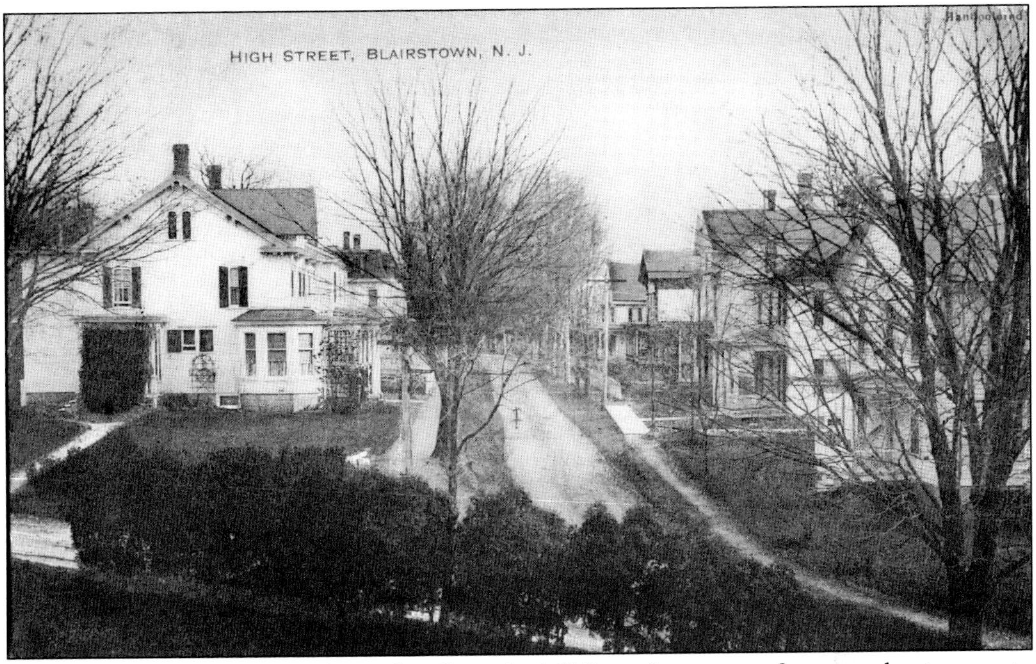

High Street was indeed high, located well up the hill from the center of town and not prone to the flooding that plagued the business area from time to time when major storms hit the area and caused the Paulinskill and its tributaries to back up. It became the setting for beautiful Victorian houses that sprang up along the unpaved road. Sidewalks were still wooden in this 1912 view.

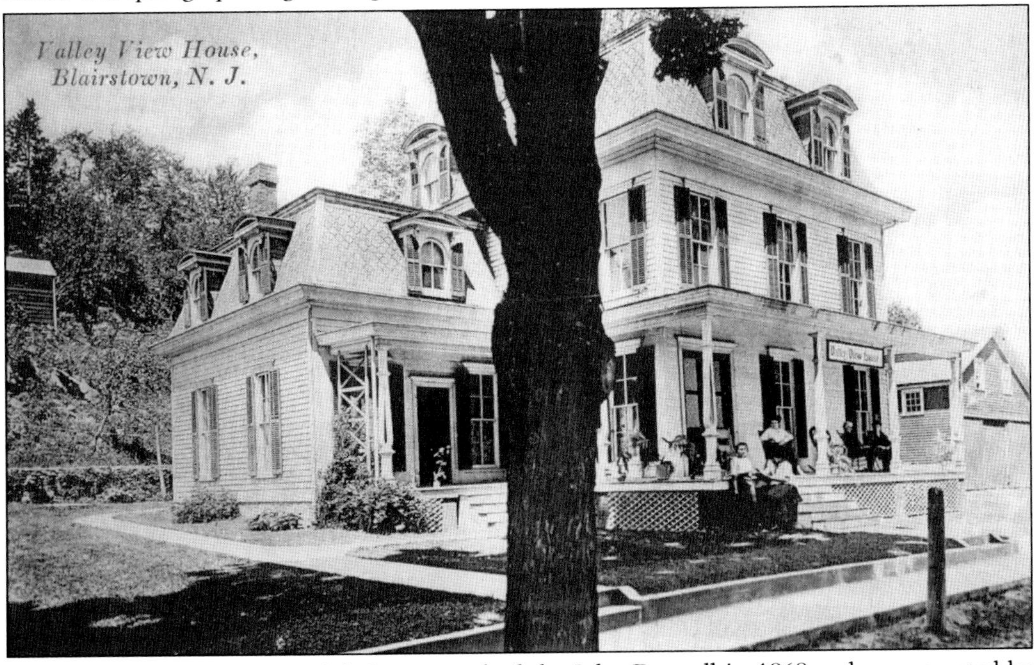

The Valley View House on High Street was built by John Bunnell in 1868 and was operated by Mary L. Albertson in 1915. It could accommodate 25 guests at rates of $1.50–$2 daily, or $7–$10 per week. Open all year, it was typical of the tourist homes that made their living introducing city folks to the benefits of fresh air and country living.

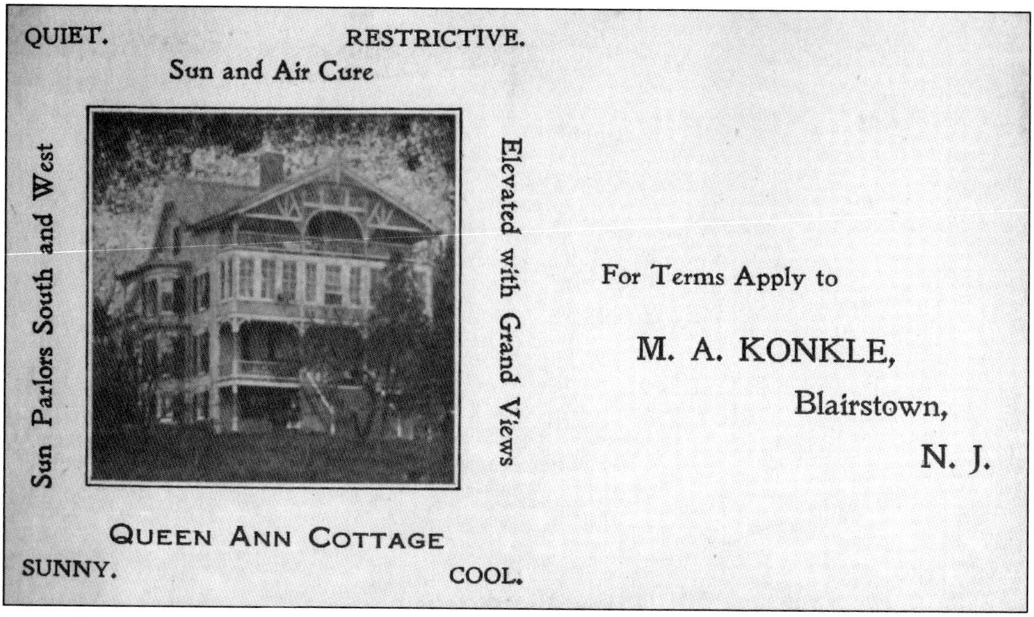

M. A. Konkle operated the Queen Ann Cottage, another guesthouse located on High Street in this beautiful Victorian home. Konkle trumpeted its sun parlors, grand views, sun and air cure, and quiet but also noted that the facility was restrictive, which in that era signaled that certain minorities and others with specific health conditions, most notably tuberculosis, were excluded.

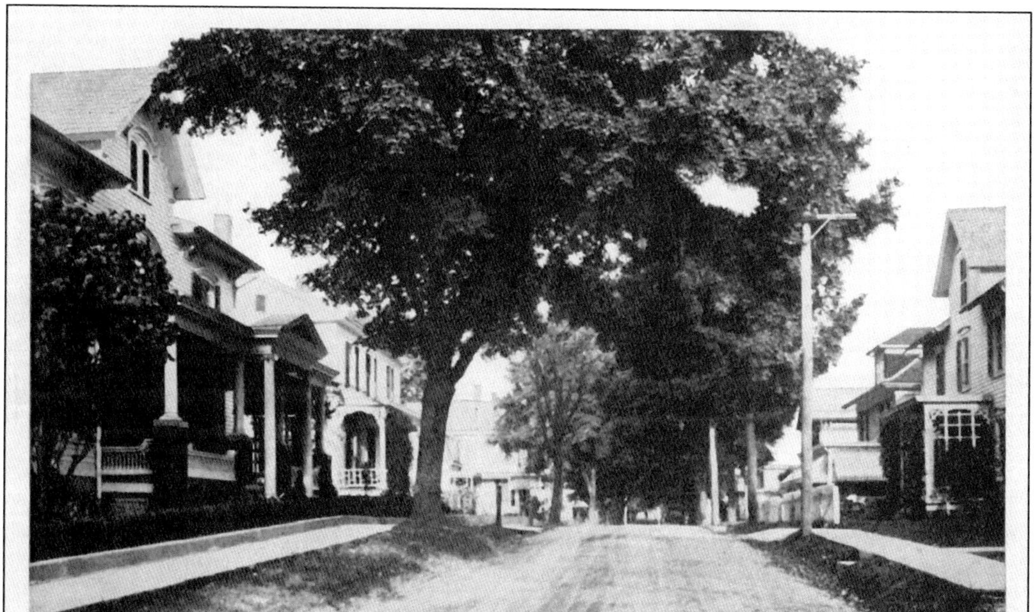

A view of High Street looking east shows some of the beautiful residences that lined both sides of the tree-shaded road. Many of these same old homesteads still stand today, a tribute to the history-minded Blairstown residents who saw fit to preserve them for future generations.

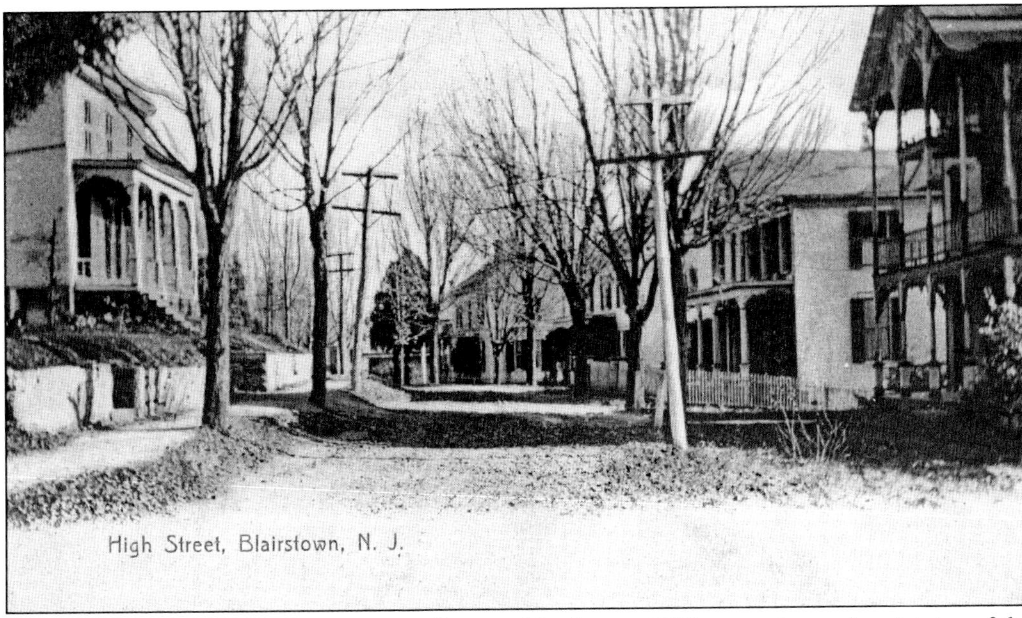

Traveling east on High Street toward Stillwater, this vintage 1908 scene shows the vicinity of the borough limits. Wooden sidewalks have given way to dirt paths, but residents still enjoy electricity, thanks to the generosity of John I. Blair, who built the area's first power plant along the Paulinskill, just east in the community of Paulina. The home at far right is that of Dr. Frank S. Gordon.

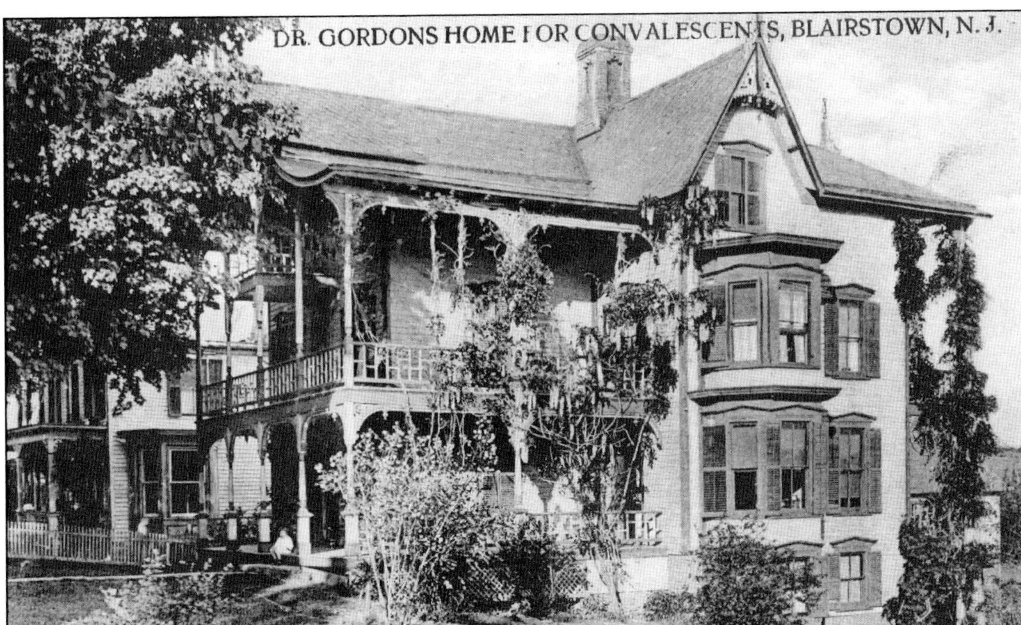

Dr. Gordon started his practice in Blairstown in 1908 and operated a convalescent facility from his combination home/office on High Street. Gordon also offered furnished bungalows for those seeking the therapeutic benefits of fresh air and sunshine in a country setting. Another notable early Blairstown physician was Dr. John C. Johnson, who arrived in 1850, practiced for over 50 years, and eventually became president of the Warren County Medical Society.

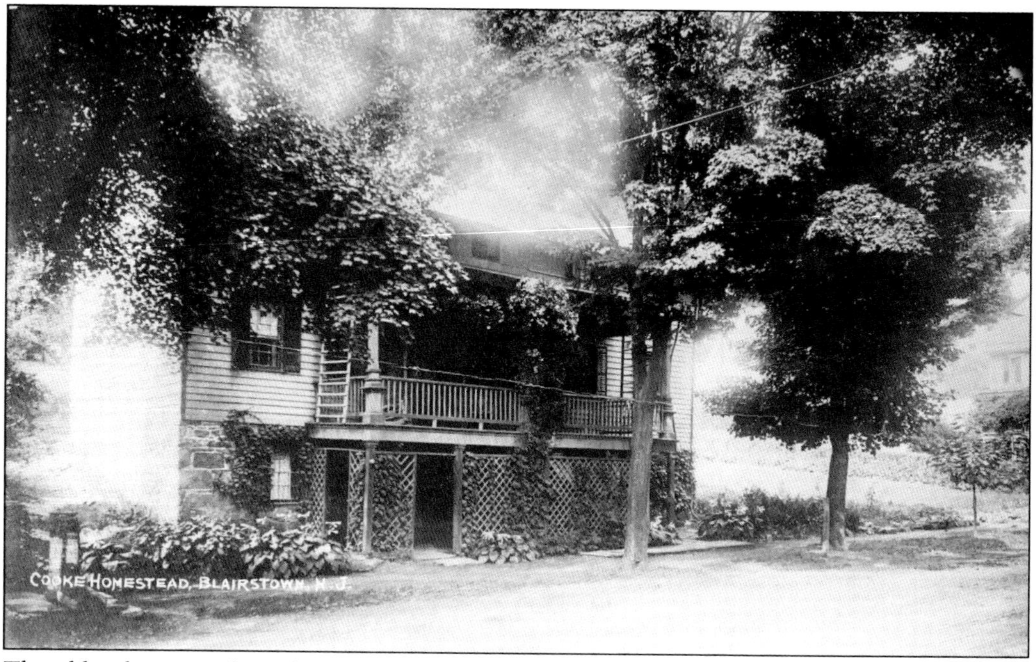

The oldest homestead in Blairstown, which still sits in its original location, is the Cooke House, located at the corner of Main and Bridge Streets just across from the Presbyterian church. This early view carried the message, "Best wishes for 1914 from the family inside. Margaret M. Cooke." Blairstown's last shoemaker had his shop here.

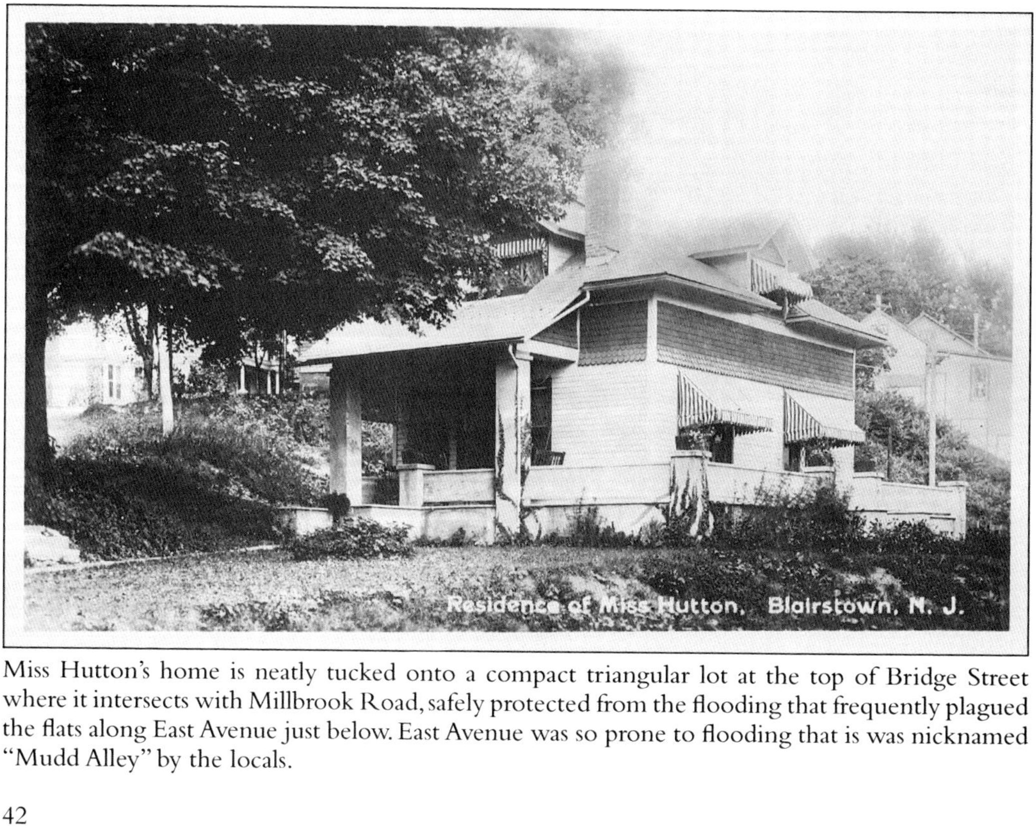

Miss Hutton's home is neatly tucked onto a compact triangular lot at the top of Bridge Street where it intersects with Millbrook Road, safely protected from the flooding that frequently plagued the flats along East Avenue just below. East Avenue was so prone to flooding that is was nicknamed "Mudd Alley" by the locals.

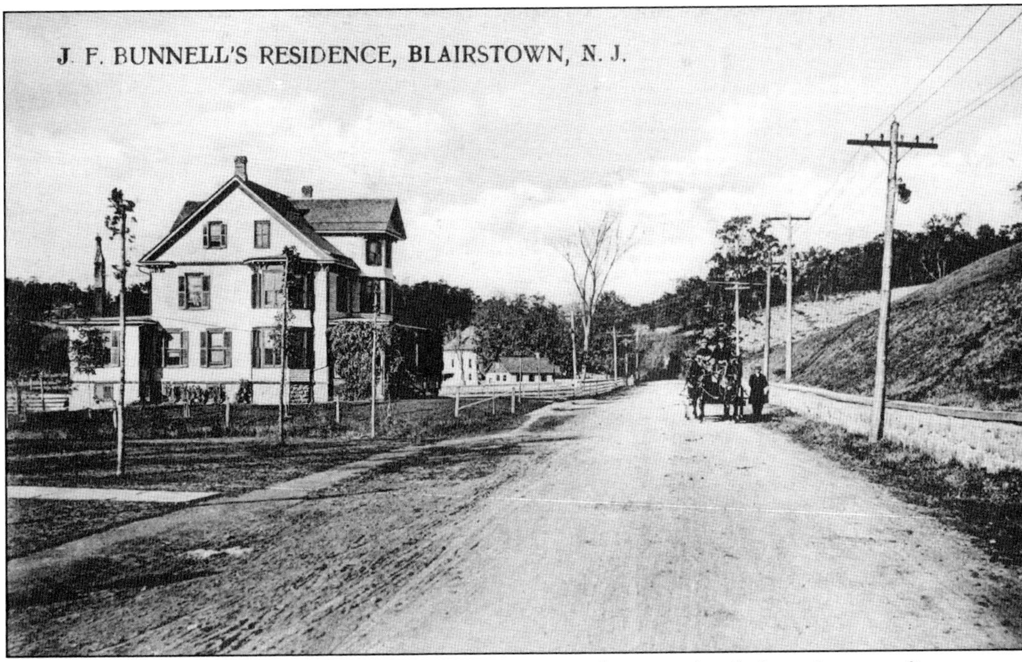

John Fletcher Bunnell lived in this opulent home on Park Street, just below the sprawling campus of Blair Academy. Bunnell had a successful carriage manufacturing business and was a ruling elder of the Presbyterian church. He also served as the first worshipful master of Blairstown Lodge No. 165, Free and Accepted Masons when it received its charter in 1893.

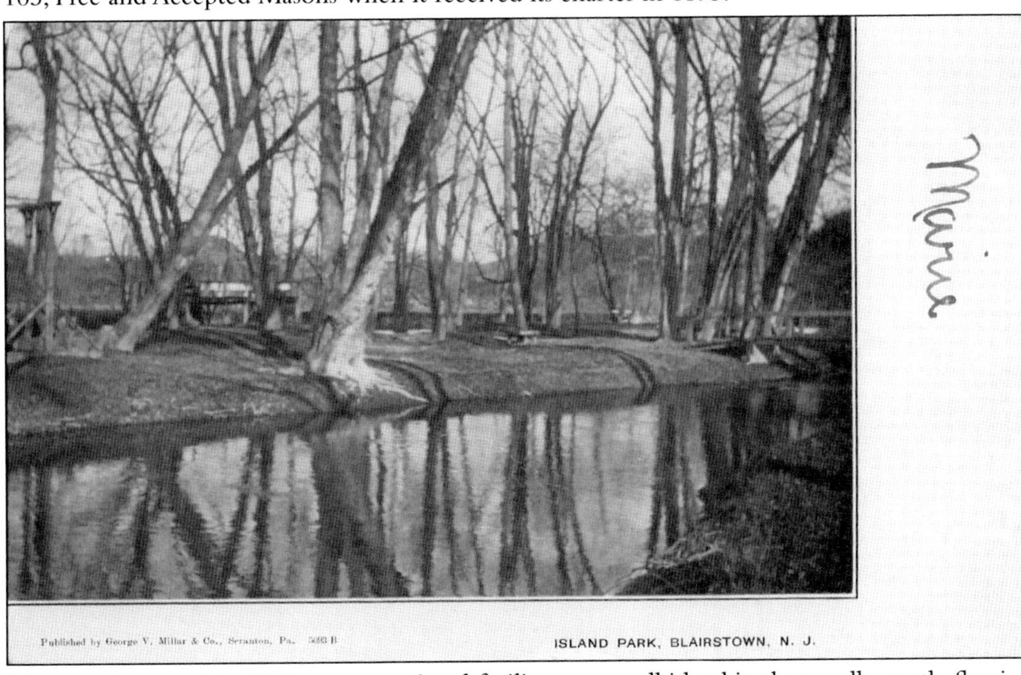

Island Park opened in 1902 as a recreational facility on a small island in the usually gently flowing Paulinskill River. Residents got there via a wooden footbridge located behind the current Blairstown Ambulance Corps building. In the early 1930s, the island was virtually eliminated when the present Route 94 was built and the highway bridge obliterated this pretty spot.

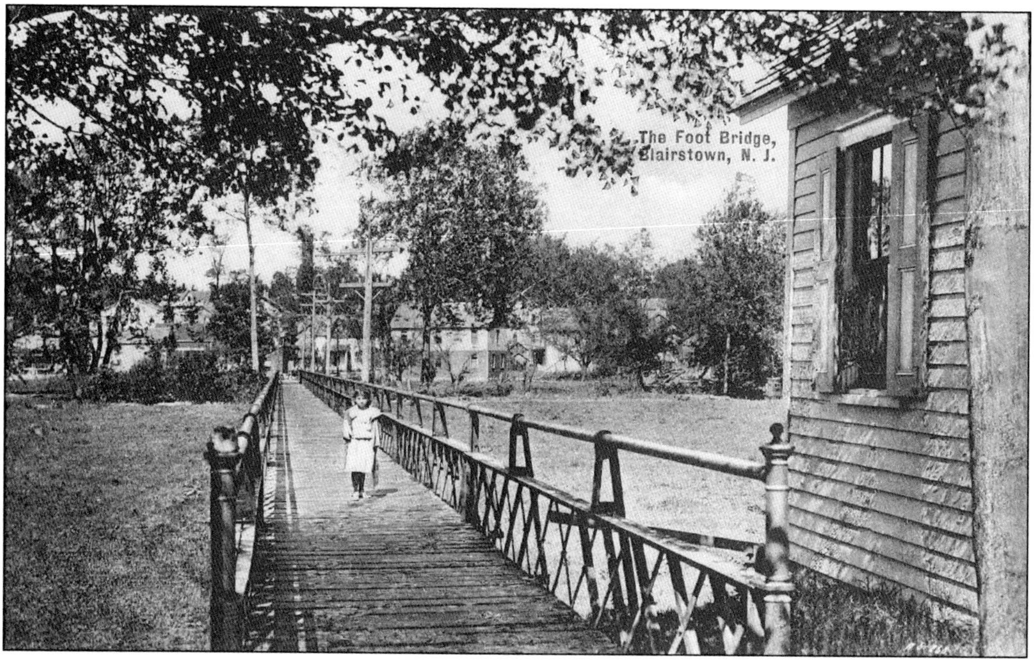

One cannot visit Blairstown without noticing the unusual footbridge that runs south from the town and crosses the meadows and the Paulinskill River. The original structure was built of wooden planks with an iron railing in 1877 by John I. Blair as a main artery between the village and his Blairstown Railway depot. Over the years, and with the help of boisterous local youths, the wooden bridge deteriorated, and a decision was made in 1892 to replace it. After heated debate over a replacement footbridge versus a new auto bridge, the former won out and, with a combination of municipal funds and a monetary gift from Blair himself, a new steel bridge was completed in 1893 and dedicated on August 22, Blair's 91st birthday. With maintenance and upgrades, the bridge has survived many floods and today guides users to Blairstown's Footbridge Park.

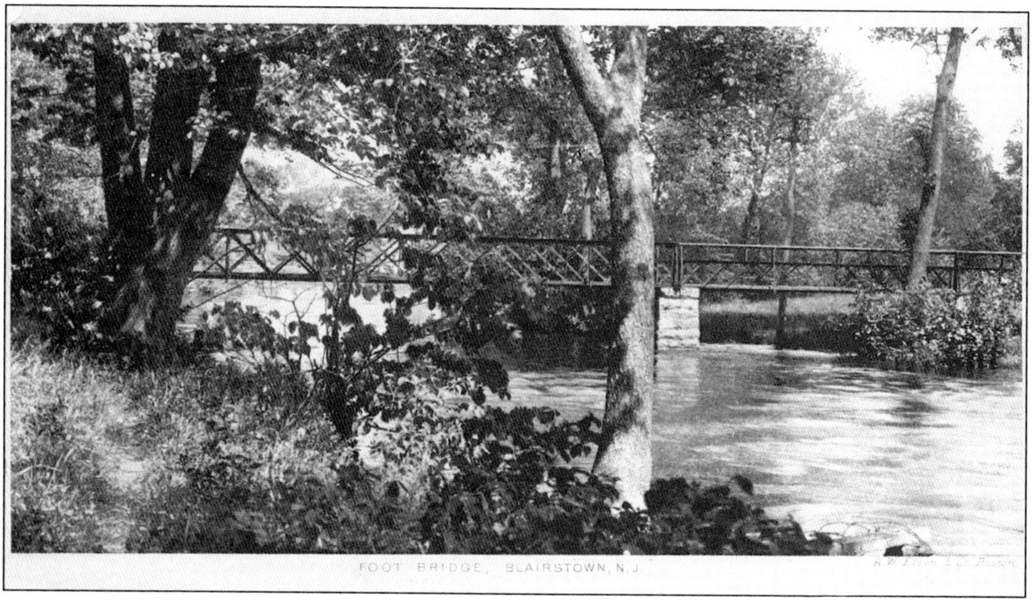

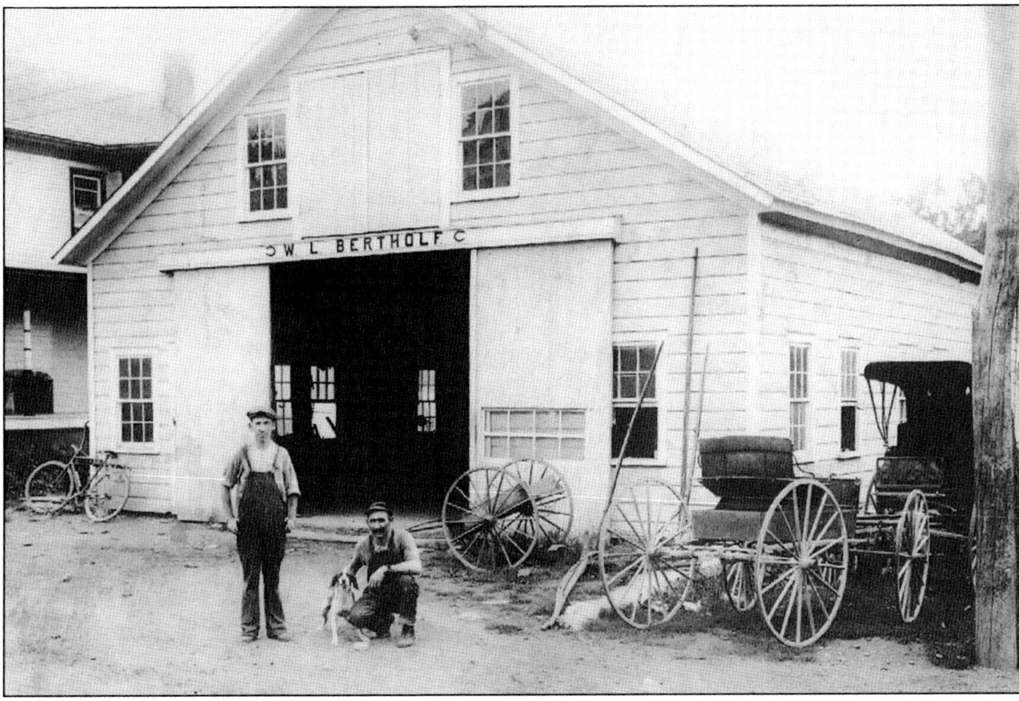

William L. Bertholf (kneeling next to his beagle hound) was born August 9, 1878, and was the owner of this blacksmith shop located just off Main Street. Standing beside him is his son Raymond H. Bertholf. When the photograph was taken, the horse was still king, but the automobile was already making inroads into the transportation business. The Bertholfs were still busy shoeing dobbin and repairing carriages, wagons, and bicycles.

JOHN H. HALL'S

LIVERY STABLE REAR OF PRES. CHURCH

BLAIRSTOWN. N. J.

LIVERY AND BAGGAGE DELIVERED 'PHONE CONNECTION

N. Y., S. & W. TRAINS—*Leave Blairstown for New York at 6:40 A. M. and 4:05 P. M. Arrive from New York at 12:08 and 6:41 P. M.*

Leave for Delaware at 9:15 A. M. and 4:30 P. M. Arrive from Delaware at 1:00 and 7:30 P. M.

DRIVES AND DISTANCES FROM BLAIRSTOWN.

Flatbrookville,	11 M	Swartswood Lake,	10 M	Hackettstown,	16 M	Stroudsburg,	18 M
Newton,	14 M	Johnsonburg,	6 M	Washington,	20 M	Hainesburg,	6 M
Millbrook,	9 M	Stillwater,	6 M	Belvidere,	15 M	Water Gap	15 M
Bushkill,	13 M	Marksboro,	3 M	Hope,	6 M	Cedar Lake,	1 M

John H. Hall operated one of Blairstown's livery stables in a building located behind the First Presbyterian Church. Hall provided baggage and livery service between the village and other nearby communities, as well as to and from the New York, Susquehanna and Western Railroad station, and even had the courtesy to include the railroad's schedule on his advertising cards.

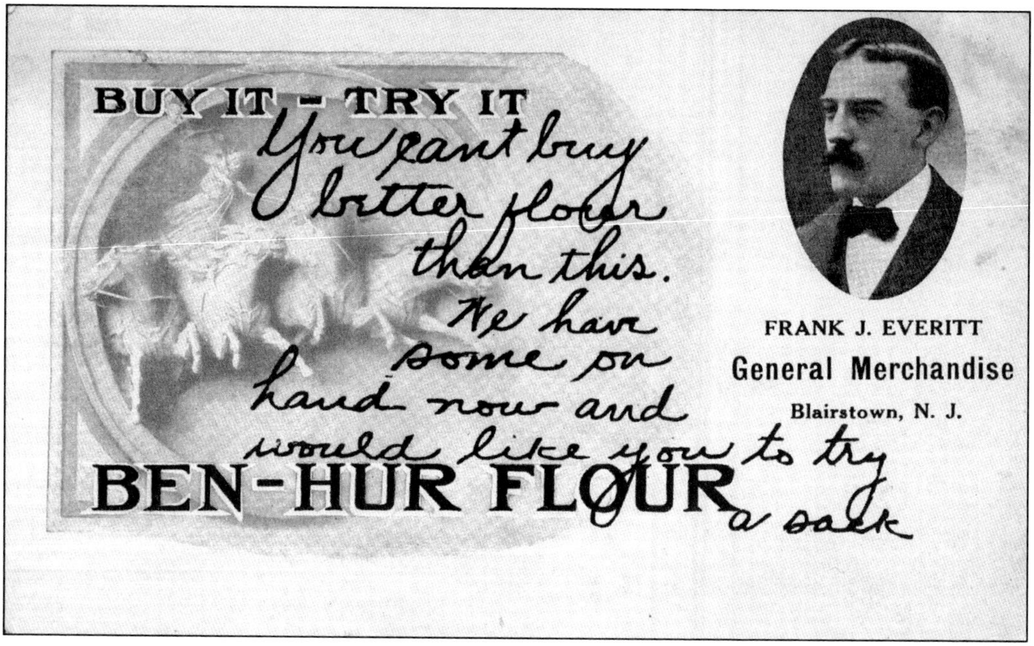

Advertising cards were an efficient way to reach rural residents and alert them to the wonderful new merchandise and services that were constantly coming into the marketplace in the early part of the 20th century. Blairstown merchant Frank Everitt sent this promotion for Ben-Hur Flour (above) to his regular customers, even taking time to add a personal note. Before Blairstown had its own dentist, the wandering Dr. J. R. Gibbs (below) was essential to the good oral health of country folks. Practitioners like Gibbs traveled the region, spending a day or so in each municipality treating the maladies of the mouth. Somnoform was primarily ethyl chloride or hydrochloric ether, a local anesthetic developed in France in 1901. Several of its minor components, methyl chloride and ethyl bromide, were considered poisonous, and its use was curtailed after 1931.

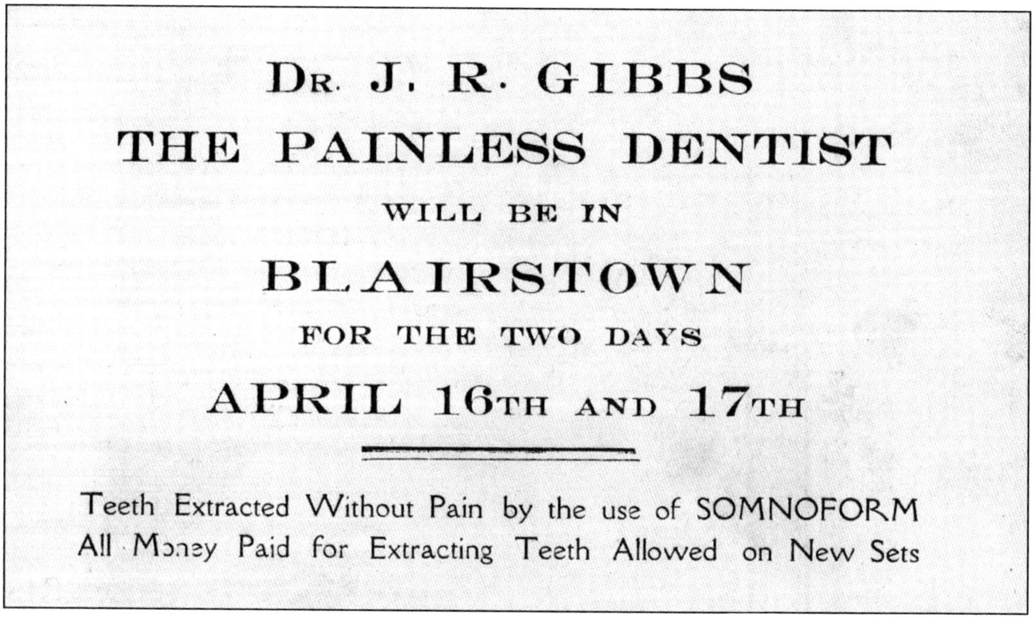

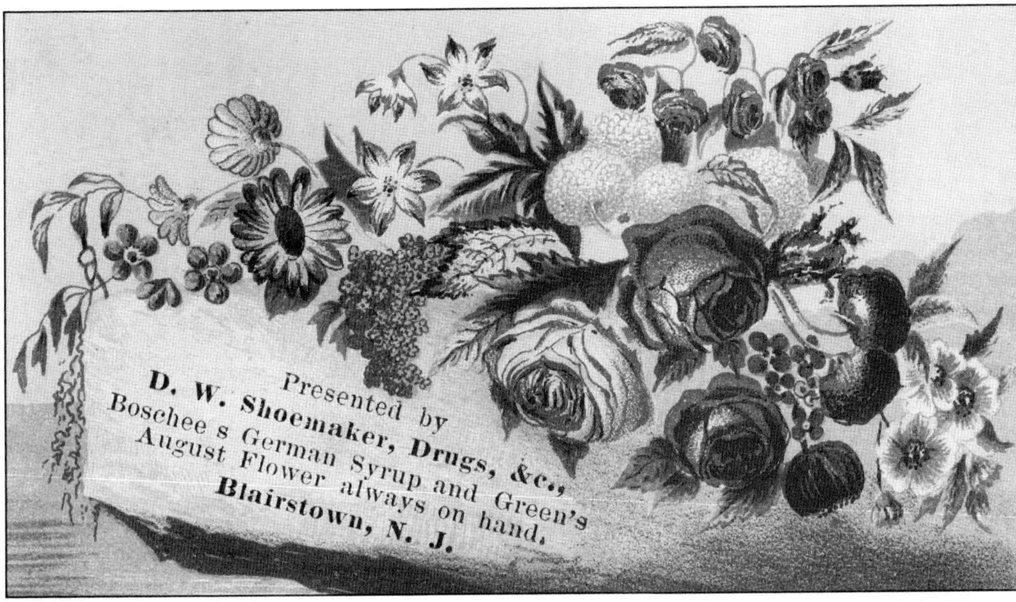

In a simpler time, D.W. Shoemaker touted the values of Boschee's German Syrup and Dr. Greene's August Flower. The syrup was promoted as a remedy for consumption, coughs, colds, croup, bronchitis, and asthma. The flower was used to treat a variety of digestive disorders. Both drugs were marketed by George Gill Green, a New Jersey native and Civil War veteran, and both were largely laudanum, a potent narcotic.

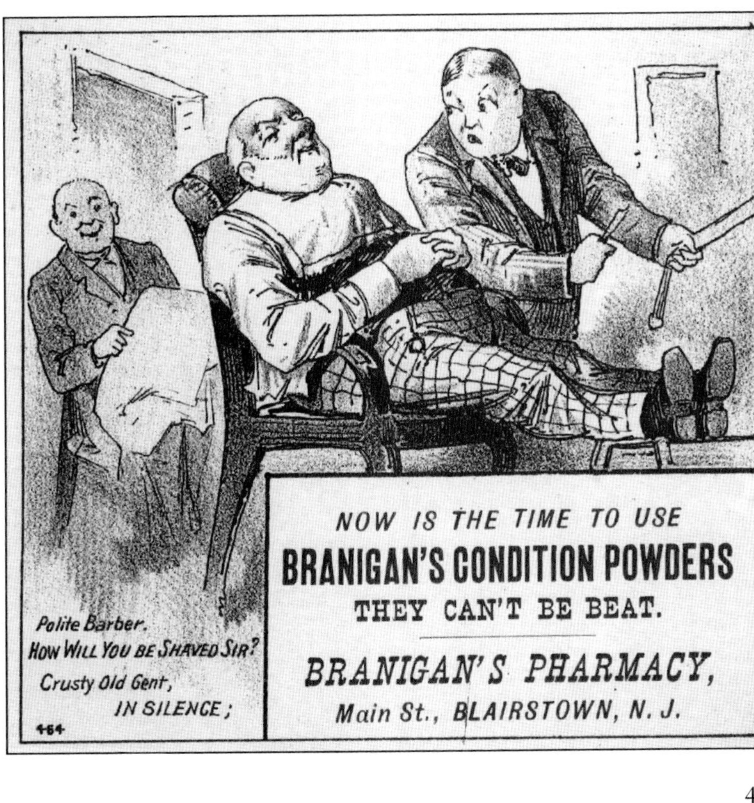

Branigan's Pharmacy on Blairstown's Main Street developed its own line of "condition powders," probably some type of effervescent bicarbonate of soda used to treat indigestion or dyspepsia. No doubt the "crusty old gent" in the barber chair could have used a dose of Branigan's Powders to cure his ill temperament.

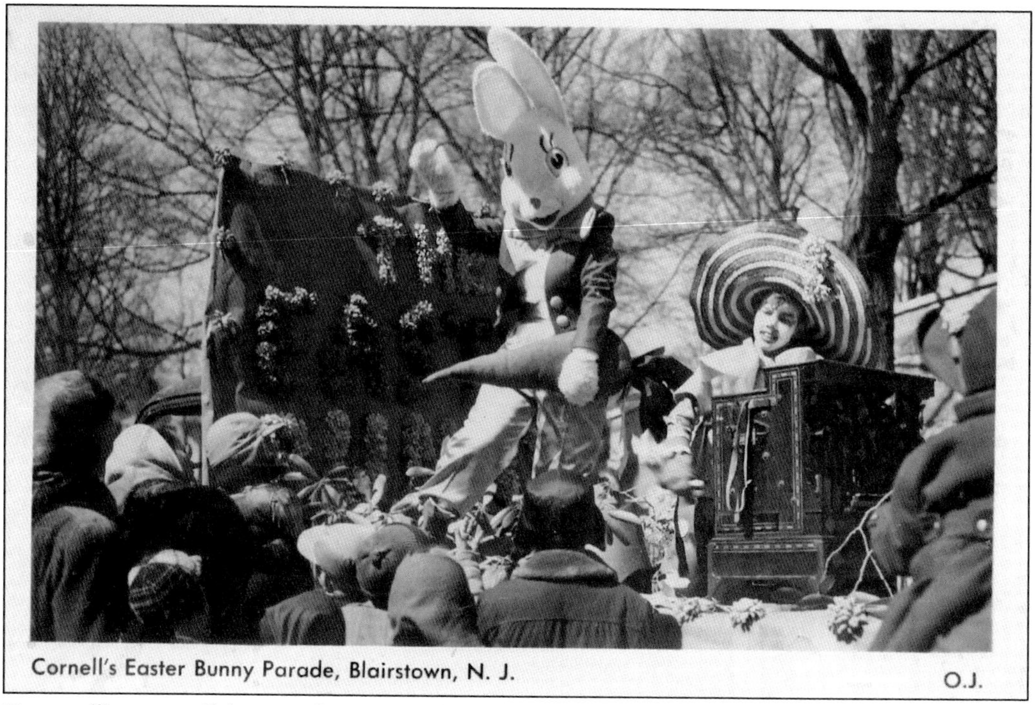

Cornwell's was well known for its 5 and 10 Cent Store on Main Street, but the firm's Easter Bunny Parade had to be one of the high water marks of the year for local children. Here Mr. Bunny himself greets a cadre of kids, whose style of dress suggests that this parade took place in the 1940s.

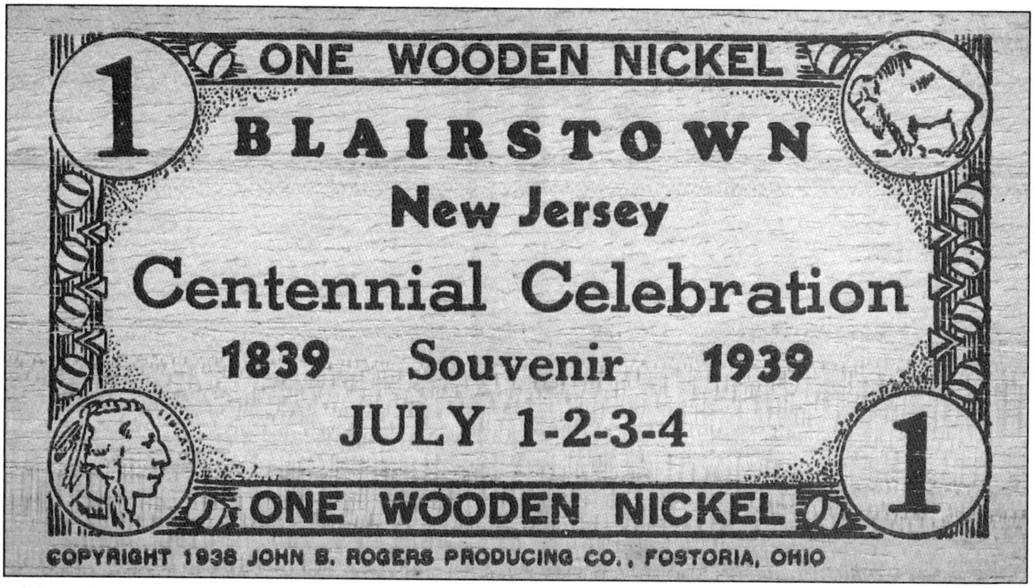

Although Blairstown was not officially incorporated until it was separated from Knowlton in 1845, local residents acknowledged 1939 as its centennial, for it marked the 100th anniversary of the renaming of the village after its patron and most famous resident, John Insley Blair. One of the souvenirs of the time was the traditional wooden nickel, actually made of thin balsa and redeemable for cash at the *Blairstown Press* office.

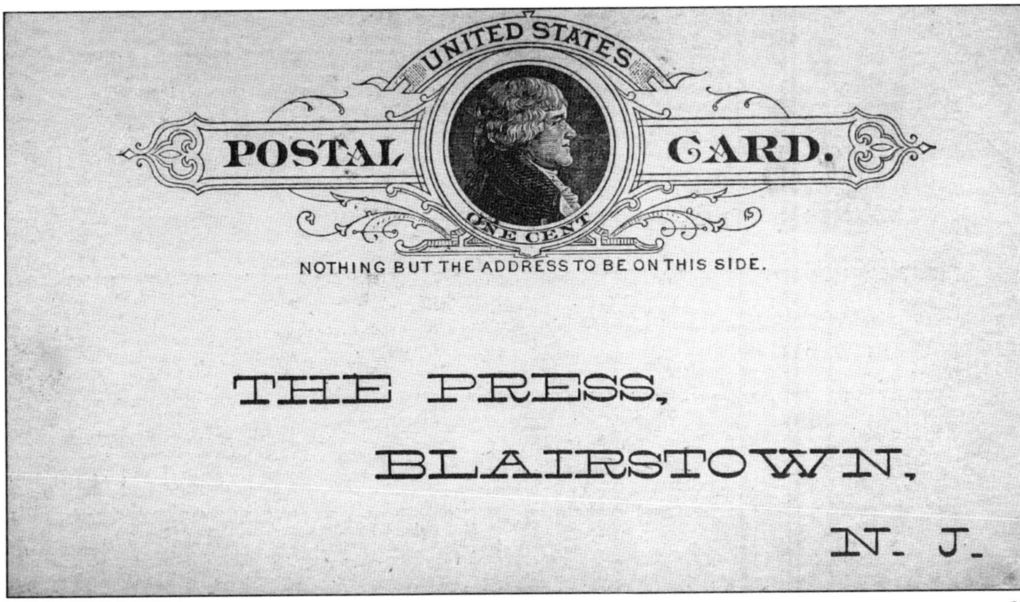

Prior to 1877, there was no newspaper serving the northern regions of Warren County. To fill that void, Jacob Z. Bunnell, a Blairstown native who had moved to Newton, published the first issue of the *Blairstown Press* on February 7, 1877. The 28-column weekly initially came out every Wednesday morning. This postcard was designed with a template back and used for the submission of wedding notices in the 1880s.

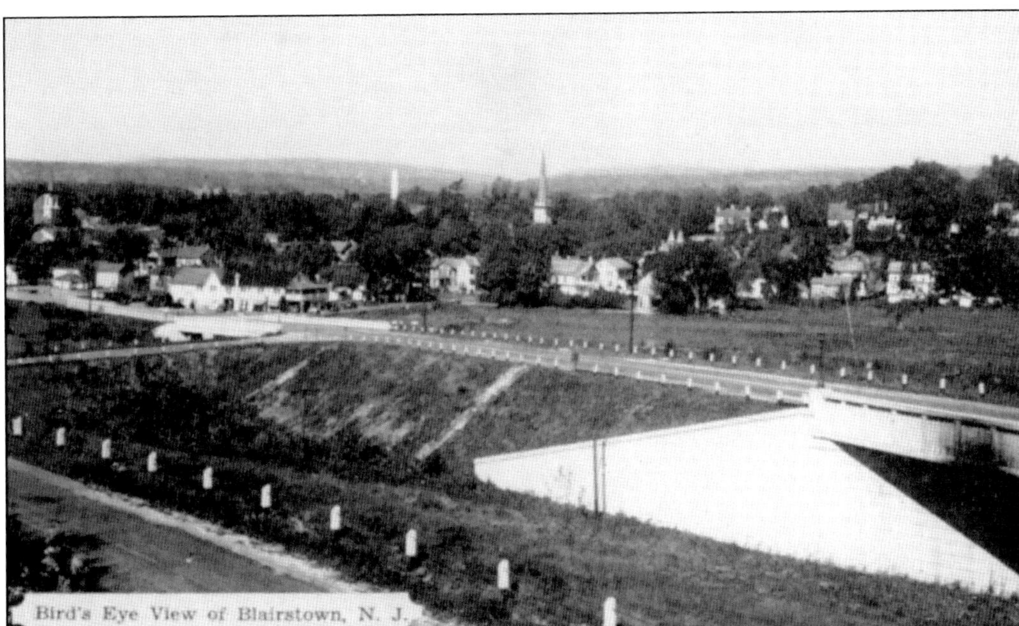

Route 94 bisects the center of this panorama of Blairstown taken sometime after May 1955, since the Methodist church spire on Academy Street is no longer visible. The smoke-stained bridge to the right crosses the main line of the New York, Susquehanna and Western Railroad while the bridge to the left crosses the Paulinskill. Within a few years, the NYS&W would abandon its line and tear up the tracks.

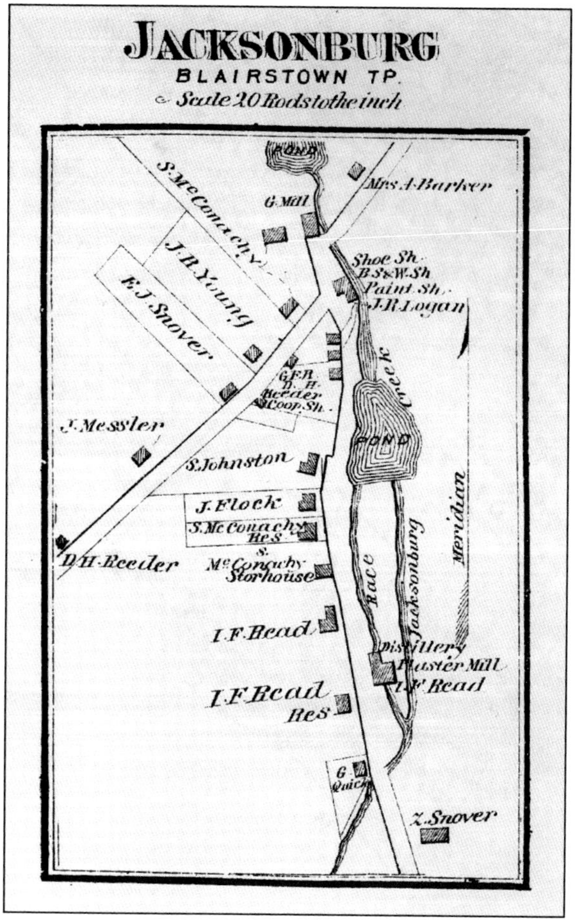

One of the suburban hamlets of Blairstown borough was Jacksonburg, located about a mile west of the village proper along the banks of Jacksonburg Creek. In 1882, Jacksonburg boasted a school, store, blacksmith shop, gristmill, wheelwright, distillery, and about 20 private residences. Applejack, or "Jersey Lightning" as it was commonly known, was made here and enjoyed by more than a few residents of northwest Warren County.

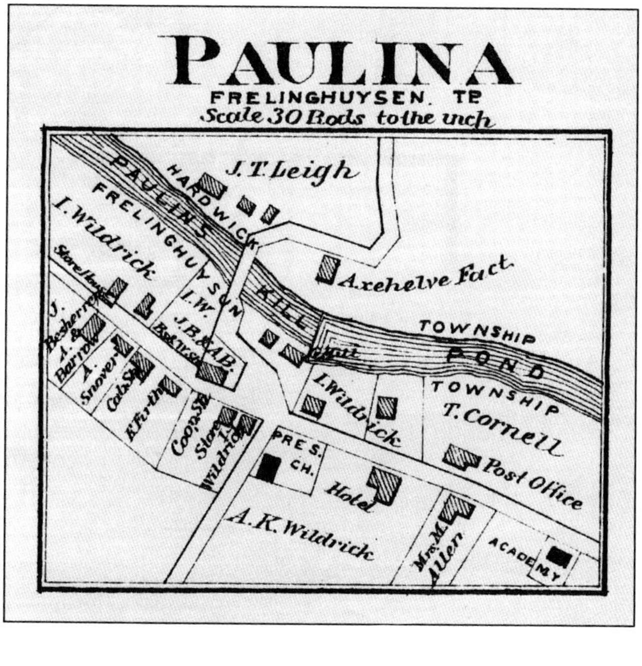

Located just northeast of Blairstown on the Paulinskill River is the settlement of Paulina, which was originally part of Frelinghuysen Township. Businessmen from Paterson dammed the river here in anticipation of constructing a large silk mill but found necessary waterpower more plentiful in Stroudsburg, Pennsylvania, thereby indirectly preserving the rural nature of this beautiful spot.

Three

The Suburbs
Hidden Treasures

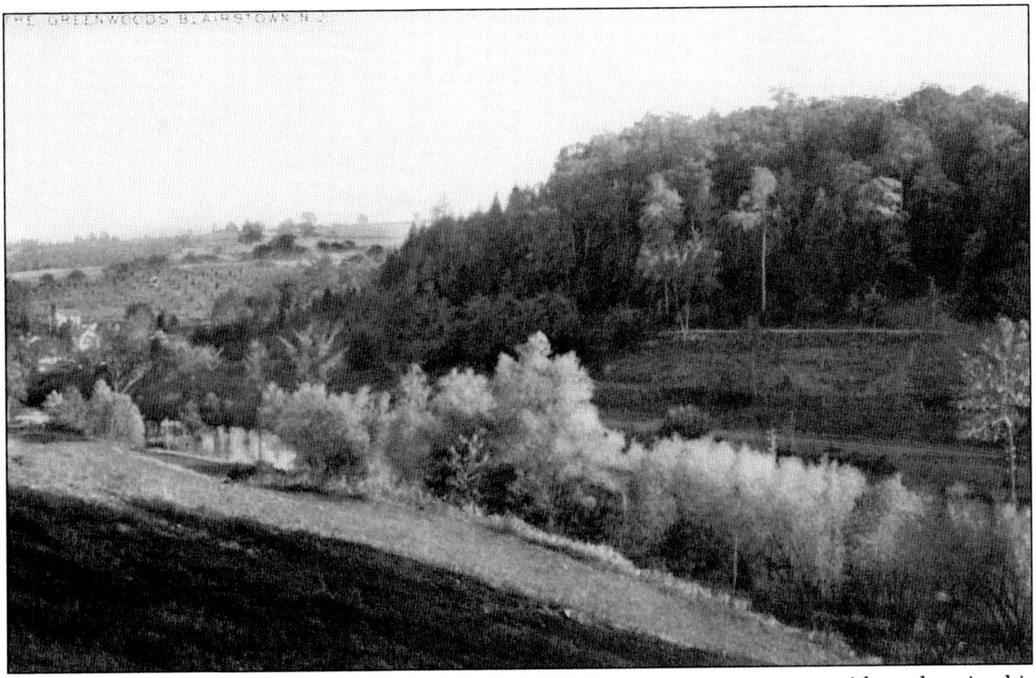

The beauty of the Paulinskill River Valley near Blairstown was never more evident than in this vintage view of The Greenwoods taken in 1908. Even in a black-and-white rendition, the unidentified photographer has managed to convey the impact of the flaming fall foliage. The Greenwoods, located at the intersection of Routes 94 and 521, got its name from the many hemlock trees that blanketed the hillside.

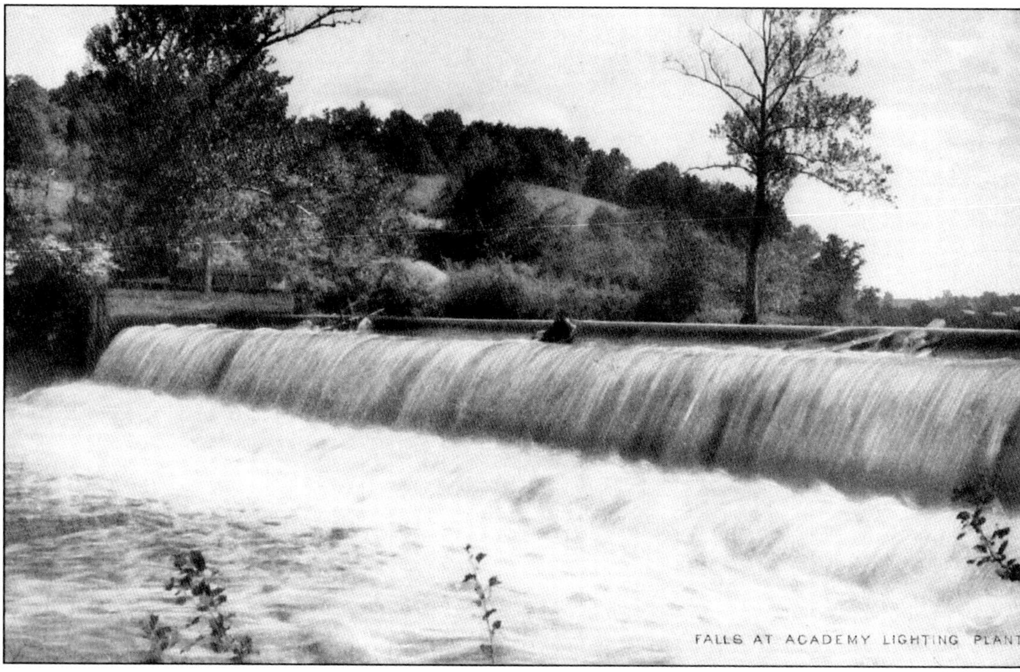

Paulina is located just northeast of Blairstown and was originally part of Frelinghuysen Township. It traces its origins to 1768, when William Armstrong built a gristmill there on the banks of the Paulinskill. In the 1890s (above), a group of Paterson businessmen constructed a dam at Paulina, hoping to harness its force to run a silk mill, but the project never materialized. In 1895, John I. Blair, desiring to bring the new marvel of electricity to the Blair Academy campus, erected a small hydroelectric plant at the south edge of the existing dam (at the right edge of the view below). Downtown Blairstown got electric service as an indirect benefit. On March 7, 1896, the 110-volt dynamo was started, delivering 50 amps of current to the village.

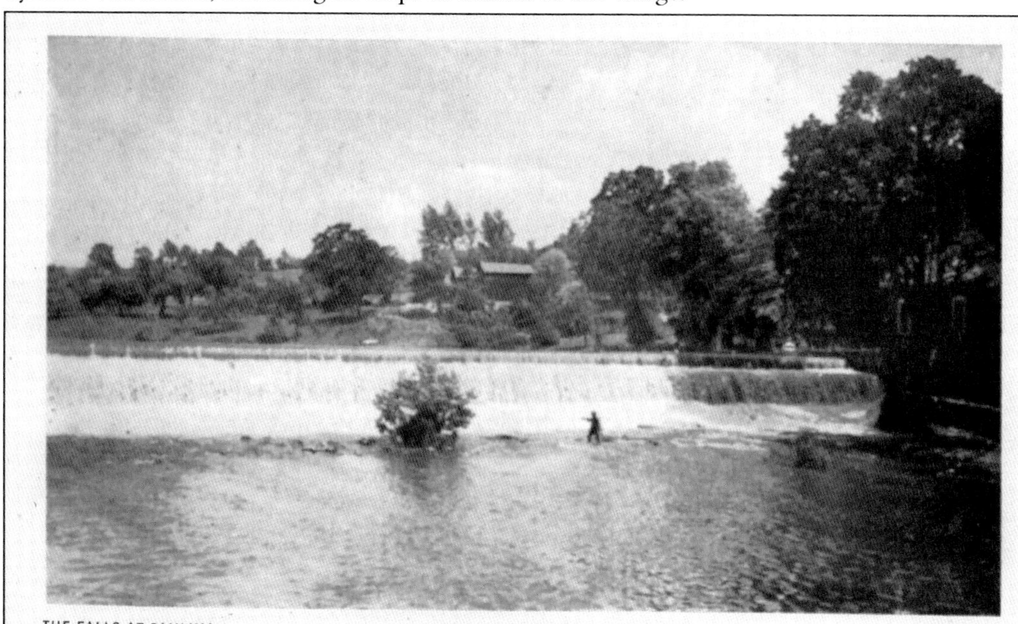

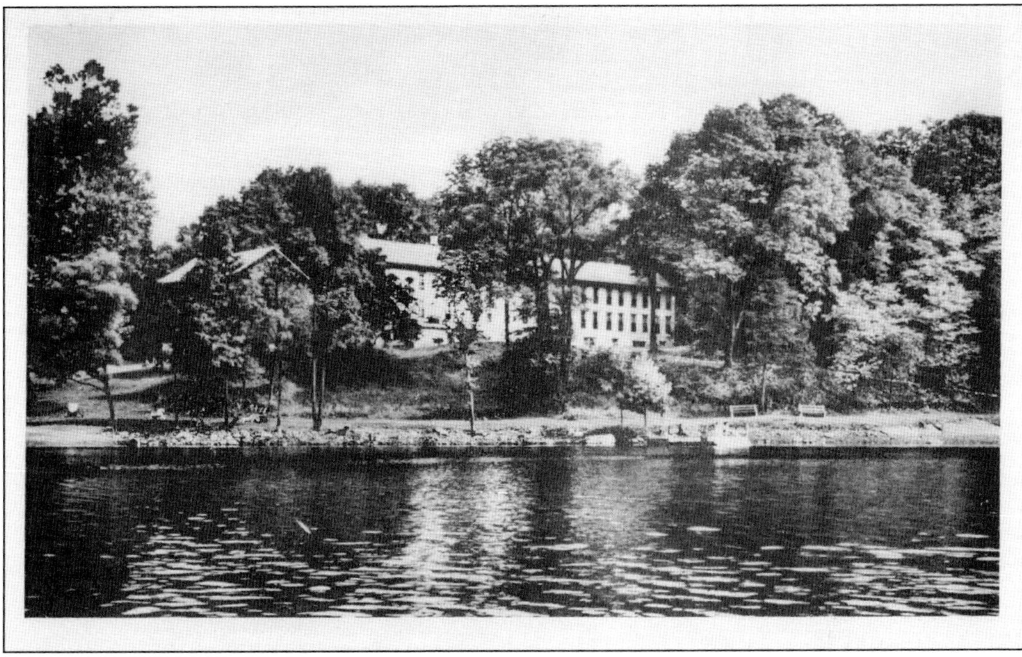

Blairstown was a popular vacation destination well into the 1900s. City dwellers, anxious to escape the urban smoke, dirt, and summer heat, would hop a train and head out for a week (or whatever they could afford) in the fresh air and open spaces of rural New Jersey and eastern Pennsylvania. Cedar Lake House, the first boarding facility in northern Warren County, opened in 1869.

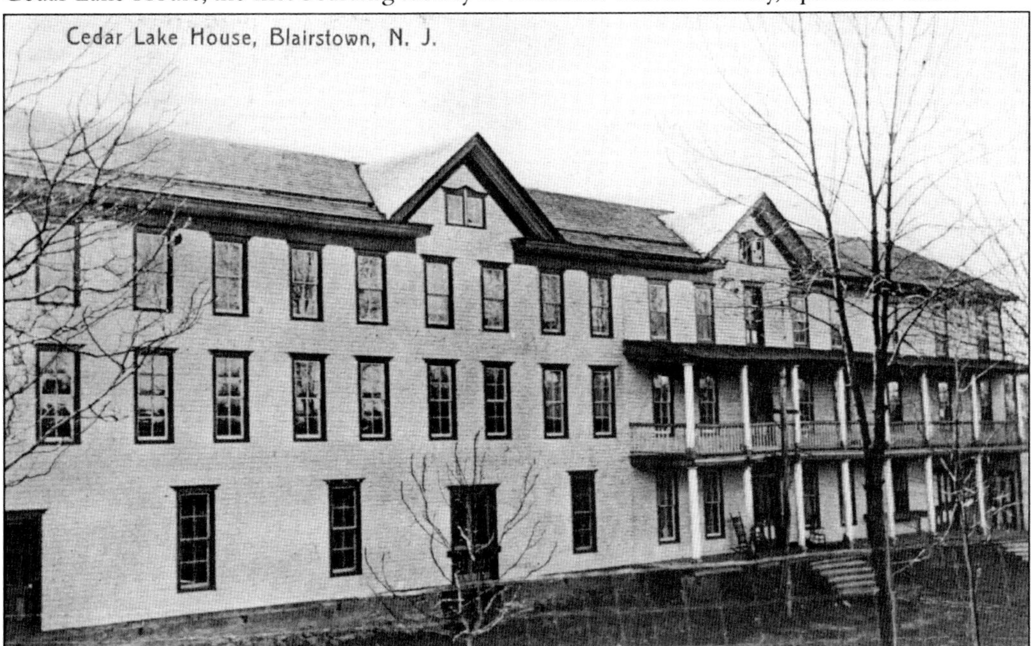

In 1903, Cedar Lake House was operated by Peter A. Lanterman, who advertised accommodations for 75 people at rates of $7 to $8 per week. It was described as a "delightful summer residence with all modern home comforts," which included well-appointed and well-ventilated rooms and electric lights. Lanterman also provided livery service to and from the NYS&W depot.

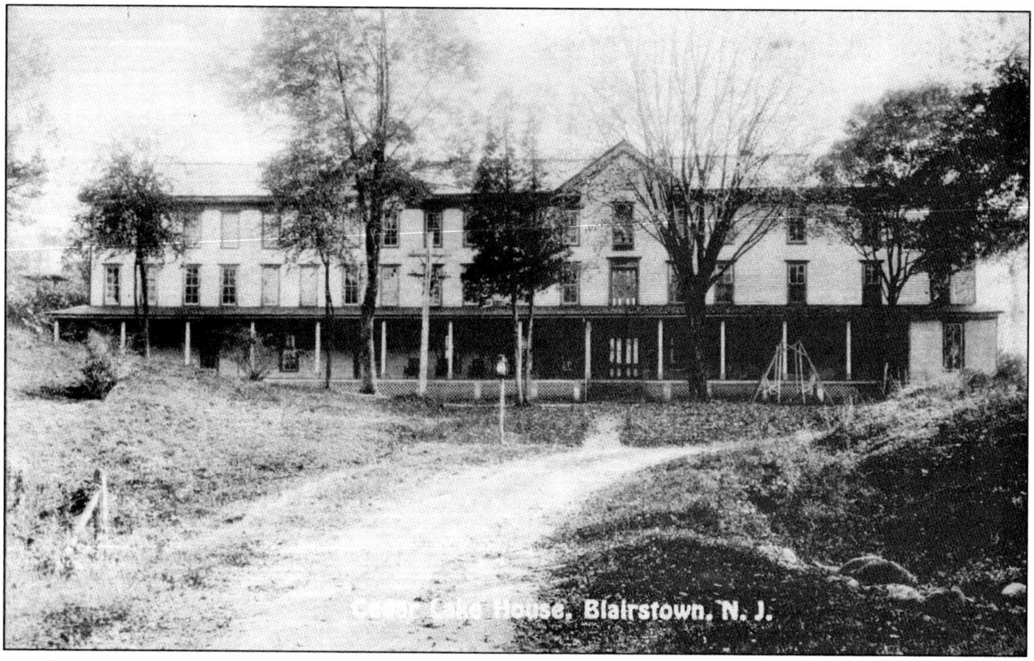

Porches waxed and waned on the Cedar Lake House like phases of the moon. Here the first floor veranda extends the length of the building while the second floor deck is missing completely (as compared to the view on the previous page). Fishing, boating, and swimming were popular pastimes at Cedar Lake. Guests could stroll on carefully constructed pathways or simply enjoy the quiet from a gazebo overlooking the water.

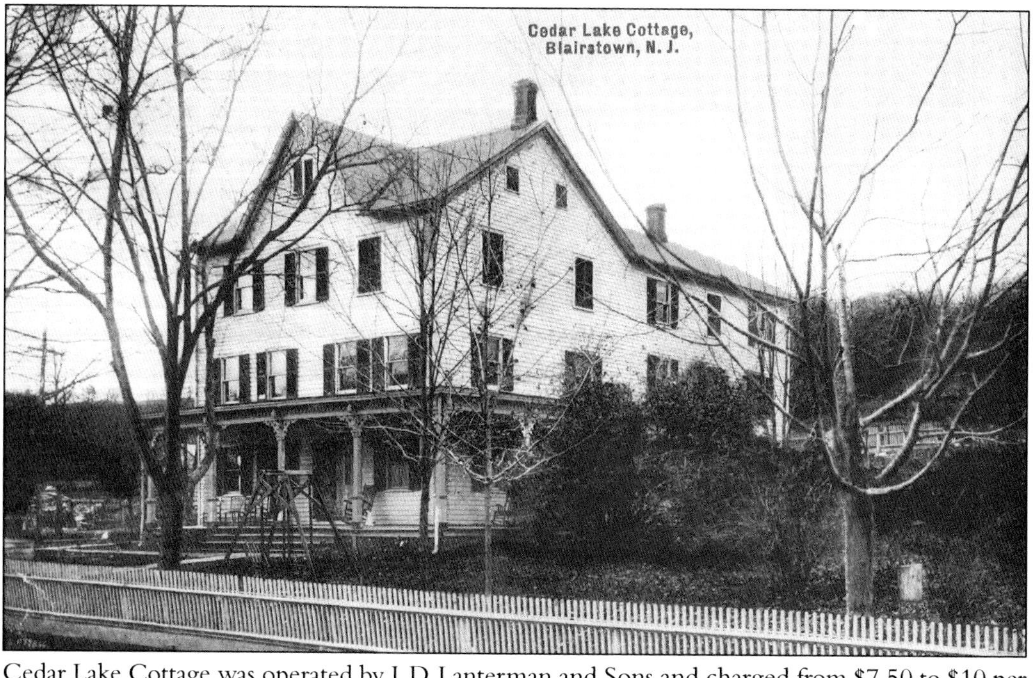

Cedar Lake Cottage was operated by J. D. Lanterman and Sons and charged from $7.50 to $10 per week. The cottage touted fresh milk, butter, and cream from the farm as well as assorted activities. A great table fare was necessary to keep guests coming back year after year.

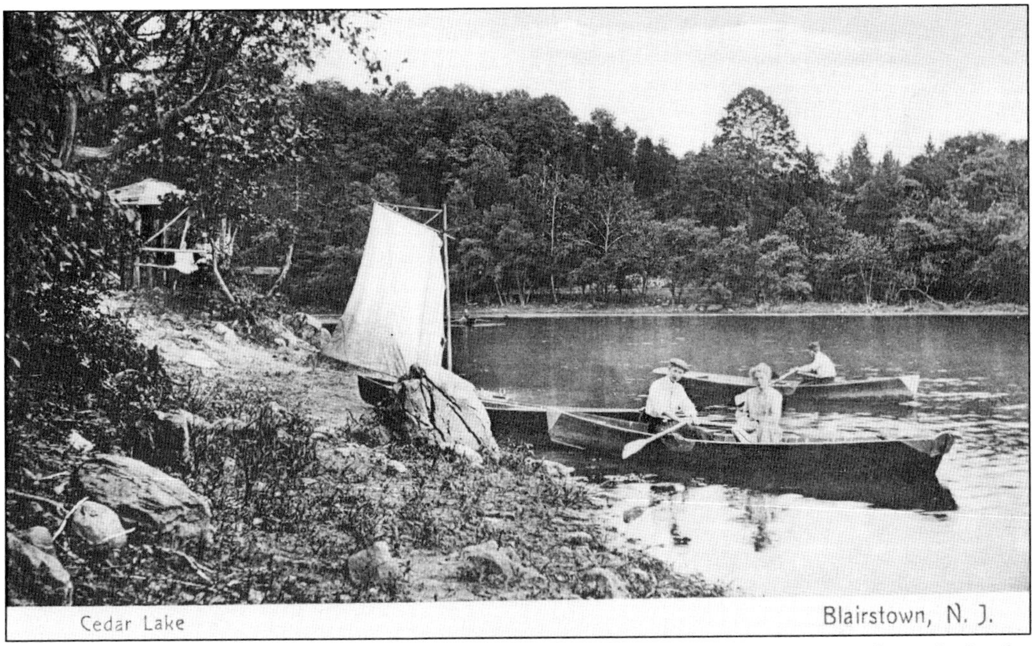

Originally known as Buttermilk Pond, the comparatively small Cedar Lake was still ample for the assortment of summer activities that it supported. Boating was always popular (above), and at one time a small steam-powered launch took guests on a leisurely tour around the perimeter. The first camp (below) was established in 1892, when a Princeton professor and some associates erected tents at the north end of the lake and roughed it for several weeks. In 1929, the Middlesex Council of the Boy Scouts of America established Camp Sakawawin at Cedar Lake and operated it there until 1947. To the left of the view is the Scouts tall, wooden watchtower. At dusk each evening, a counselor climbed to the top and bellowed, "All boats in," the sound echoing across the placid lake as the sun set slowly behind the Kittatinny Ridge.

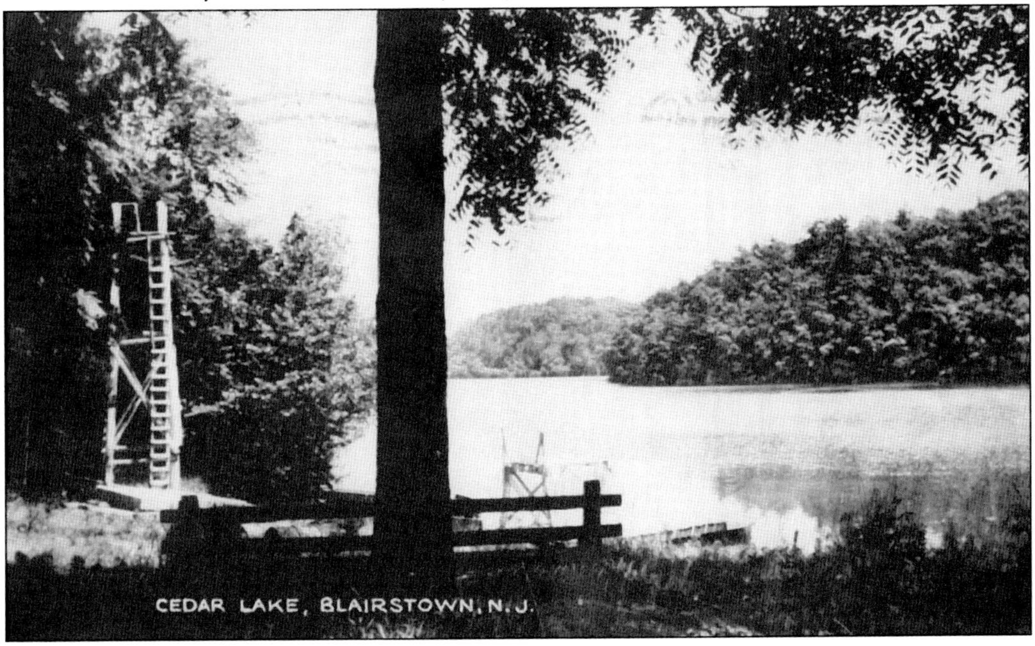

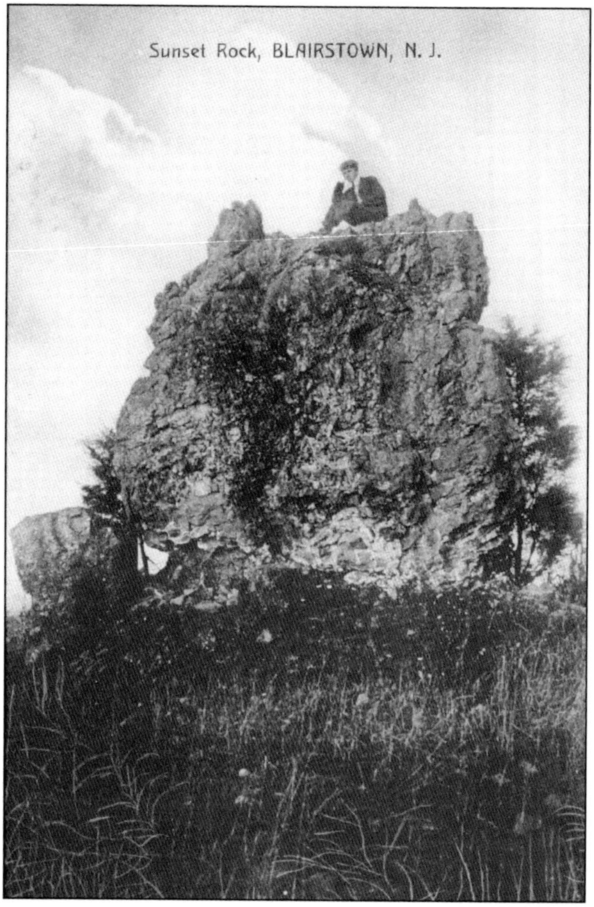

Sunset Rock, or Sheep Rock, as it was sometimes called, is a stack of stones located in a field between Cedar Lake and the former New York, Susquehanna and Western right-of-way. It stands almost perpendicular, approximately 25 to 30 feet high, but its many crevices and small ledges make it easy to climb. Local legend maintains that Native Americans used it as a signal rock.

Lake Susquehanna was created in 1928 when a local entrepreneur, Rocco Bunino, dammed a stream at the west end of Kalarama Meadow just off Cedar Lake Road to create a recreational facility. Kalarama was a stop on both the Blairstown Railway and the NYS&W and even boasted a tiny depot. When the stop was downgraded, an ill-advised attempt was made in 1891 to move the station to Vail.

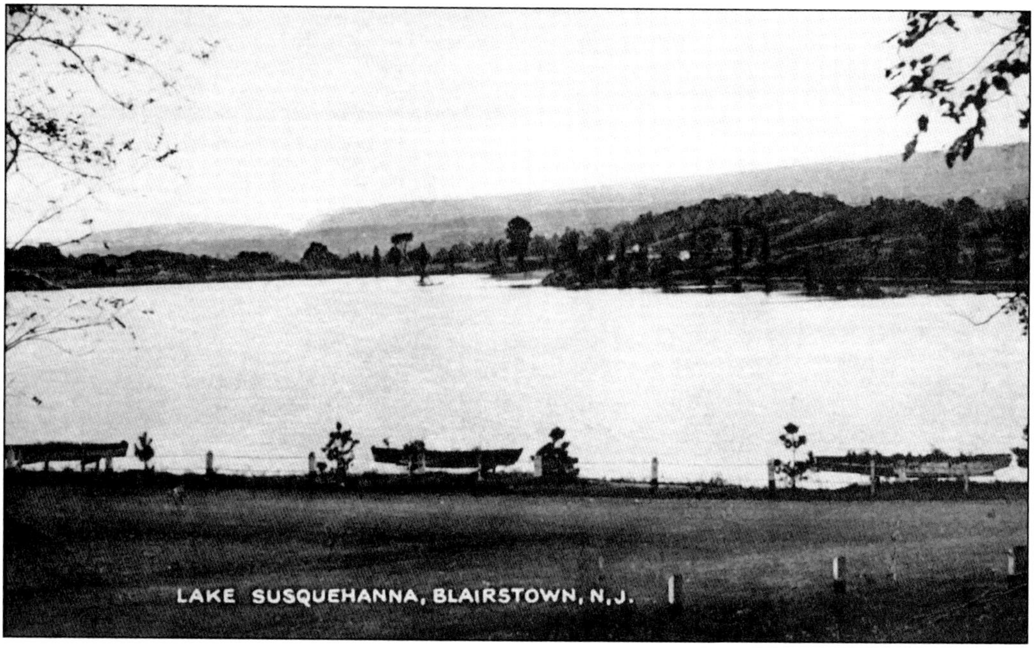

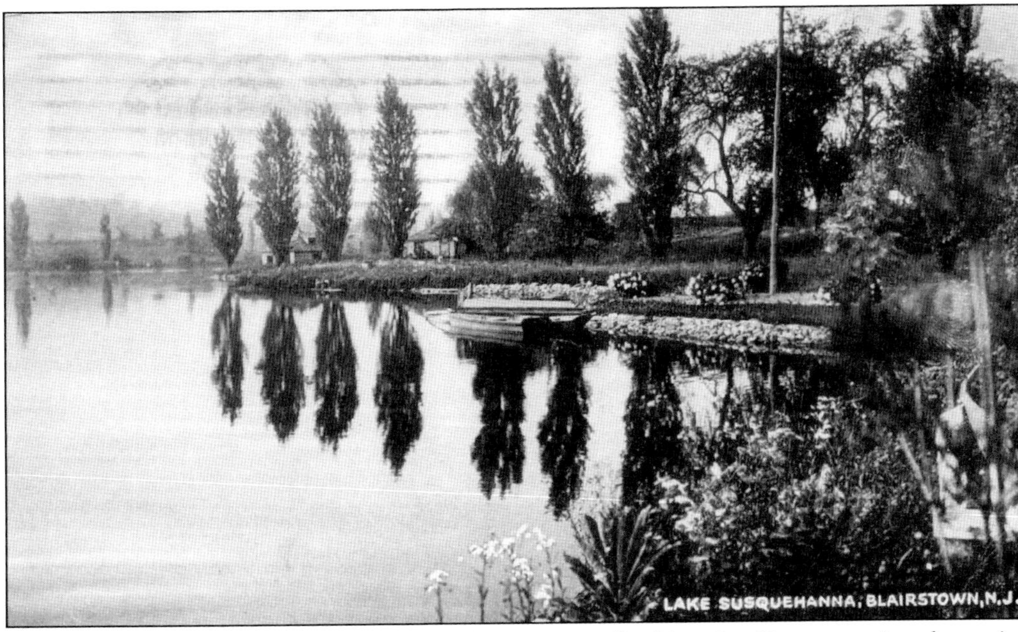

The NYS&W building department, remembering an earlier historic effort at moving the station in North Hawthorne, New Jersey, by jacking it up and sliding it down the rails, tried the same procedure with Kalarama but met with disaster as the depot toppled over and collapsed. For years, the NYS&W ran employee picnic trains to Blairstown Airport at Lake Susquehanna but ceased the practice in 1956 due to economic downturns.

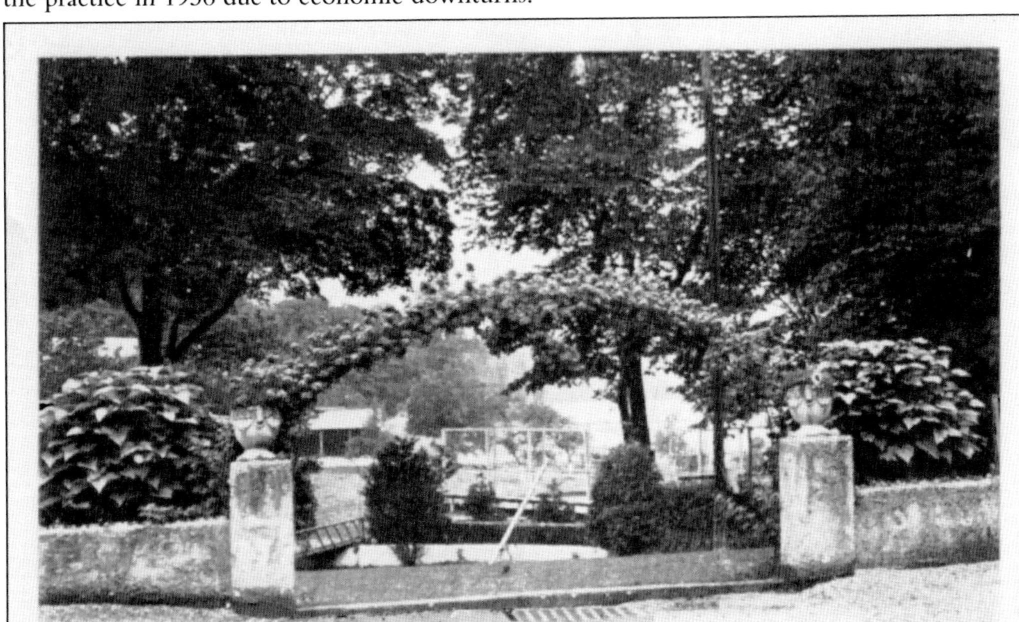

Bunino purchased acreage around Kalarama in 1920 and opened the popular Rocco's Villa Sunset resort in early 1927. This view, looking toward Lake Susquehanna, shows the area containing tennis courts and a swimming pool. The dining room specialized in Italian food, and old-timers remember going there with empty food pails to be filled with spaghetti for the family supper.

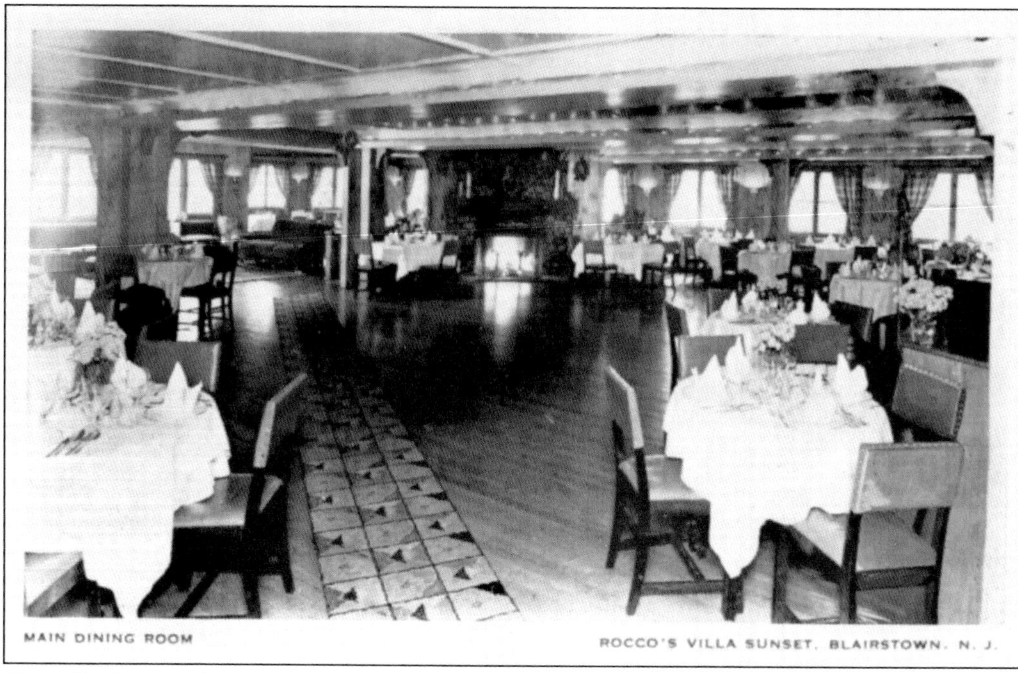

The Villa Sunset (above) eventually expanded to become a year-round attraction when Bunino cleared ski trails for winter activity, and it became so popular that he added an airport to serve his guests who could now fly in with their private planes. After World War II, Bunino expanded the airport by adding a fueling facility and even a flight school, using war surplus aircraft that he purchased from the federal government. In 1953 (below), Bunino sold the resort and moved to Milwaukee, Wisconsin, to become president of the Blatz Brewery. The new owners changed the name to the Sunset Lodge but still touted it as a year-round resort and aggressively sought out the catering and banquet business.

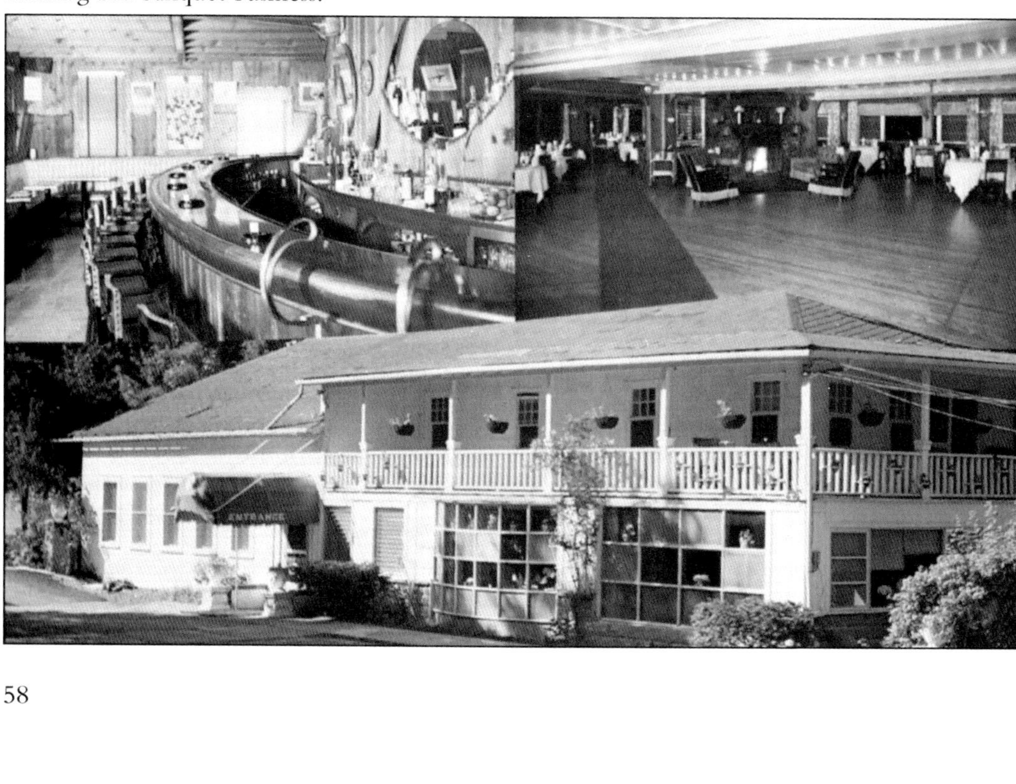

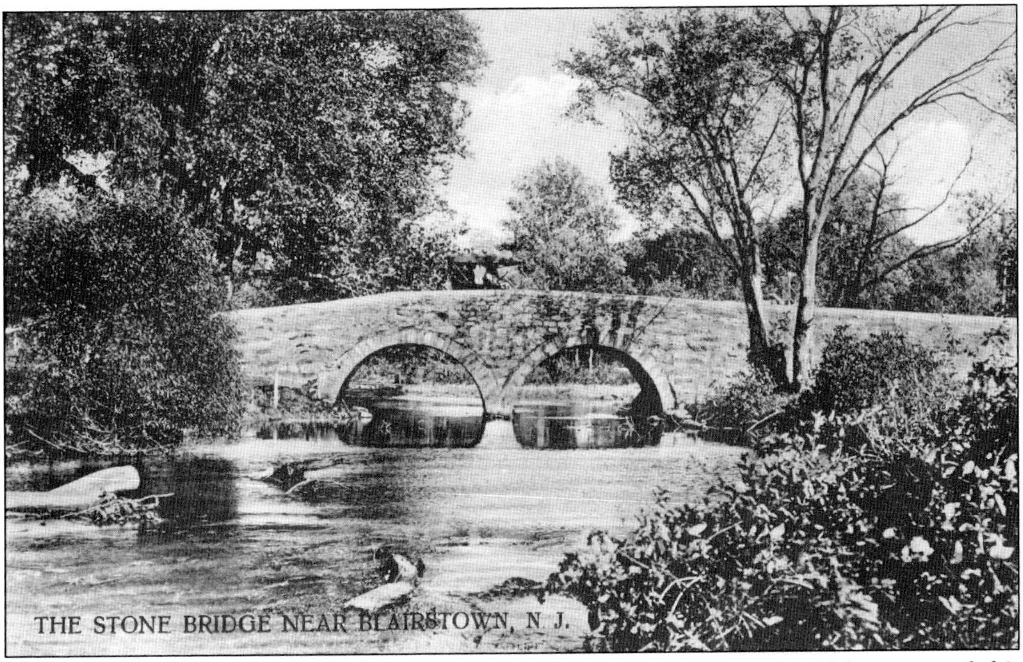

Driving from Rocco's to the present Route 94 via Lambert Road, one would have crossed this beautiful stone arch bridge, which once spanned the Paulinskill between the Blairstown Airport and today's North Warren Regional High School. The bridge survived into the 1980s but was removed to accommodate the widening of Lambert Road. Similar examples survive at Paulina and at Warrington in Knowlton Township.

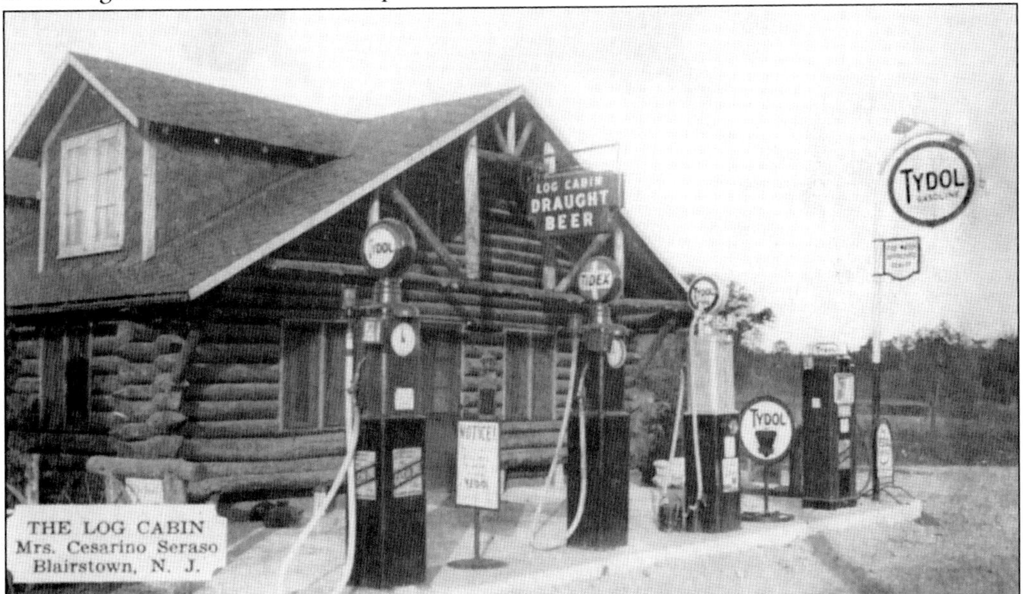

Tourists in need of fuel, either for their vehicle or themselves, could stop at the Log Cabin at the intersection of Route 94 and Mohican Road, where both gasoline and draft beer were sold. Mrs. Cesarina Seraso was the owner when this photograph was taken in the 1940s, and three grades of Tydol gasoline were available, with ethyl selling for 19.9¢ per gallon.

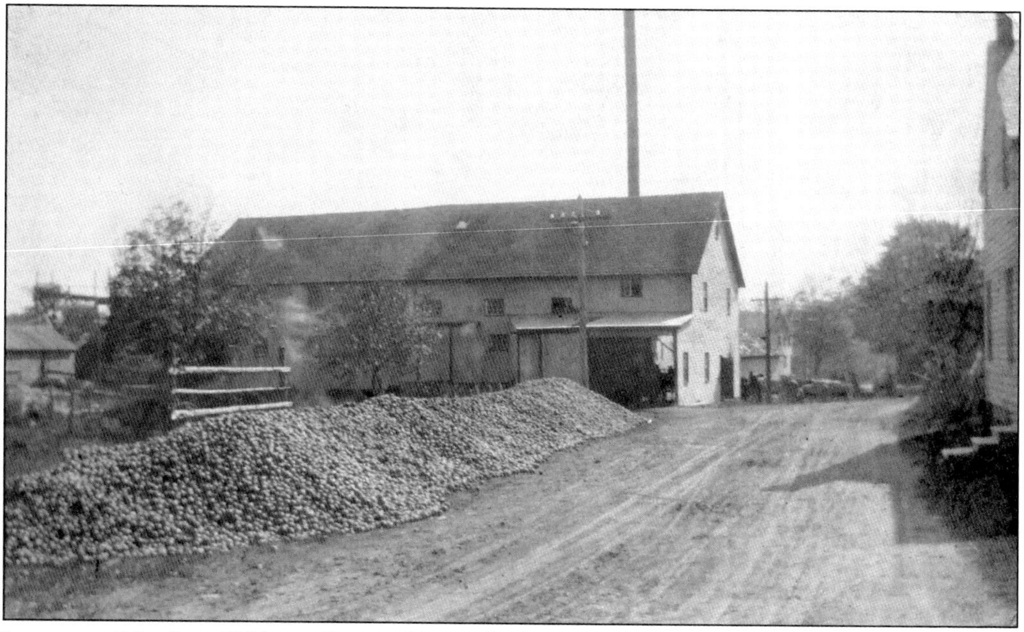

Just west of the Log Cabin on Route 94 was the hamlet of Jacksonburg, site of I. F. Read's Apple Distillery. Read's was the largest facility of its type in the state until Prohibition forced it to close in 1920. Farmers from as far away as Allamuchy delivered as many as 5,000 bushels of apples per week, resulting in the fruit being piled high behind the building on Jacksonburg Road.

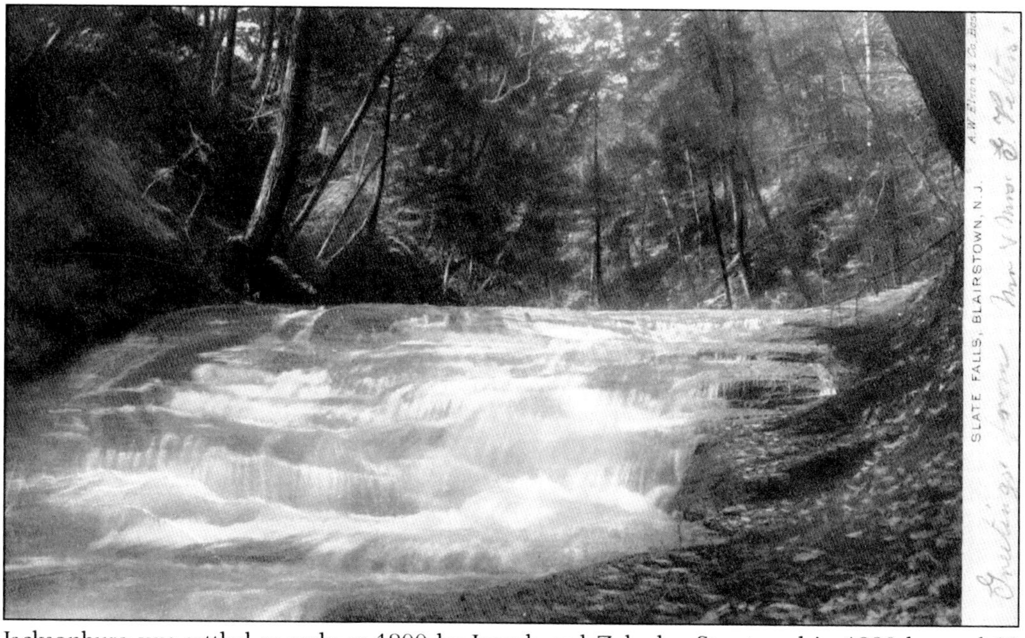

Jacksonburg was settled as early as 1800 by Joseph and Zebedee Stout, and in 1880 boasted 20 dwellings, a mill, Read's distillery, and a public school. Following Jacksonburg Creek north, the traveler finds Slate Falls, a beautiful scene surrounded by hemlock trees that takes him back to a simpler era.

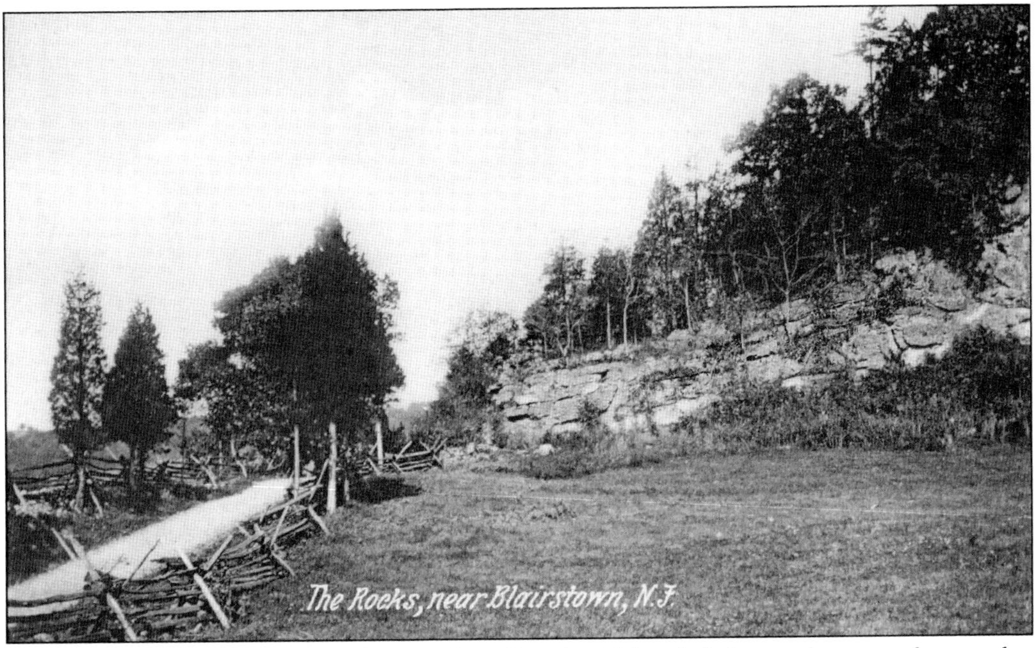

"The Rocks" are located alongside Bear Cave Road, which winds its way between the wooden fences seen at the left. The road was so christened because of the many crevices in the rock formations that were supposedly inhabited by local bruins. Whether it was true or not, the road still retains its unusual name today.

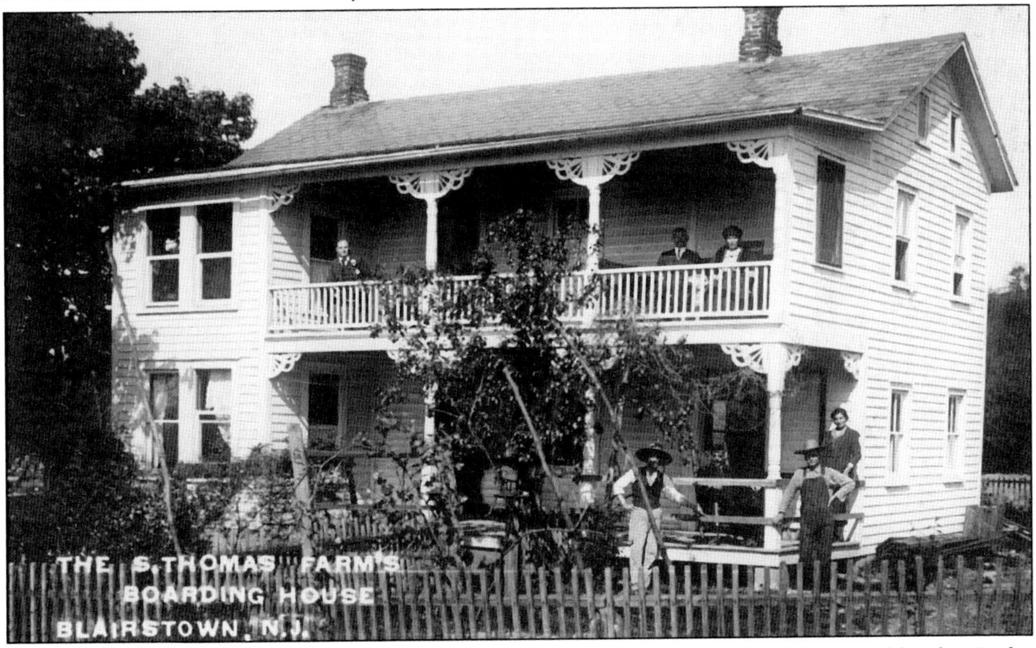

Vacationers seeking to escape the hot, dirty cities were not limited to larger resorts like the Cedar Lake House or Rocco's Villa Sunset. Local farmers also got a piece of the tourist pie by offering rooms with board at prices that were often much less expensive than the larger facilities. The S. Thomas Farm was one of these retreats that offered wholesome, delicious farm fare with all the rural amenities.

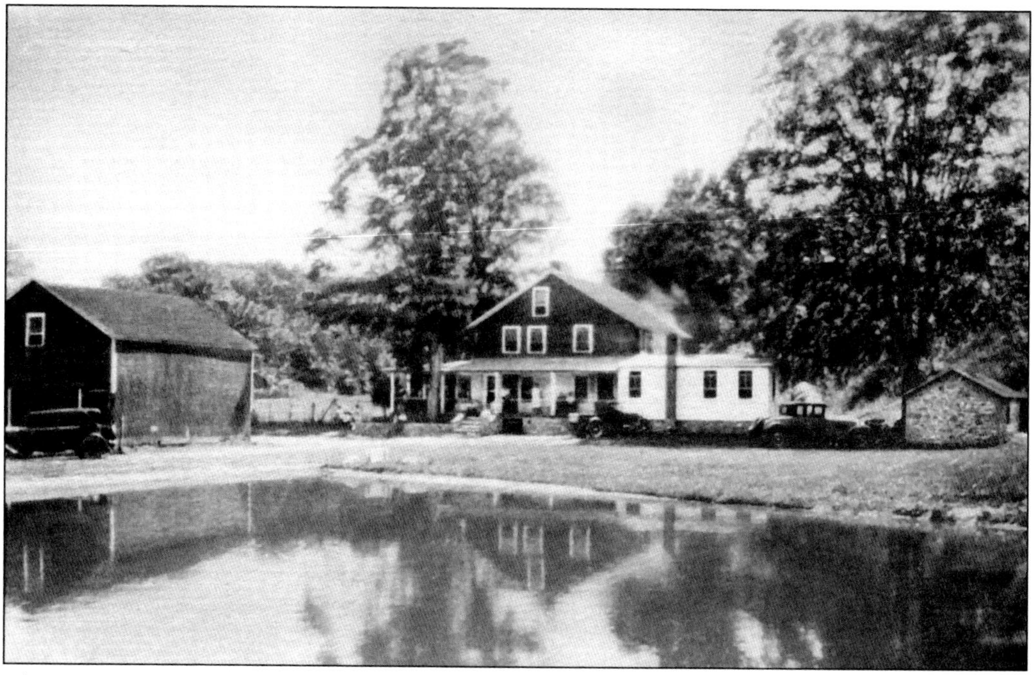

The Cecconi Farm on Mohican Road also rented rooms with meals at daily or weekly rates and offered weekend getaways. Guests could spend their time fishing, hunting, swimming, or just relaxing on the front porch. Cecconi's was one of the few local accommodations that was open year-round.

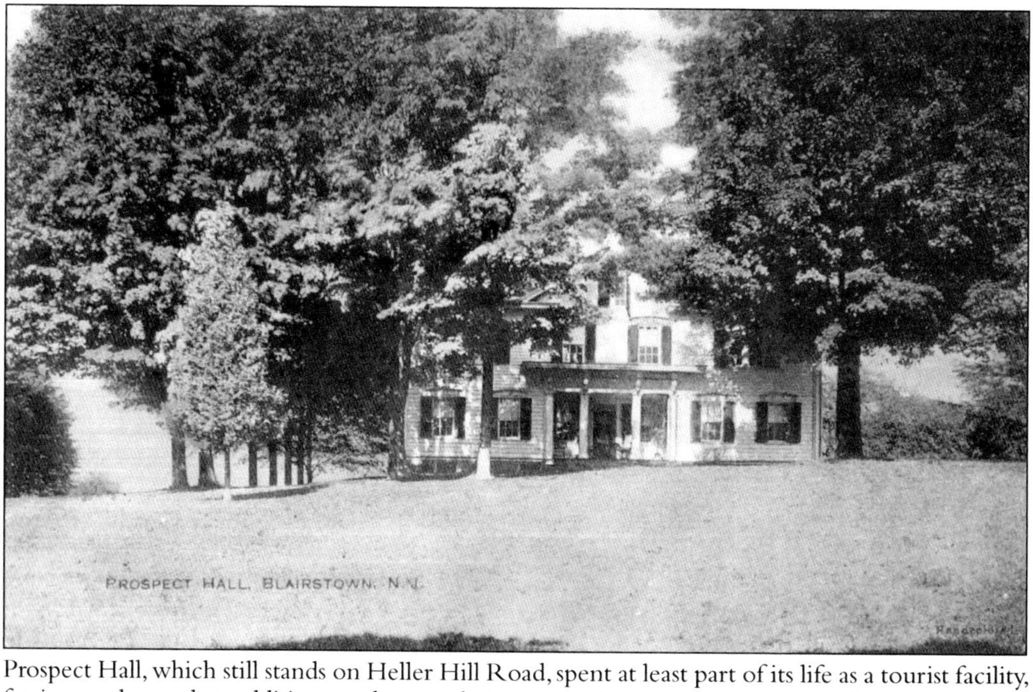

Prospect Hall, which still stands on Heller Hill Road, spent at least part of its life as a tourist facility, for it once boasted an addition on the rear that contained over 20 guest rooms. The sender of this card, Emma, says, "Alf and I are spending a few weeks up here having a dandy time."

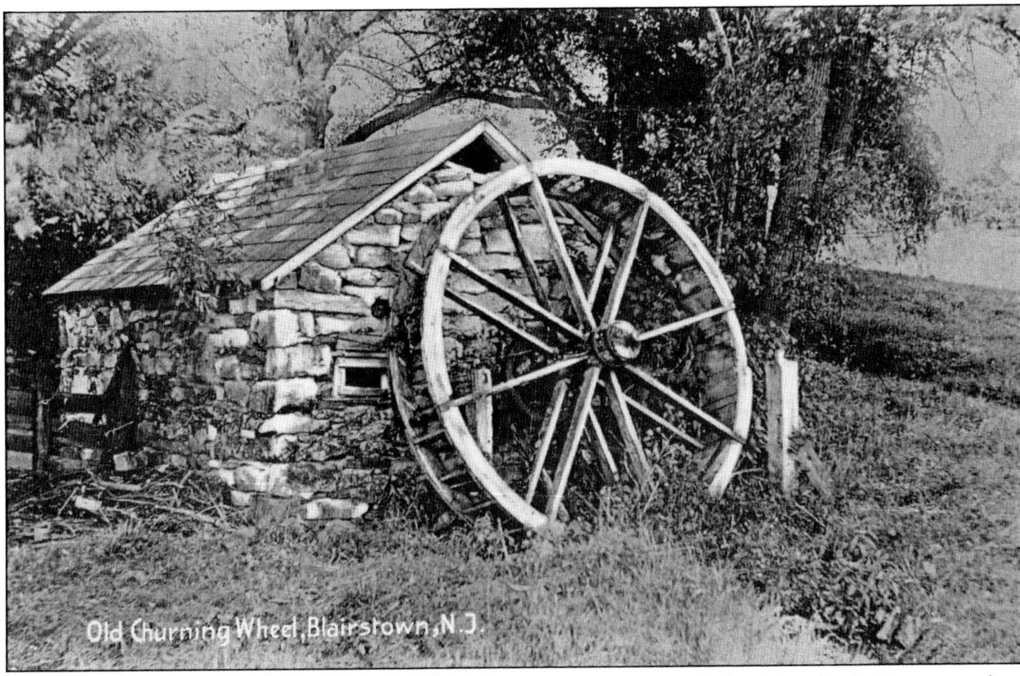

A vintage view shows the old springhouse on the property of the Hoagland Homestead on Hoagland Road. The sturdy limestone structure still stands, although the wooden waterwheel has long since disappeared. Local limestone was a favorite building material of early settlers because of its strength, durability, and insulating properties.

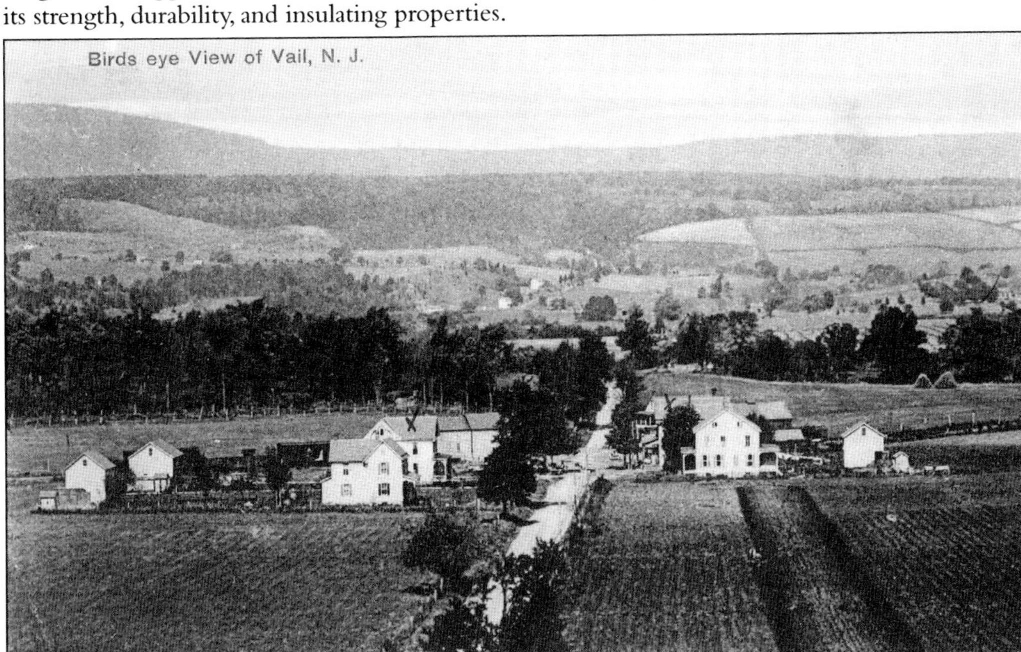

The suburb of Vail, four miles west of Blairstown borough, was a stop on the Blairstown Railway, and later the New York, Susquehanna and Western. The card's author, Lizzie, writes that the two *X*s mark the location of her house and store. The *Blairstown Press* reported on June 20, 1888, that I.W. Smith had opened a general store in Vail. Perhaps Lizzie was either his wife or daughter.

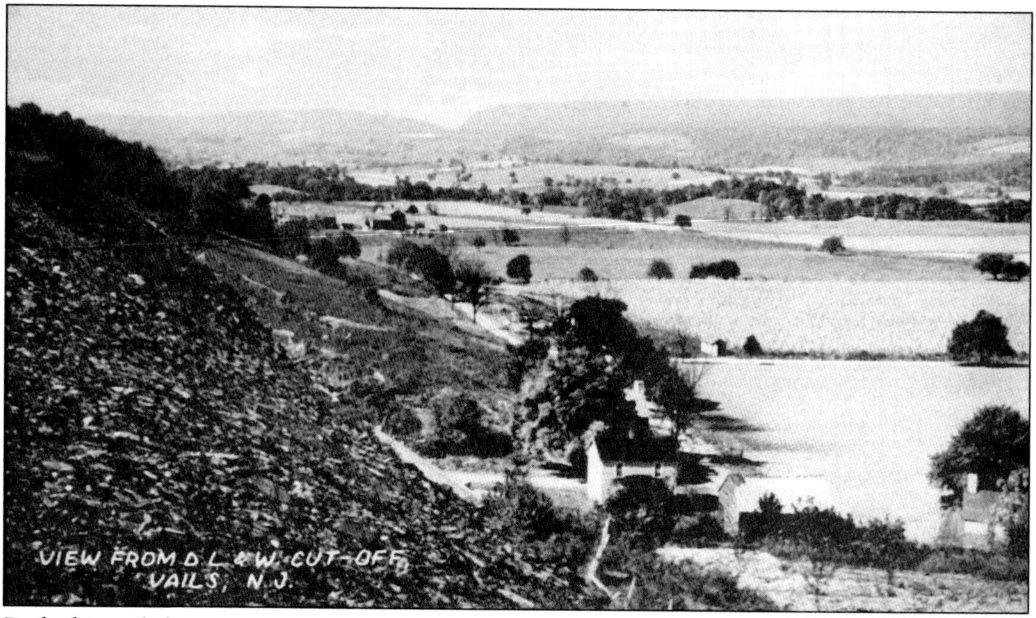

Both this and the previous view were taken from the immense fill of the Lackawanna Railroad cutoff at Vail. While appearing sparse, the picture tells a story. The stone house at lower right center was the home of Samuel Youmans on Mount Hermon Road. He was reportedly swindled by two city slickers who sold him a "formula" for making molasses from rhubarb. The intersection became known as "Molasses Junction."

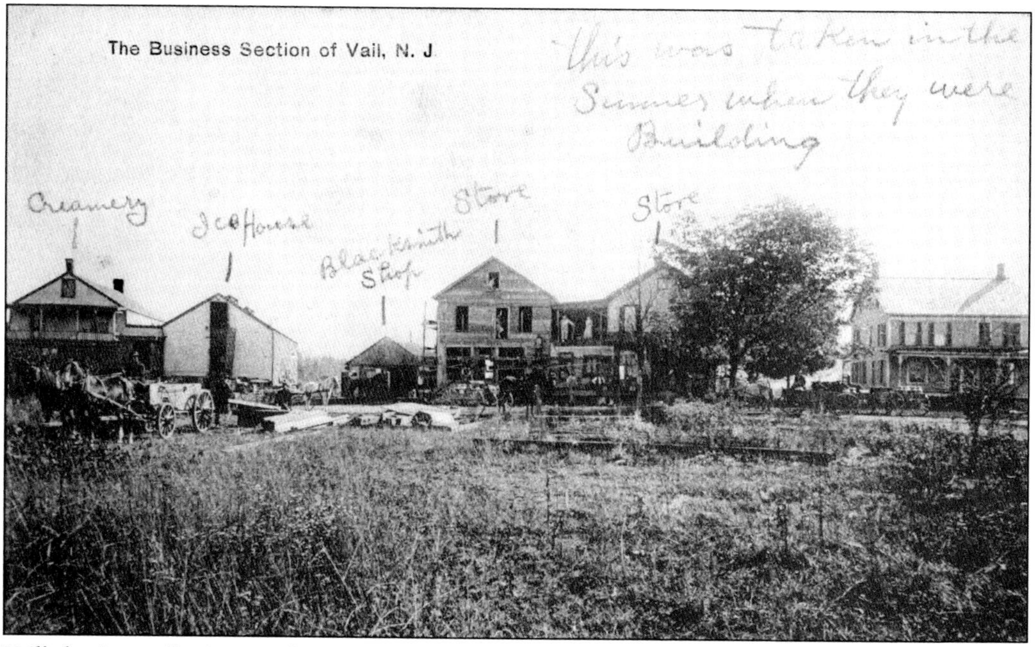

Vail's business district was busy in 1910. From left to right are the Keystone Dairy Company creamery, icehouse, blacksmith shop, store, and a private residence. The activity is likely caused by the construction of the Lackawanna Railroad Cutoff under way several hundred yards to the south. Vail took its name from John D. Vail, superintendent of the Blairstown Railway and nephew of John I. Blair's wife, Ann Locke.

Four

Blair Academy
John I. Builds a School

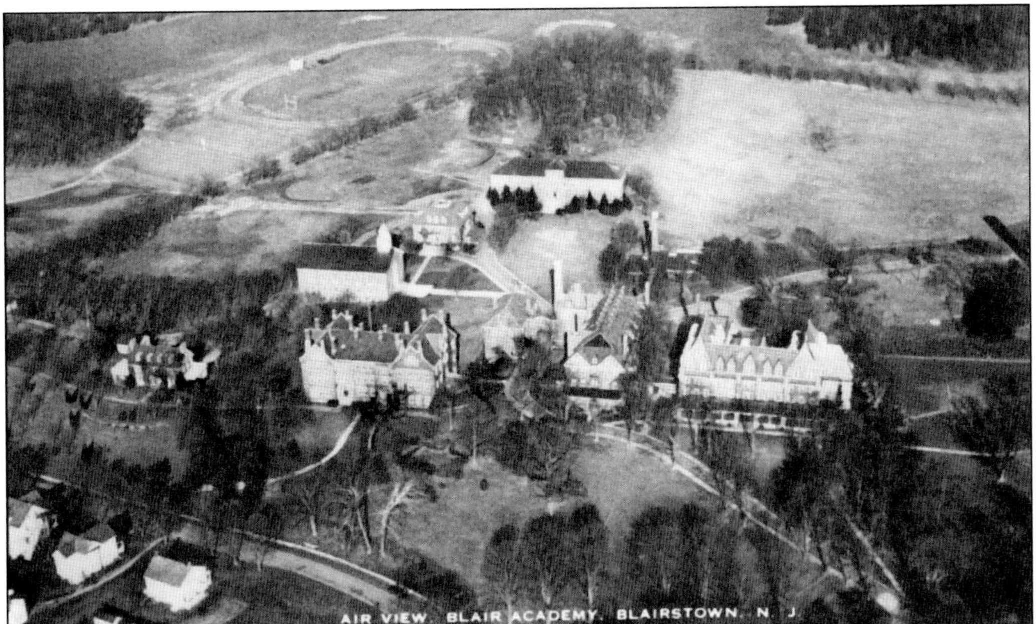

In 1848, the Blairstown town fathers and officials of the Presbyterian church agreed that it was time to establish a school. On April 6, a meeting was held to determine an appropriate site, with John I. Blair; John A. Reiley, minister of the First Presbyterian Church; and John Bunnell, a local carriage maker, in attendance. Blair agreed to the donation of a small building, referred to as the "Old Academy."

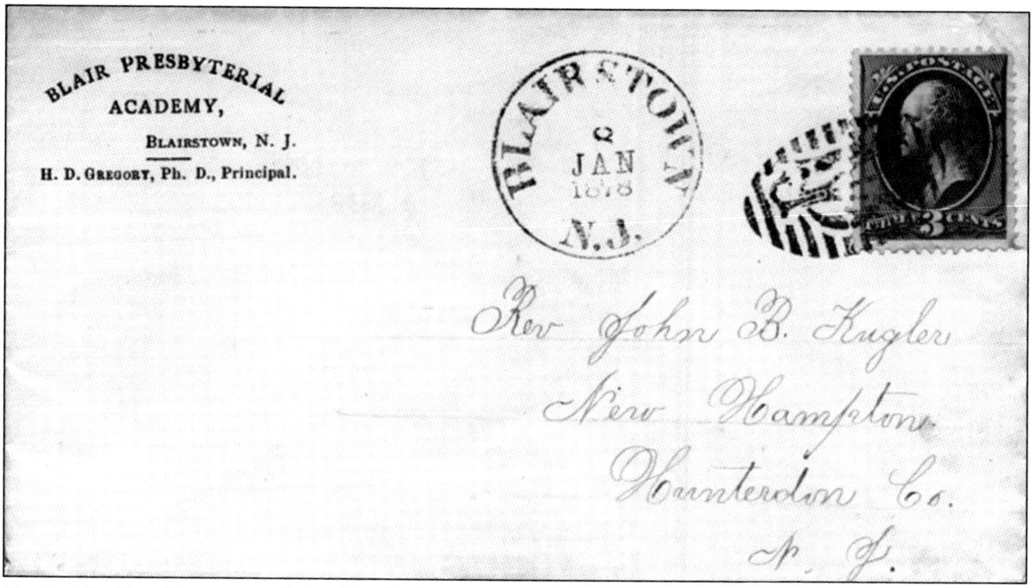

Dr. Isaiah Condict, a practicing local physician, was the first principal of what was named Blair Presbyterial Academy and served for a year. Dr. Henry D. Gregory was in charge of the school in January 1878 when he sent this letter to Rev. John B. Kugler in Hunterdon County. The cancelation is "John D. Vail." Reverend Kugler was later the historian of the First English Presbyterian Church of Amwell, New Jersey.

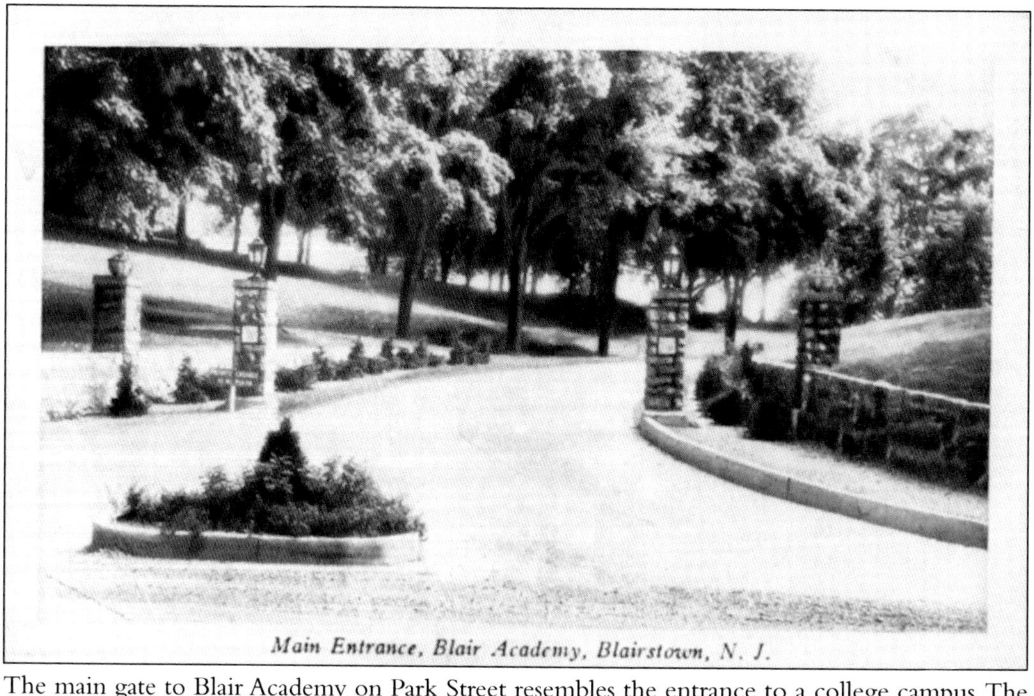

The main gate to Blair Academy on Park Street resembles the entrance to a college campus. The school was well attended from the outset with many students coming from surrounding towns to be educated. Those traveling significant distances were boarded locally. In the summer of 1849, the school was officially given over to the Presbytery of Newton and operated under its jurisdiction as a religious institution for many years.

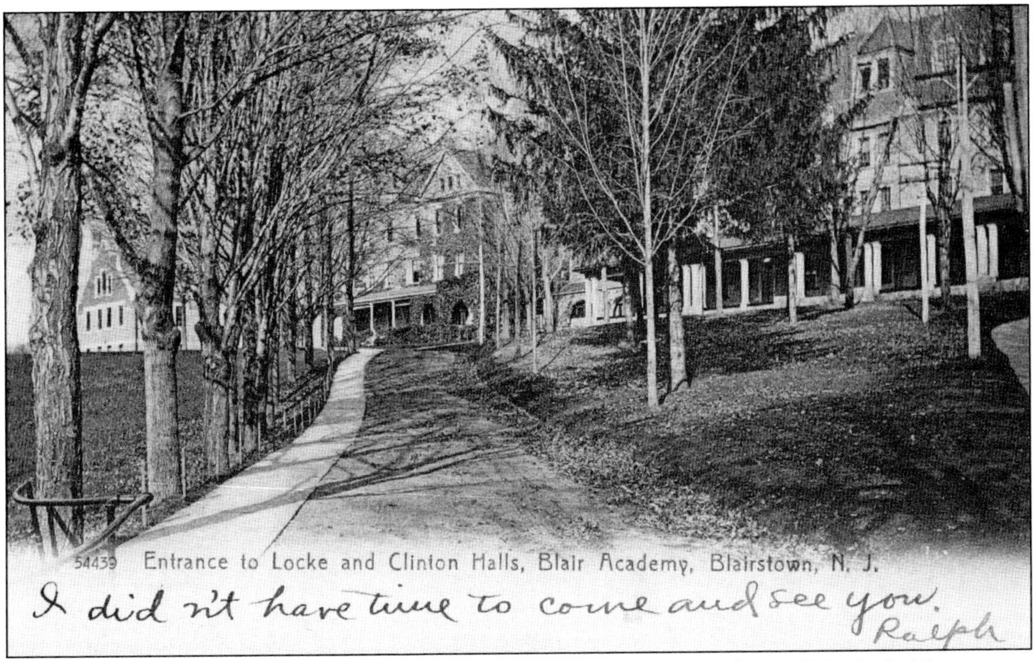

The driveway to two of the earliest buildings, Clinton Hall and Locke Hall, is shaded by mature trees. John Blair donated Locke Hall, but it was not named for his wife, Ann Locke, until 1900. DeWitt Clinton Blair, their longest-surviving child, donated Clinton Hall, thereby continuing the tradition of family generosity.

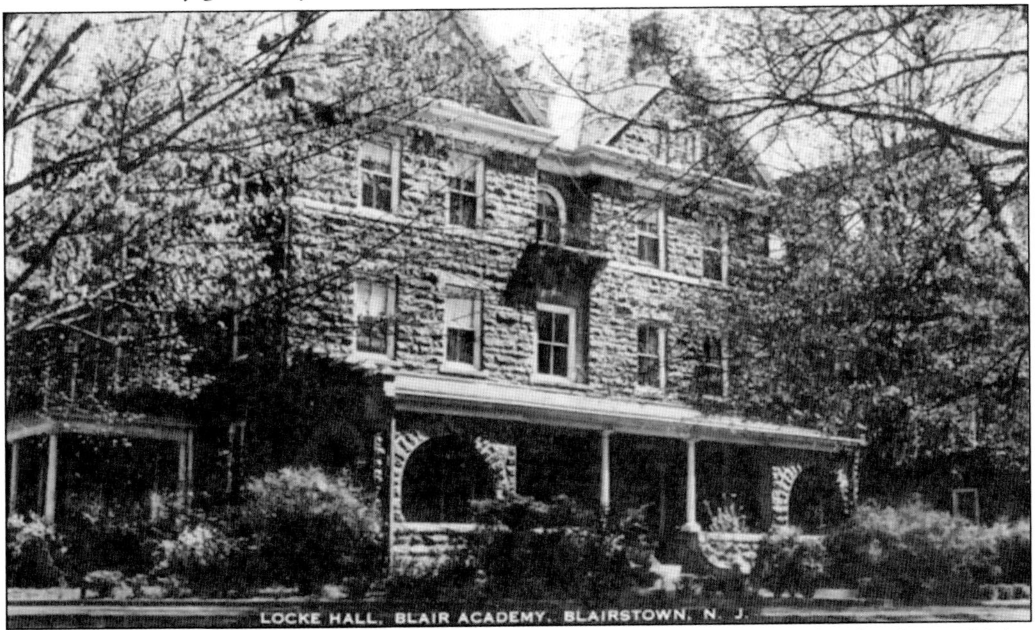

Ann Locke, memorialized by Locke Hall, was born November 13, 1804, the daughter of John Locke of Frelinghuysen Township and granddaughter of Capt. Francis Locke, who died in a skirmish at Elizabethtown (now Elizabeth), New Jersey, on September 15, 1777. She married John Blair on September 27, 1827. Remembered as generous to the poor, Ann died October 12, 1888, and is buried at Blair Academy.

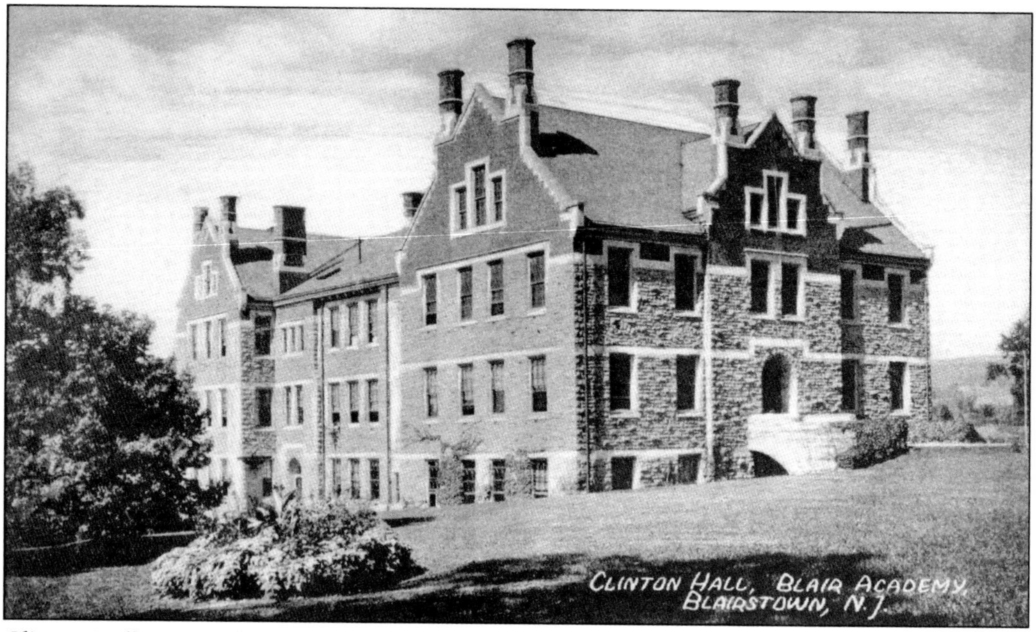

Clinton Hall was a gift from the Blairs' son DeWitt Clinton Blair in 1900 and was completed in two sections. At 5:40 a.m. on December 8, 1922, a fire started in a rear storage closet and gutted the entire structure. It was rebuilt the following year, as the sturdy stone walls survived. Today it serves as the location of administrative and business offices, the campus bookstore, and the art gallery.

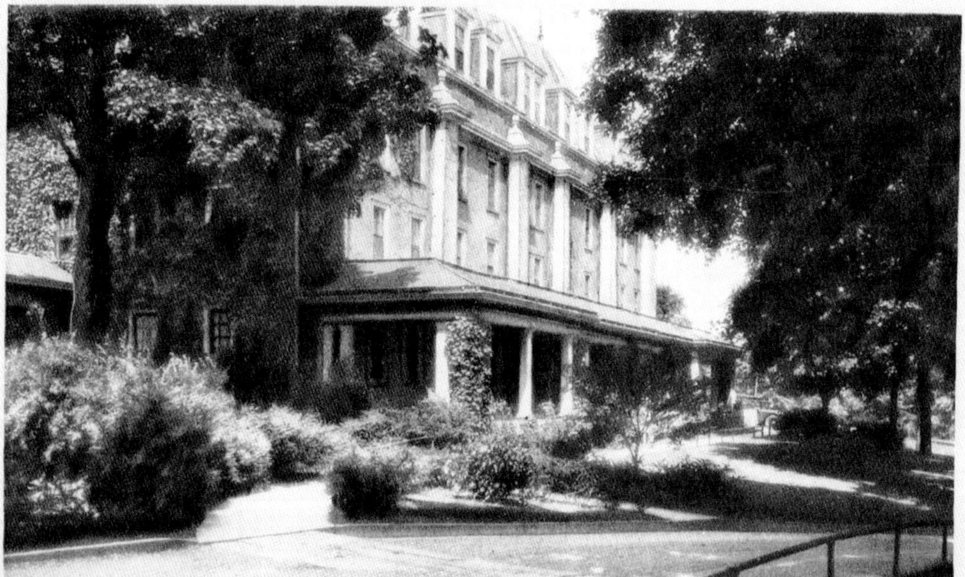

Insley Hall, Blair Academy, Blairstown, N. J.

Insley Hall was another gift from John I. Blair and named in honor of his mother, Rachel Insley. Built in 1898, it housed dining facilities in two spacious double dining rooms dotted with small tables that conveyed a homelike atmosphere. By the time of his death in 1899, Blair had donated the equivalent of $600,000 to the academy by way of endowments, property, and buildings.

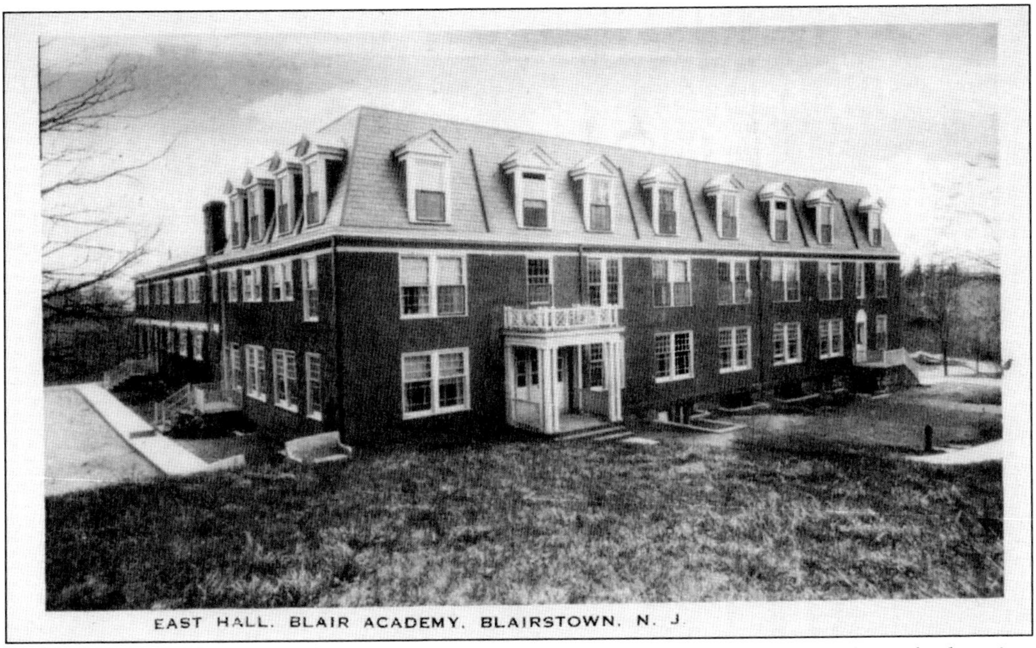

East Hall (above), another gift of John I. Blair, accommodated classrooms and physical education programs until a new gymnasium was completed in 1915, at which point East Hall became a dormitory. This view shows the new entrance built in 1926 using a donation from the Blair family. West Hall (below) was built in 1912 as a dormitory for the younger boys. The school, which officially became Blair Academy in 1904, began as a coeducational facility in 1848 but became an all-male school in 1915. Coeducation was resumed in 1970, and the school has been so ever since. Dr. John C. Sharpe (1898–1927) and Dr. Charles H. Breed (1927–1946) were headmasters during the time that many of the photographs of the school seen in this book were taken.

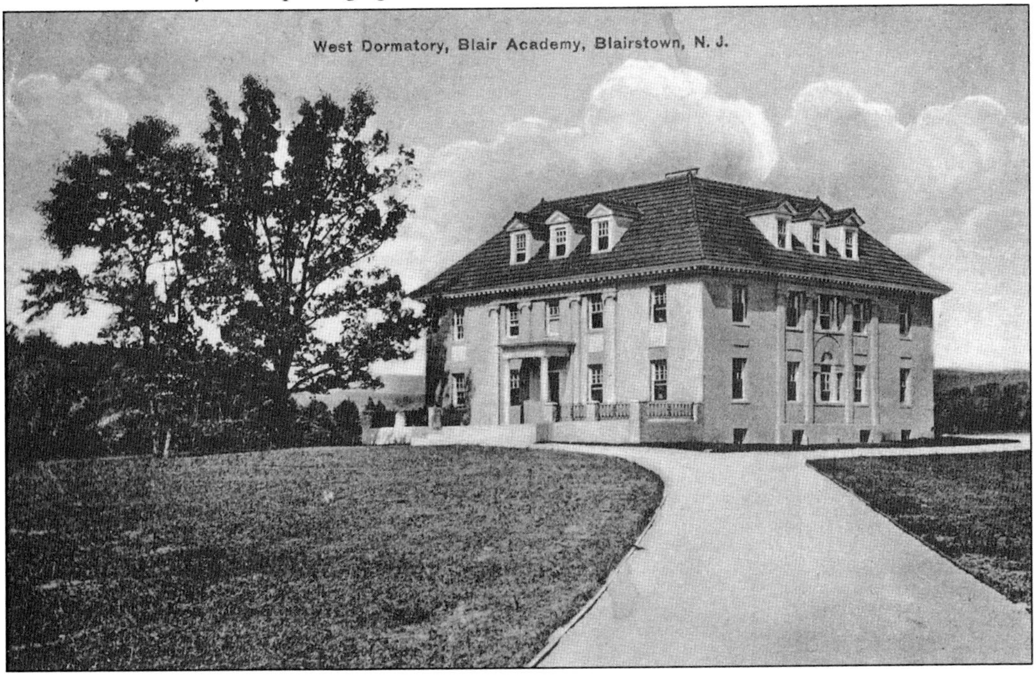

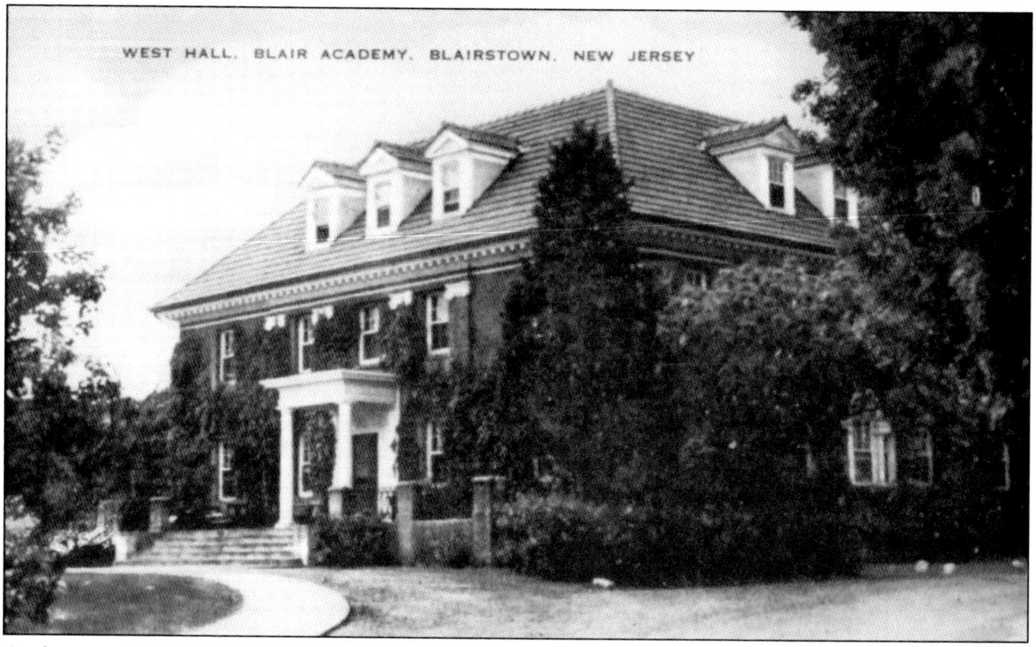

A close up of West Hall in the 1940s reveals the graceful aging that has taken place since the previous view was snapped some 25 years earlier. Trees and shrubs have matured nicely, and a thick, green blanket of climbing ivy now covers the facade.

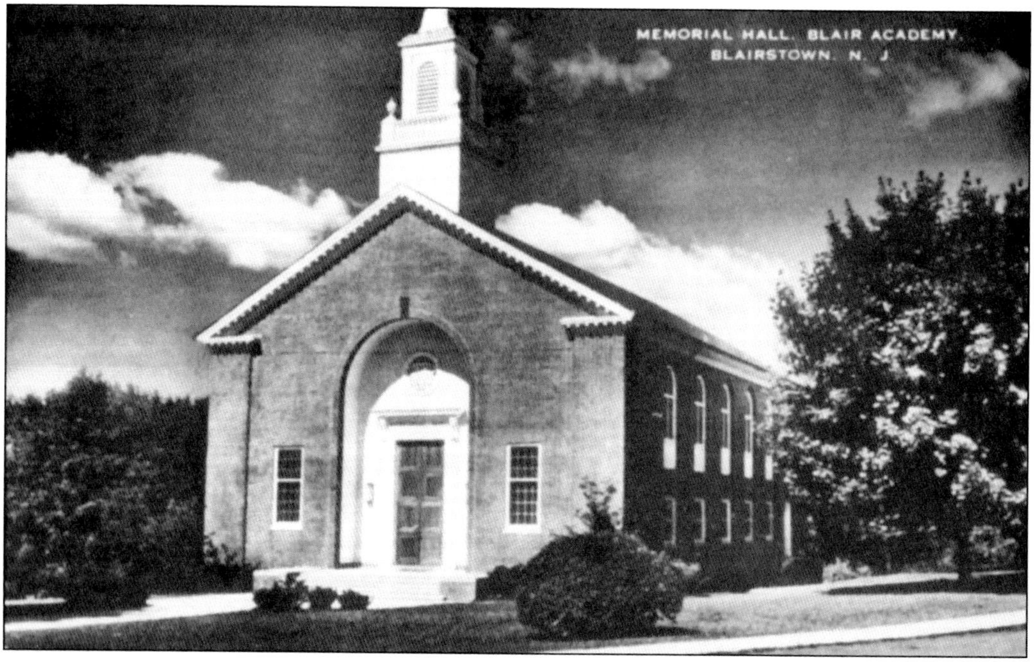

Memorial Hall was originally built as a combination chapel and library facility to commemorate Blair alumni who served in the military and were lost in one of the two great world wars. It was dedicated with much fanfare on Alumni Day, May 10, 1952, with New Jersey governor Alfred E. Driscoll giving the keynote speech. It still serves the campus today as the remodeled Timken Library.

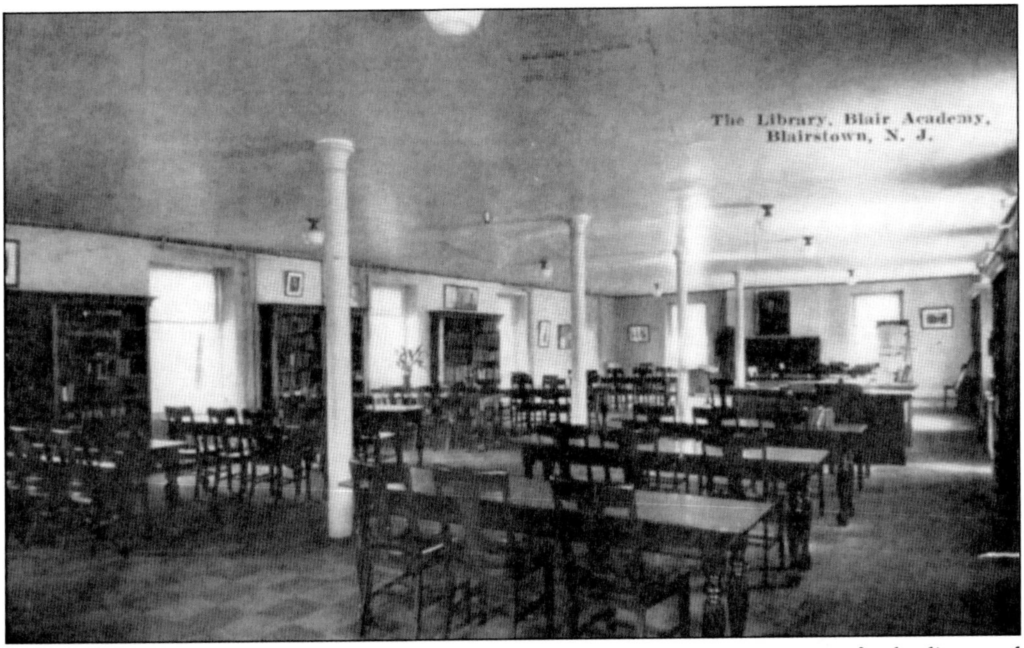

A look at the earlier Blair library reveals a facility typical for its era: spartan, foreboding, and designed to convey a serious, studious atmosphere. Pupils dared not talk, or they ran the risk of being silenced by a stern librarian. As a testimony to its prestige, the library received a donation of 1,000 volumes in 1849 from supporters in Princeton, Trenton; New Brunswick, New Jersey; and Philadelphia, Pennsylvania.

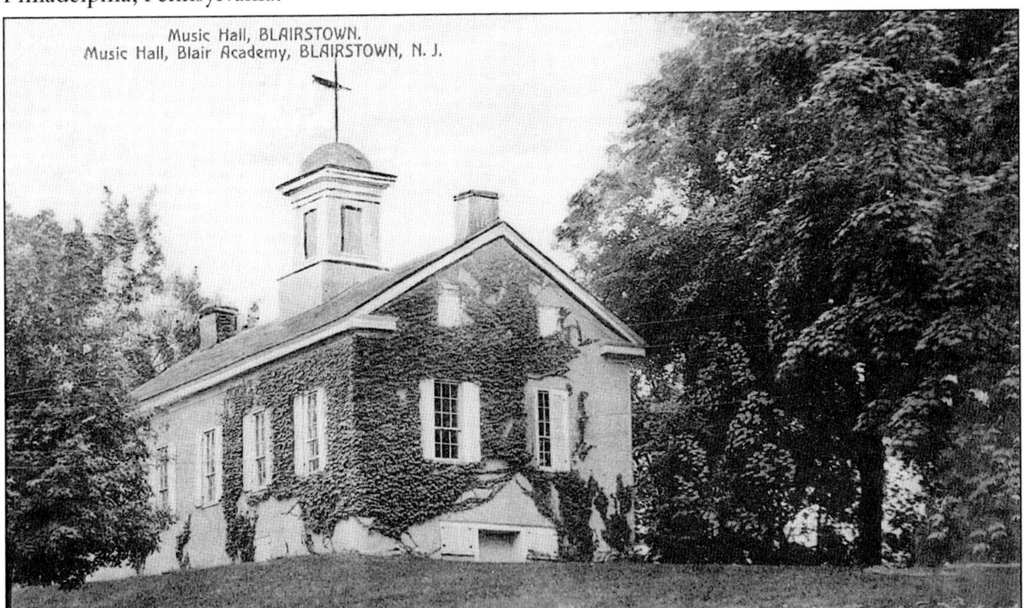

In the summer of 1848, a 48-foot-by-24-foot foundation was laid on property donated by John I. Blair, and construction of the first academy building began. This stone edifice was ready for occupancy that November 16 and contained two classrooms—for the primary and secondary schools. By 1896, it had deteriorated and was restored and remodeled for use as the Music Hall.

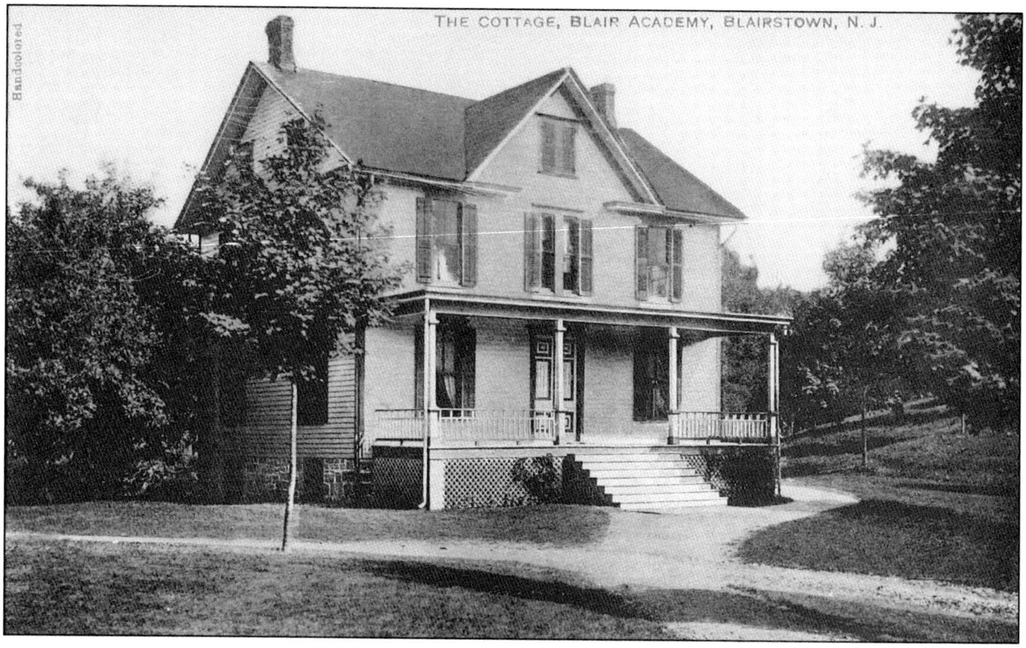

The Cottage (above) and Millbrook Cottage (below) are two campus buildings used as dormitories to house both staff and students. Students began boarding at Blair in 1848 when the school was first opened and continue to do so today. In 1848, a boarding student might come from Newton, New Jersey; in 2010, a student might come from Nigeria.

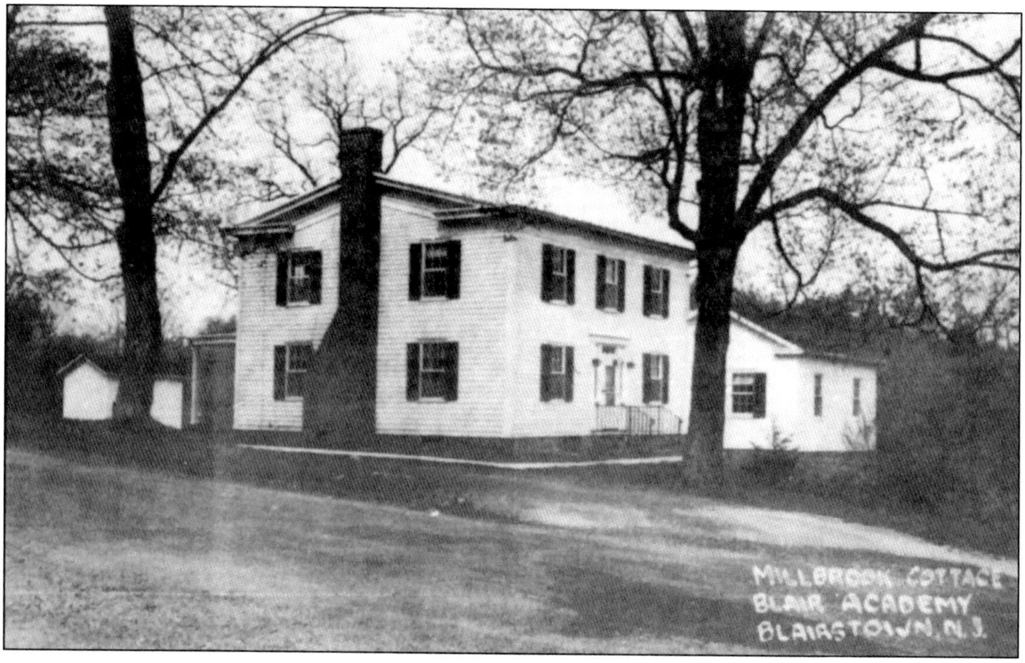

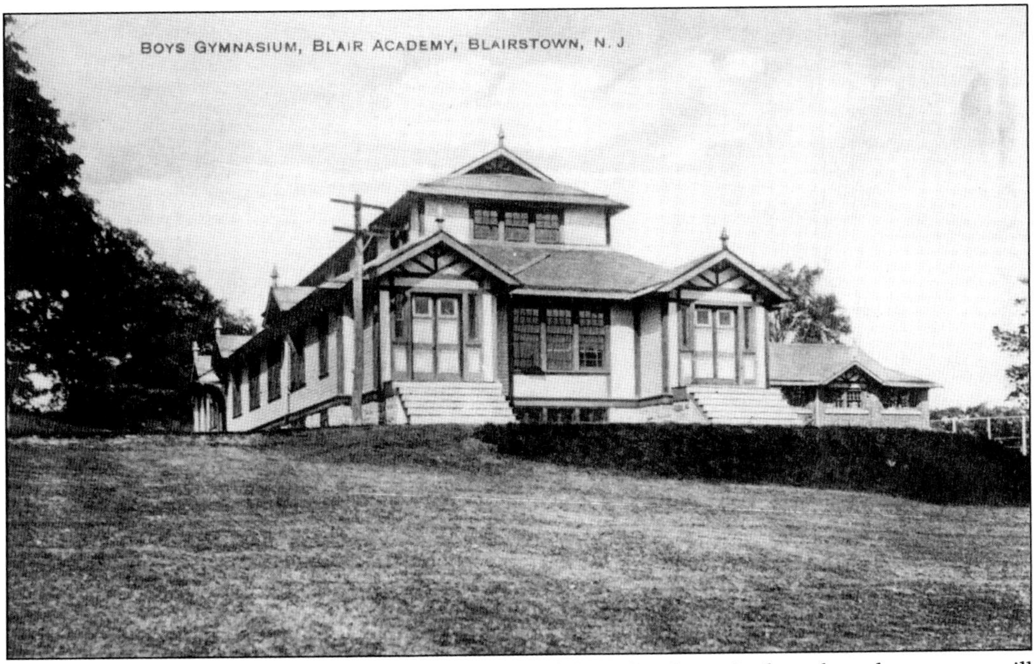

Physical education was always an important part of the school curriculum, but classes were still segregated around 1900. This Boys' Gym was erected in 1885 and served the campus for 30 years until it fell into disrepair. With an emphasis on building a healthy body and the emergence of the interscholastic sports program, this little facility became quickly outmoded and was replaced in 1915.

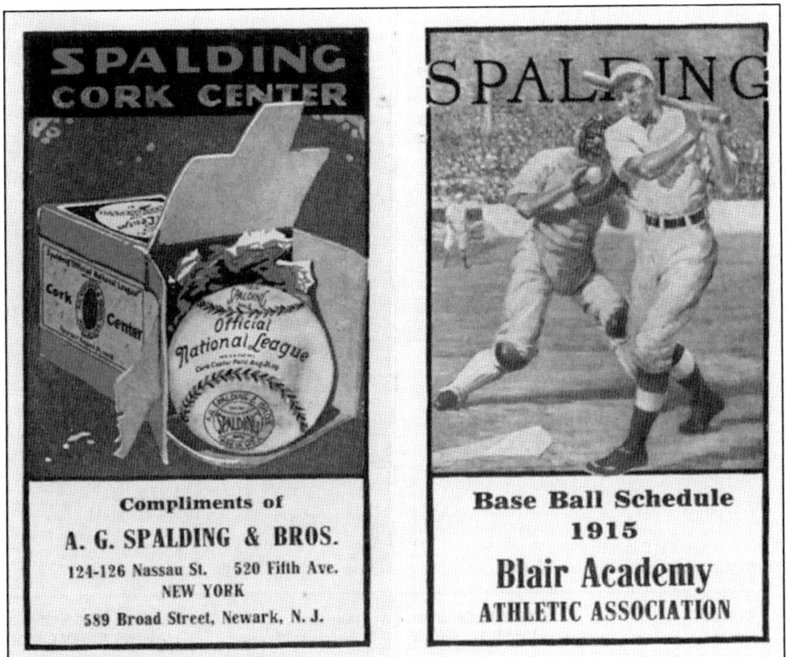

Baseball was indeed "America's Game" in 1915, and schools all over the country were competing at the interscholastic level. Playing only three games on the road, the Blair nine went 10-4 that season under coach Jesse Gace but lost to archrival Peddie by a score of 3-0. John Gibson was the team captain. A. G. Spalding Company, noted manufacturers of baseball equipment, provided the colorful schedule.

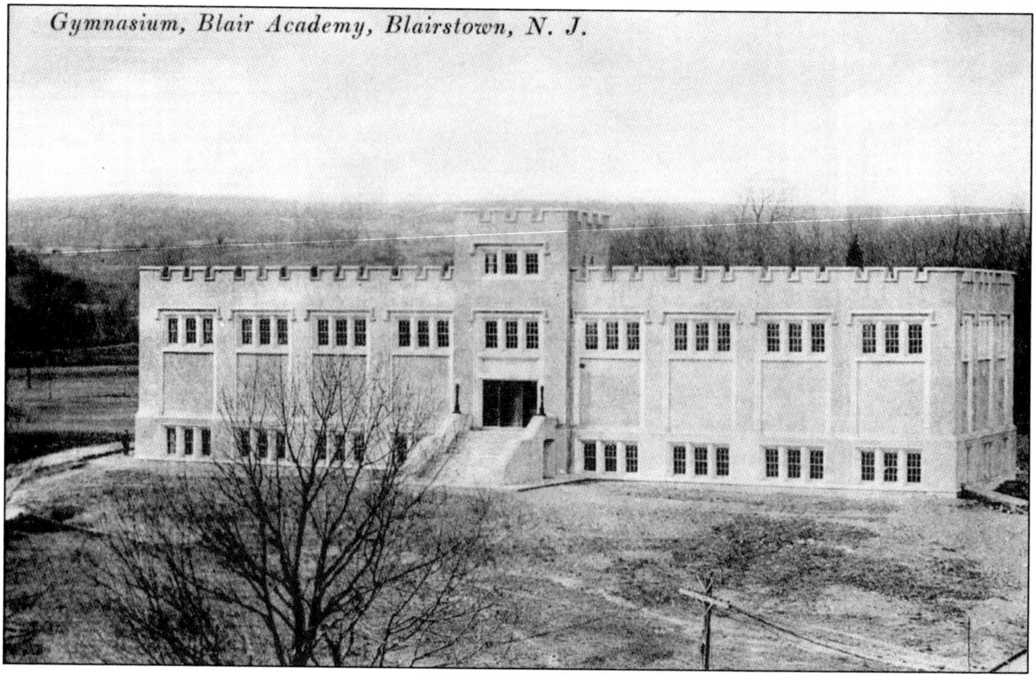

Construction of the new gymnasium began in 1913 and took almost two years to finish. Shortly after completion, the building (above) has the appearance of a medieval castle, and the landscaping had not yet been done. In a later view (below), the roof has been rebuilt from a flat variety to a hip design, and shrubs and trees have noticeably grown and matured. The building still functions as a physical education facility today, surviving as the Walker Gymnasium, and is attached to the Hardwick Hall field house complex.

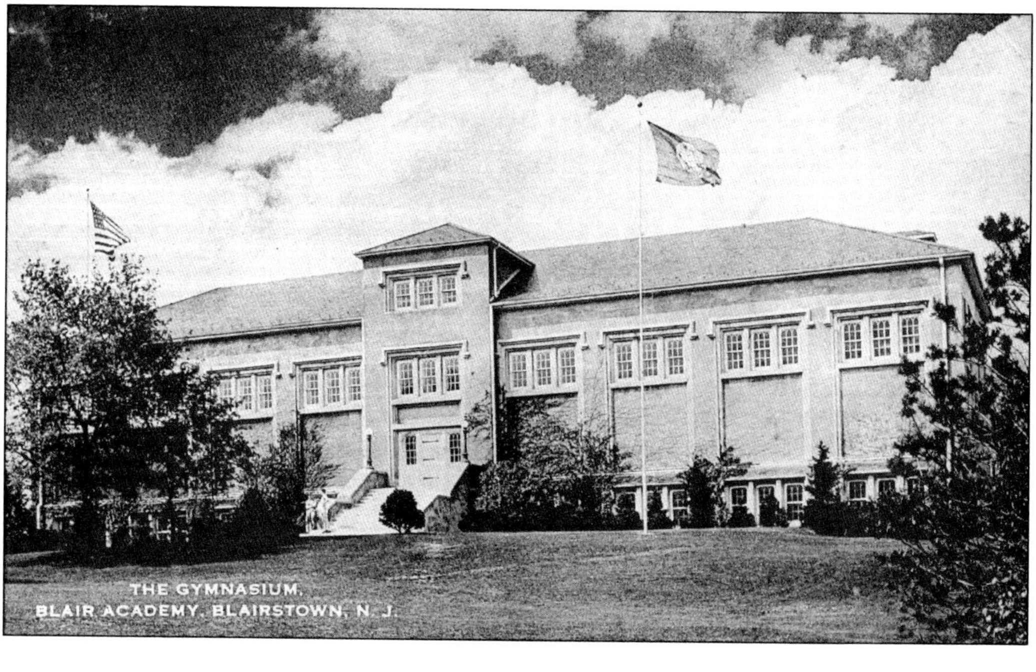

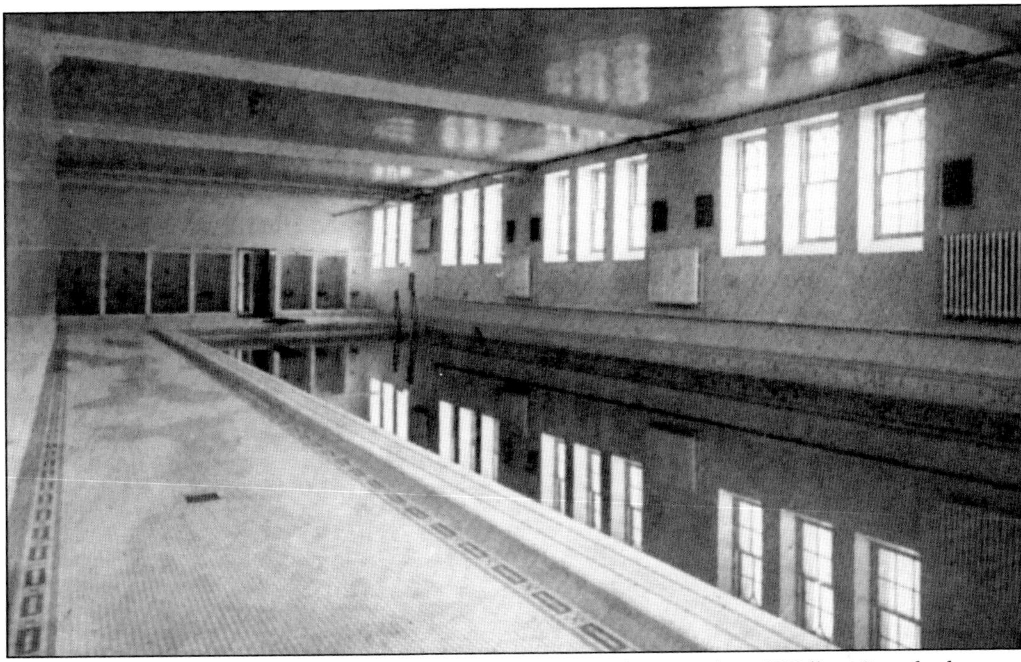

A necessary component of any new gymnasium was an indoor pool, and Walker Gym had a state-of-the-art facility in 1915. The old Boys' Gym had a pool added in the summer of 1901, much to the delight of students who returned from their vacation to find a natatorium in operation.

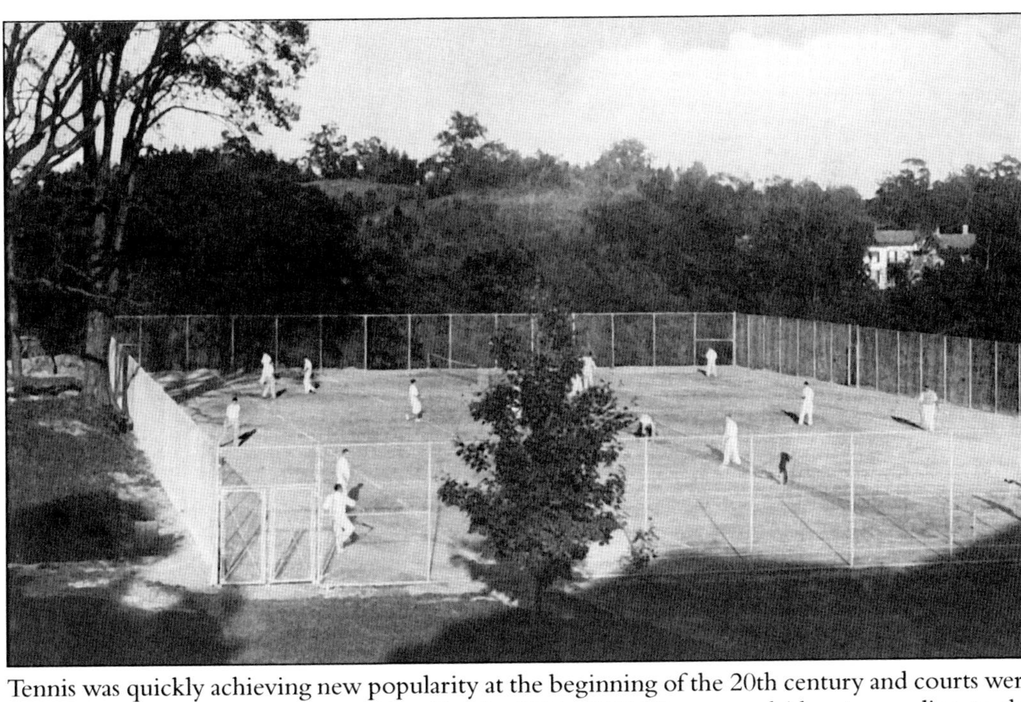

Tennis was quickly achieving new popularity at the beginning of the 20th century and courts were added to the property just east of East Hall in 1901–1902. They were laid out according to the standards of the time and actually made larger than required.

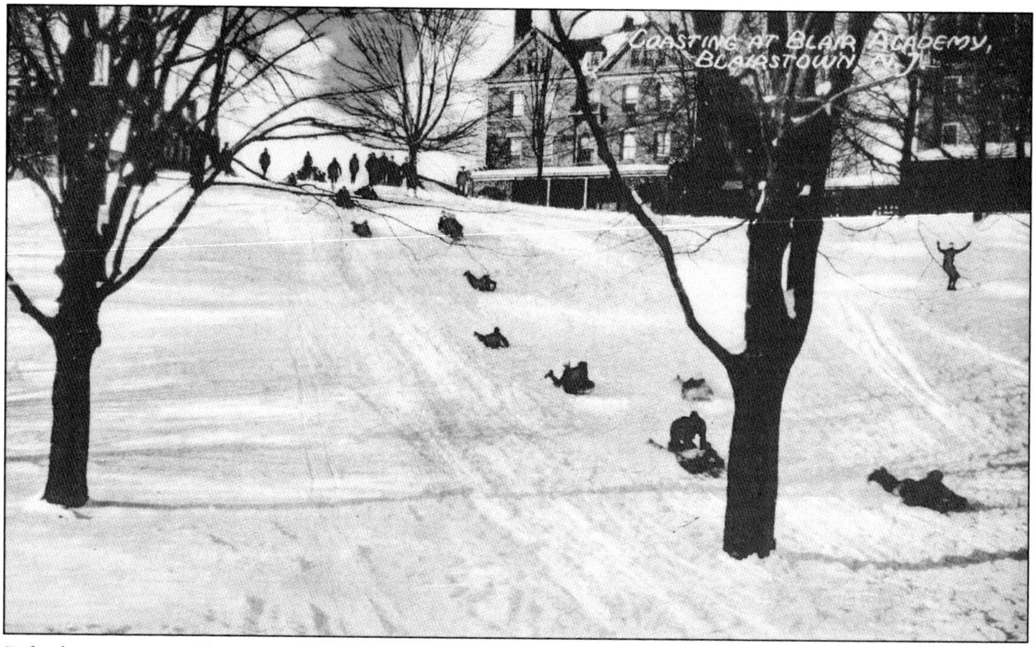

Baby boomers recall winters being harsher when they were young, with snow coming in December and staying until March. What better way to spend a morning than to hear John Gambling proclaim on WOR radio that school was closed and then rush outside to build snowmen or spend the day sledding? In an earlier era innocent of radio, a cadre of Blairstown youths practices the timeless sport.

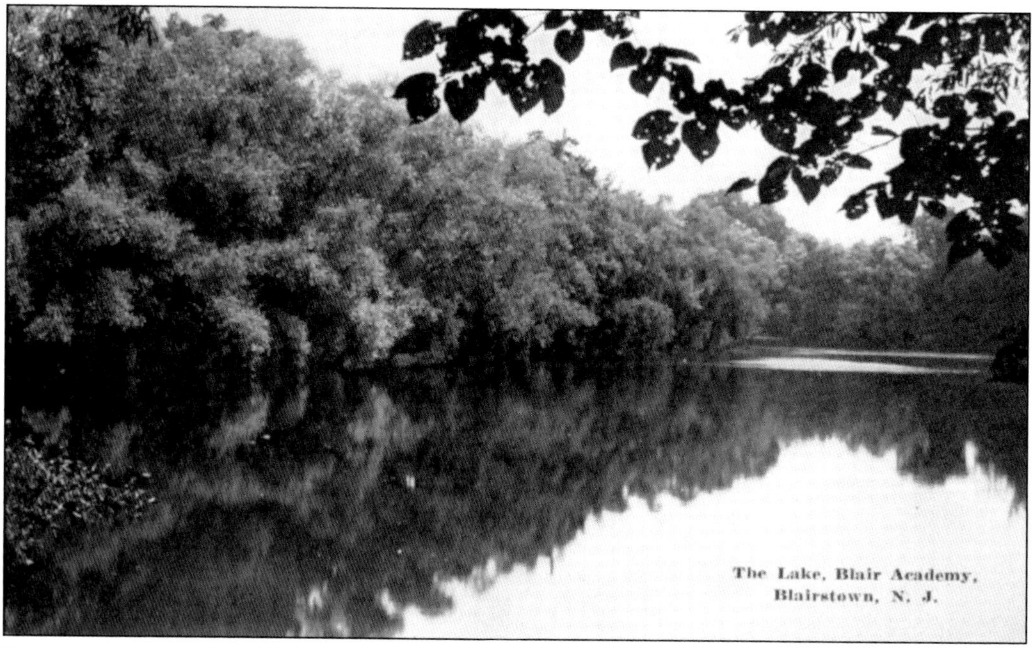

Whether someone is a Blair Academy student or a Blairstown resident, Blair Lake, located at the southeast end of the campus, is a beautiful spot to relax and unwind. The lake is actually a millpond, created by the construction of the dam that was designed to provide a source of water to power the mill on Main Street.

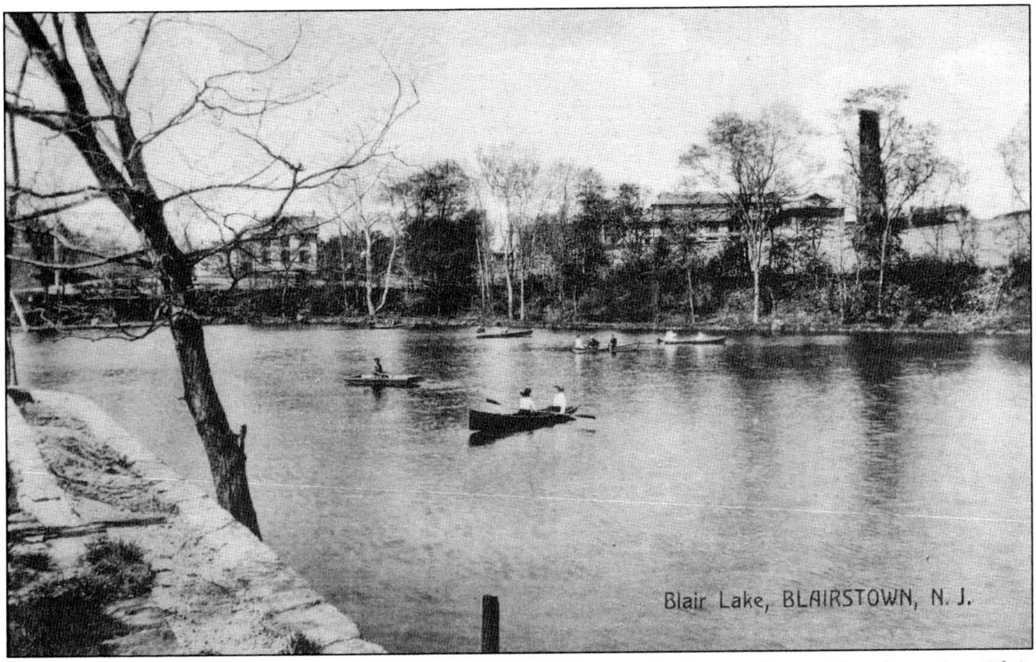

Boating and ice-skating were once permitted on the lake, which was formed by damming Blair Brook at the south end of Brook Meadow. The waters backed up, covering the meadow and creating the lake as well as the attractive falls that tumble over the dam under a footbridge that crosses the waterway. Blair Brook also provided waterpower for the gristmill on Main Street.

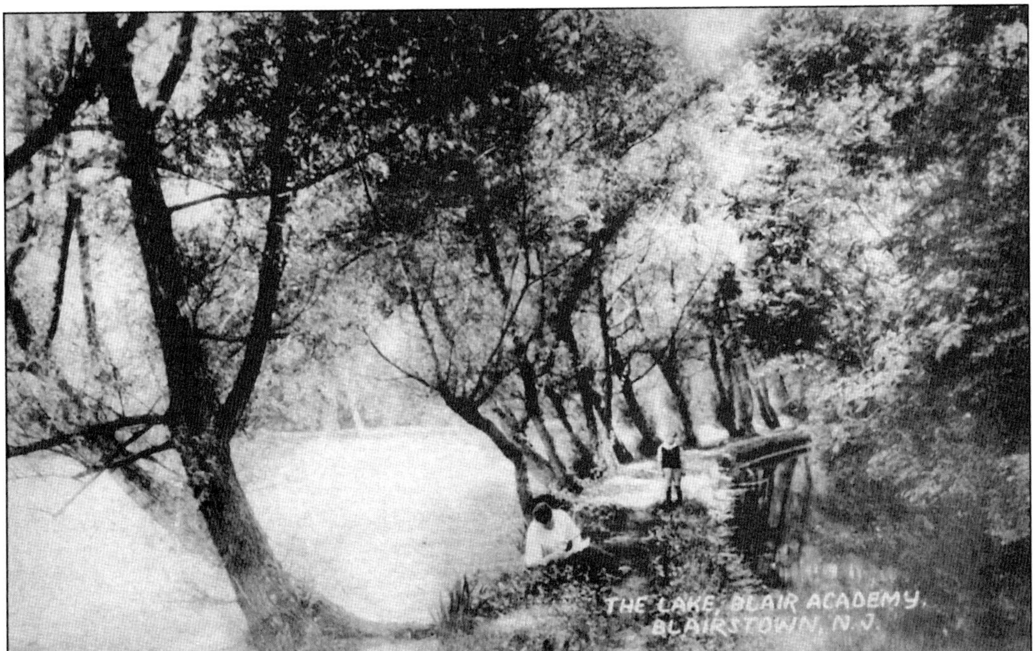

An interesting view of the walking path surrounding Blair Lake shows a watercourse to the right that may very well have been the raceway that once supplied power for the mill. It was often said that young men asked their sweethearts to marry them while taking a leisurely stroll on this path.

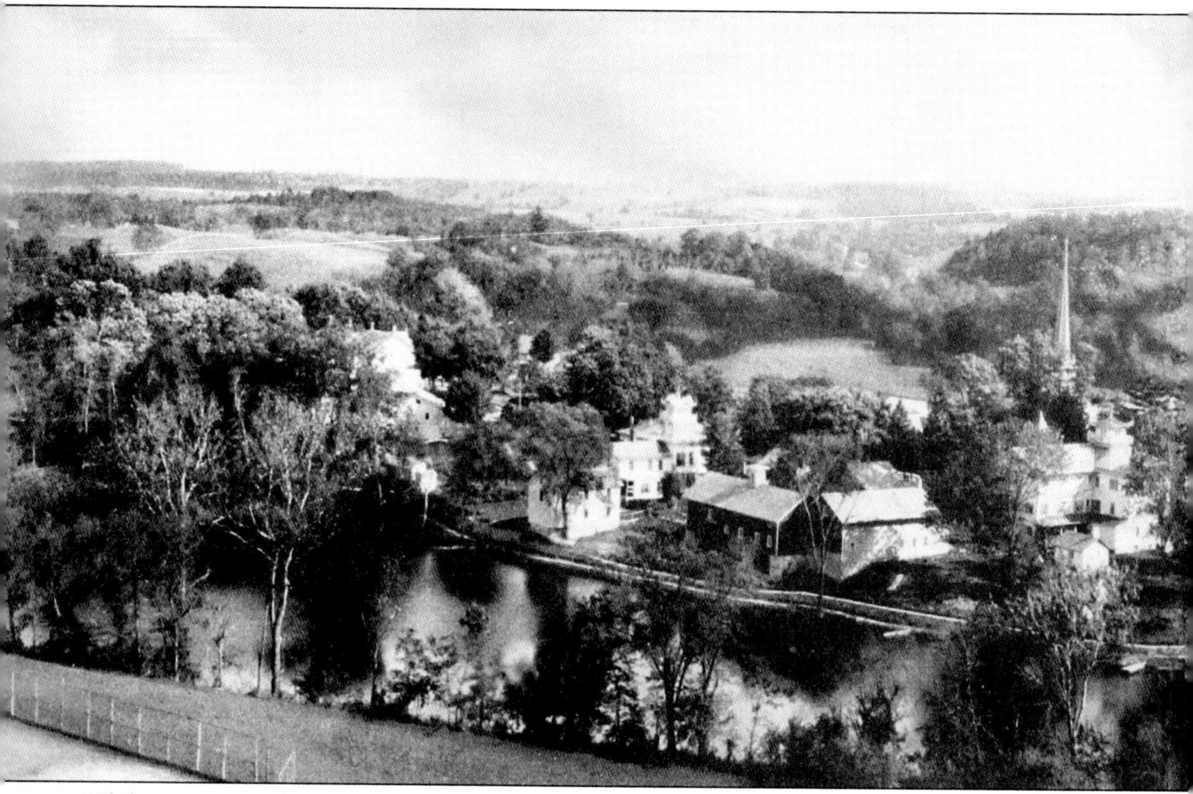

While most typical panorama postcard views of Blairstown village have been taken from the Edgehill Road area, this unique variation shows a perspective of the town from the hill at Blair Academy. The pristine body of water at the lower left is Blair Lake. The spire of the Methodist

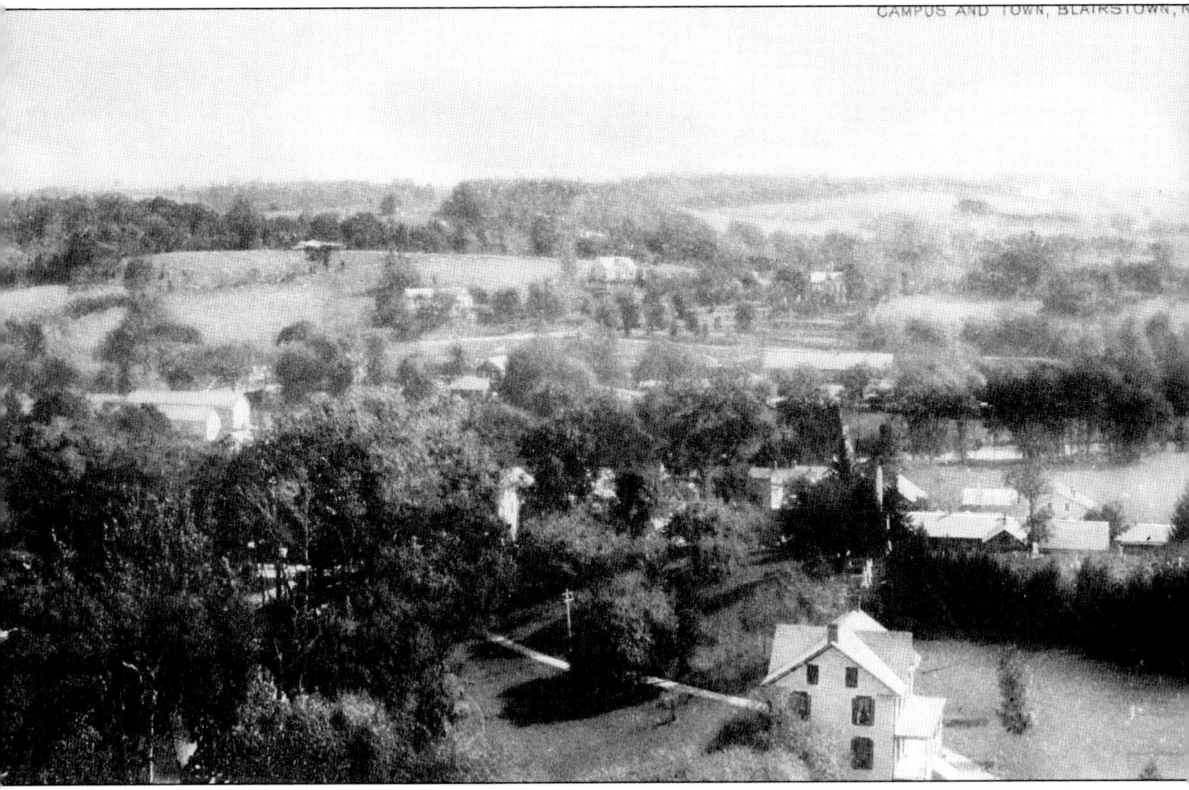

Episcopal church dominates the scene to the left center, and in the distance to the right center is the gray roof of the New York, Susquehanna and Western Railroad station on the south side of the Paulinskill River.

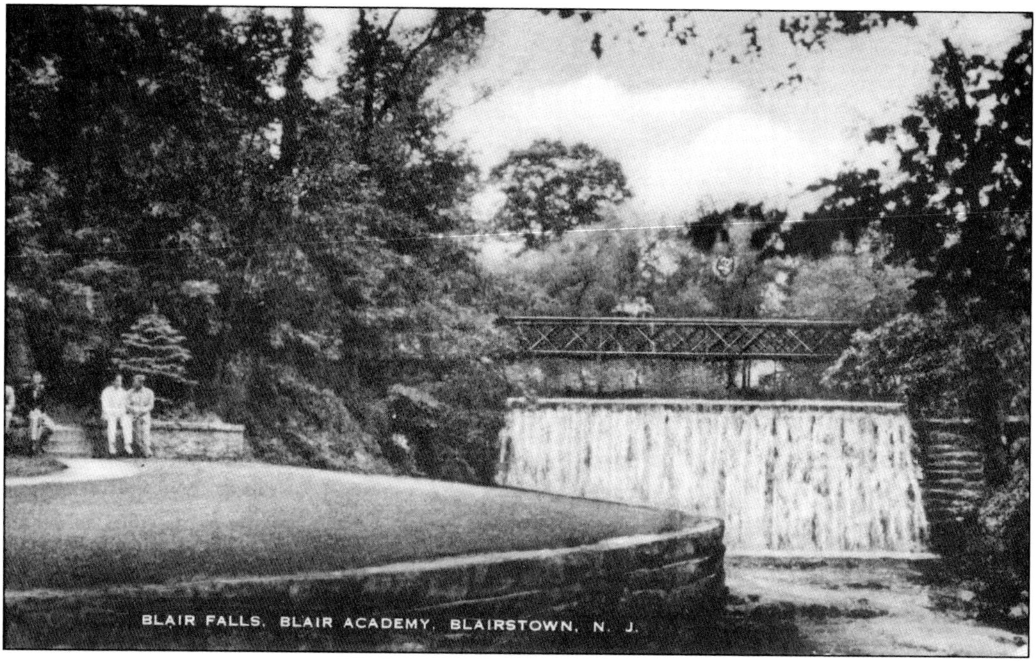

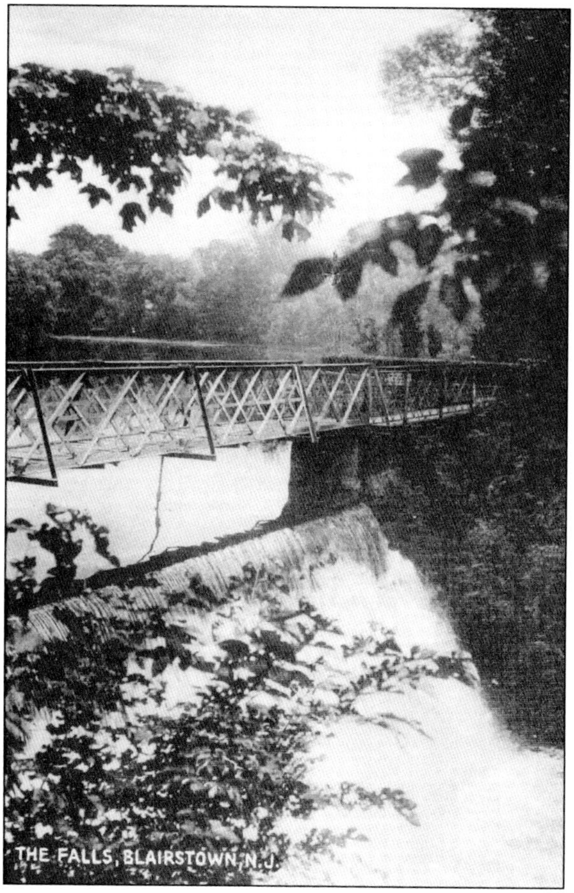

Two views of the dam and Blair Falls at the southern outlet of Blair Lake give a better perspective of the area. The dam (above) was built about 1903 from native limestone and has never had to be replaced. The attractive stone stairs at the left lead to the pathway around the lake and to the footbridge that crosses above the falls. They were designed by Dr. John C. Sharpe, who was headmaster from 1898 to 1927. The photographer provides a closer look at the footbridge (left), which was completed in 1904. On hot summer days, it was the place to go to catch the cool breezes and spray from the water as it tumbled over the dam and ran down past the mill.

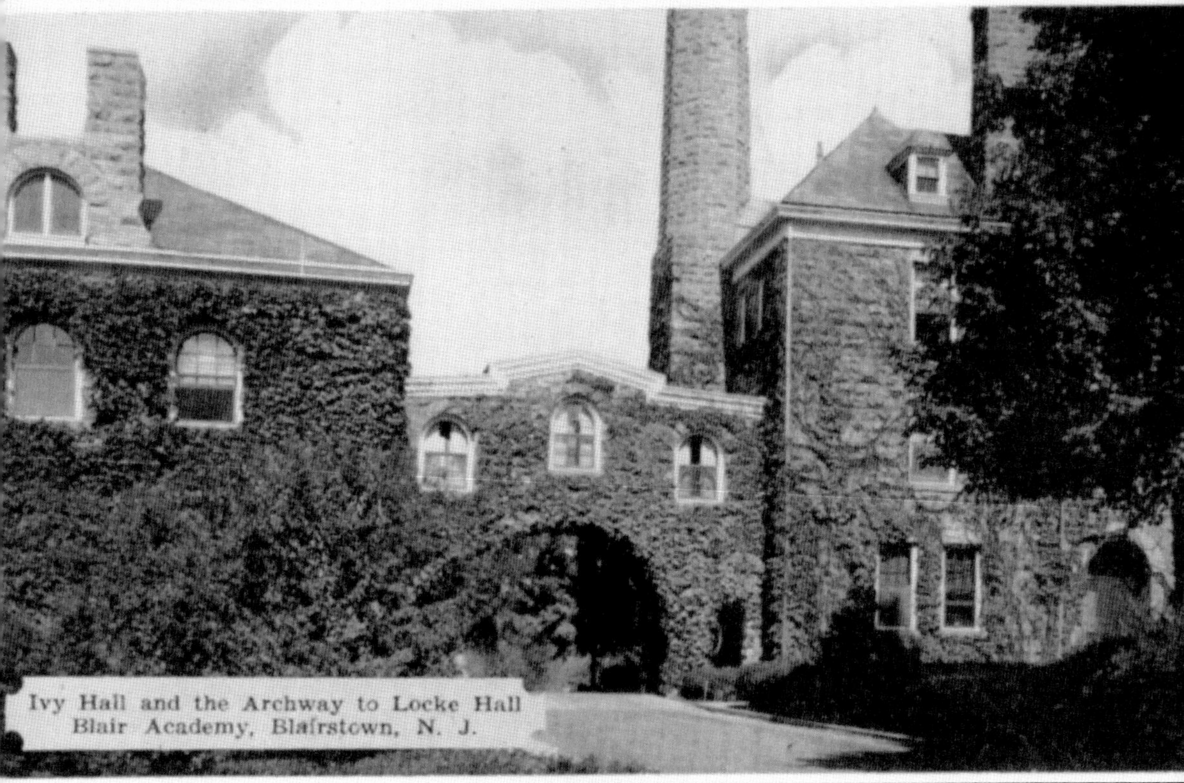

A fitting place to take leave of Blair Academy is the ivy-covered archway that joins Ivy Hall (left) with Locke Hall (right). The arch was constructed in 1904 by Italian stonemasons and connects the two buildings via an enclosed hallway. It once spanned just another roadway through the campus but now has become a significant point of interest. Adjacent to the arch is the Meerwarth Courtyard, a favorite gathering spot for Blair students. At graduation each year, the entire class marches out through the arch, signifying their leaving the protective environment of the school to face the demands and challenges of an ever-changing world.

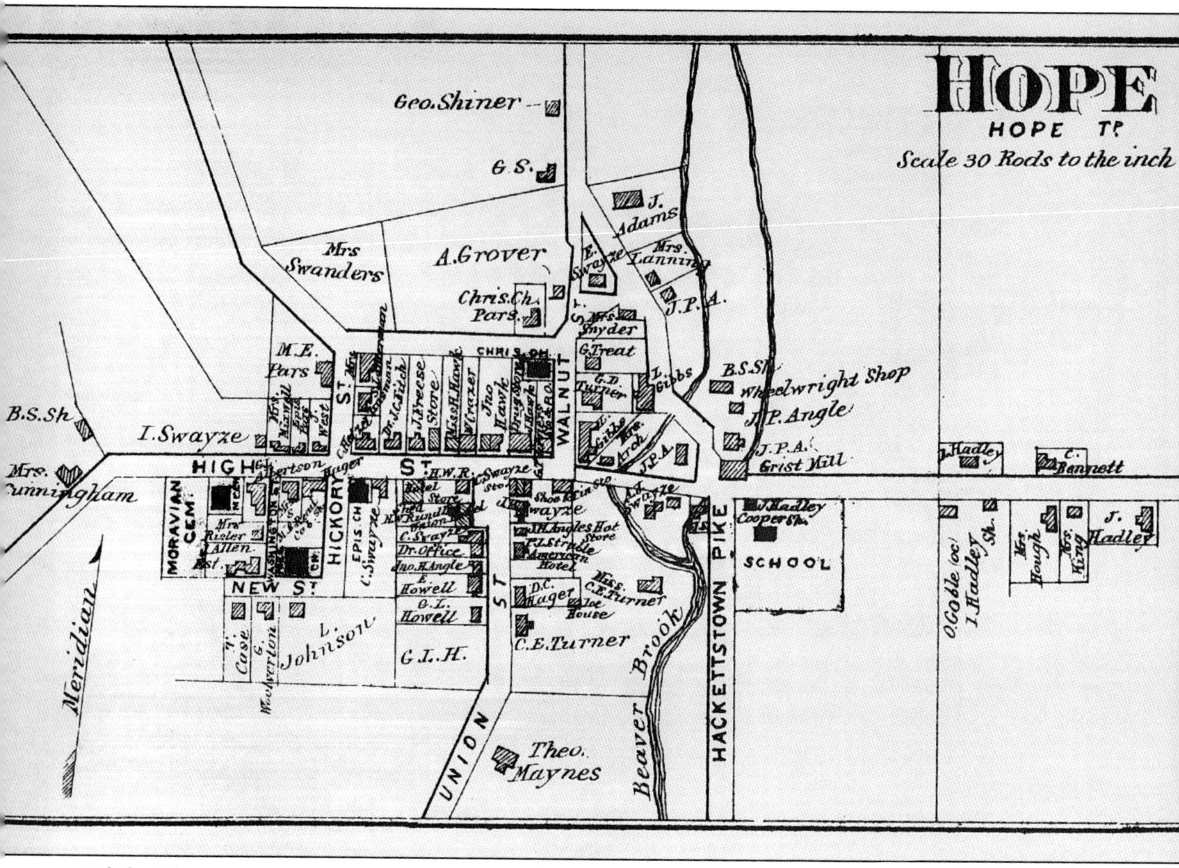

While Blairstown owes its existence to a financial wizard and entrepreneur, Hope's history is steeped in the quest for religious freedom by a people who lived a communal lifestyle and held property in common. Moravians driven from their European homelands by persecution found peace and liberty in Pennsylvania, and missionaries of the order who traveled far and wide to convert Native Americans, discovered the beautiful area that they eventually called Hope.

Five

Hope
A Moravian "Experiment"

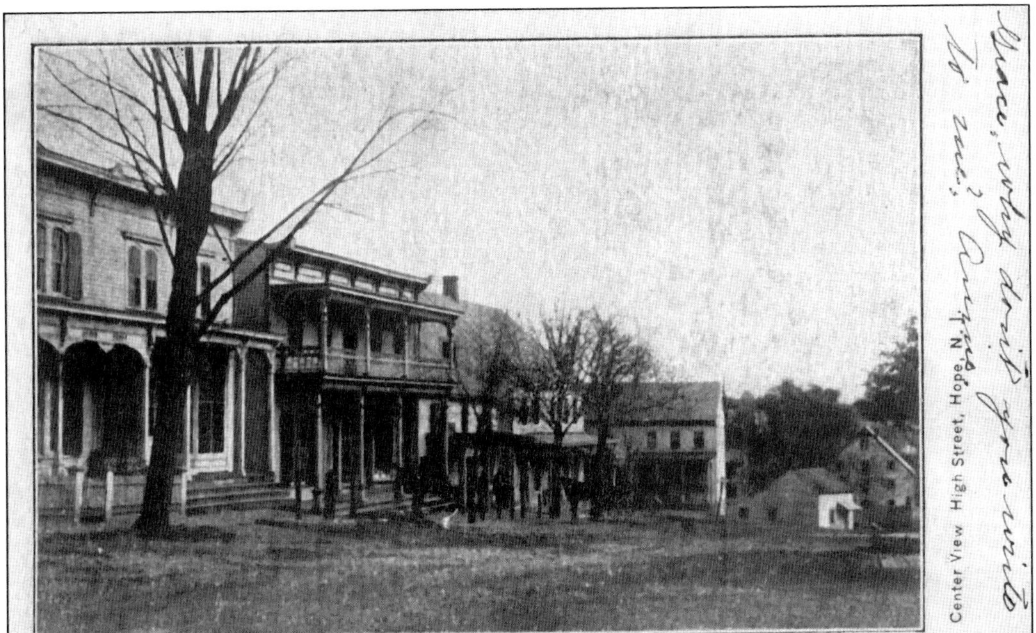

This was High Street in Hope before the great 1918 fire that forever altered the village's profile. Moravian missionaries Joseph Powell, Bruce Shaw, and others from Bethlehem, Pennsylvania, frequented the region as early as 1740, as they traveled northeast into Minnisink territory, preaching and converting the Native Americans. They were welcomed at the log farmhouse of the first settler, John Samuel Green Jr., who owned extensive property in the area.

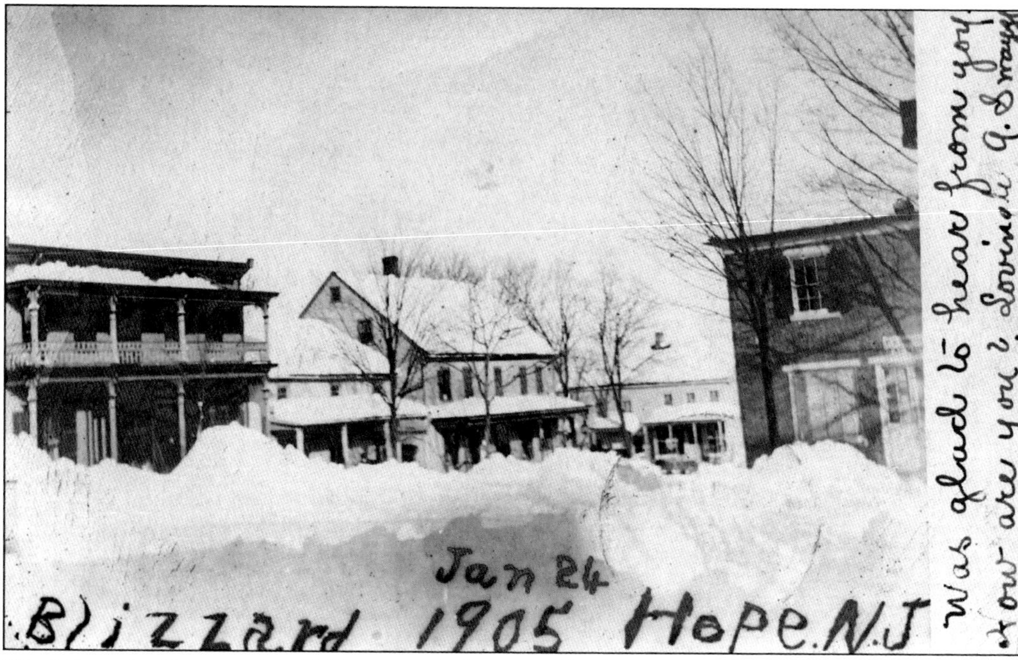

The blizzard of January 26, 1905, covered the same block with a white blanket. In 1768, Green, whose parents converted to the Moravian faith during the French and Indian War, offered the order 1,000 acres gratis to establish a permanent settlement. Declining to accept it as a gift, they paid £1,000. The following year, Peter Worbass became the first settler on the tract, which was christened Greenland in 1770.

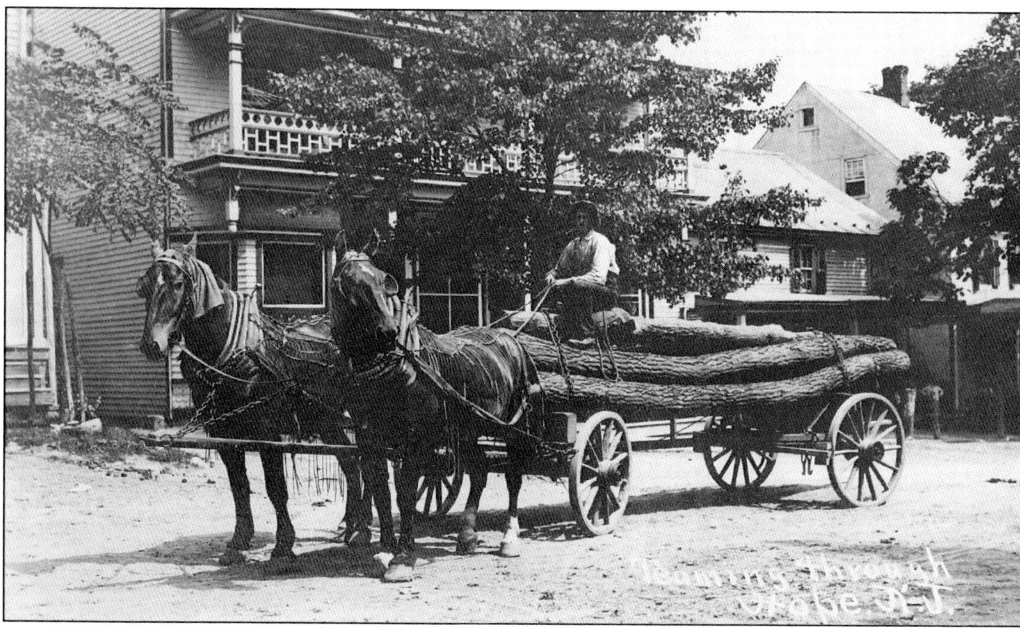

Clark Wilson and his team pose on High Street on their way to the sawmill. Greenland was considered an "experimental community" until 1774, when the property was finally surveyed and a plot of the village proper drawn up. On February 8, 1775, it was decided by drawing lots to change the name from Greenland to Hope, at that time geographically part of Sussex County.

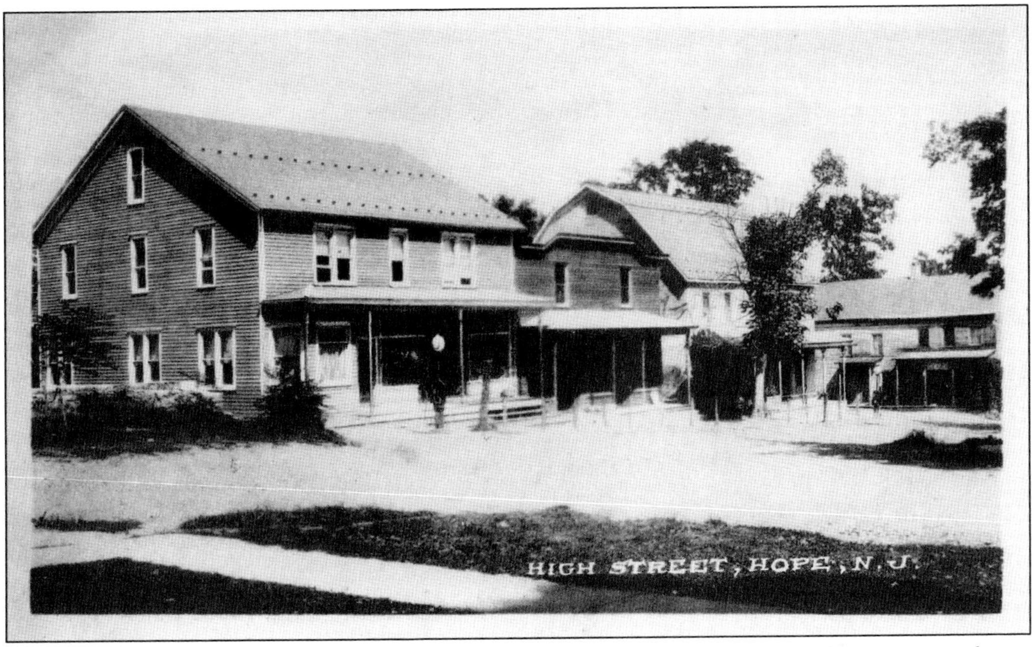

Alvah Howell leased the stone building at the corner of High and Walnut Streets for use as a residence, store, and post office. On September 28, 1918, a fire broke out in the frame warehouse located behind it and consumed the entire block, which was longer than it is today. In this 1920s view, the Howell building has been reconstructed and two new wooden structures stand to its left.

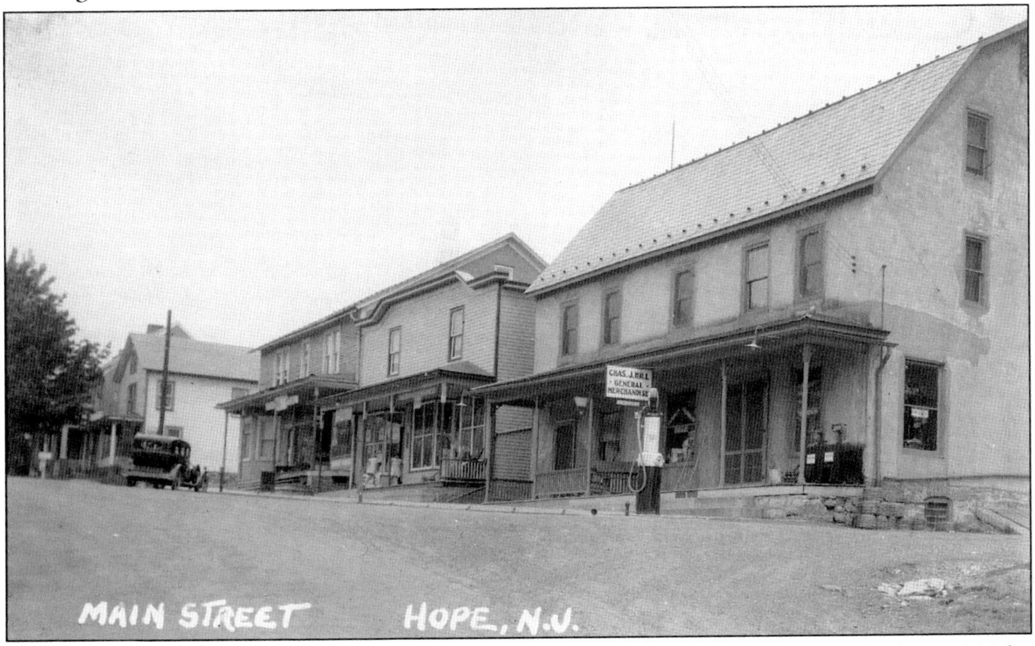

This view looks west at the same location some years later. Howell's store was rebuilt in 1919 by its owner, Fletcher Turner, and sports a redesigned roofline. The building was originally erected in 1777 by Moravian settlers using local limestone and was used as a store. All Hope properties were held in common by the congregation, which was totally self-sufficient and governed according to the regulations of the church.

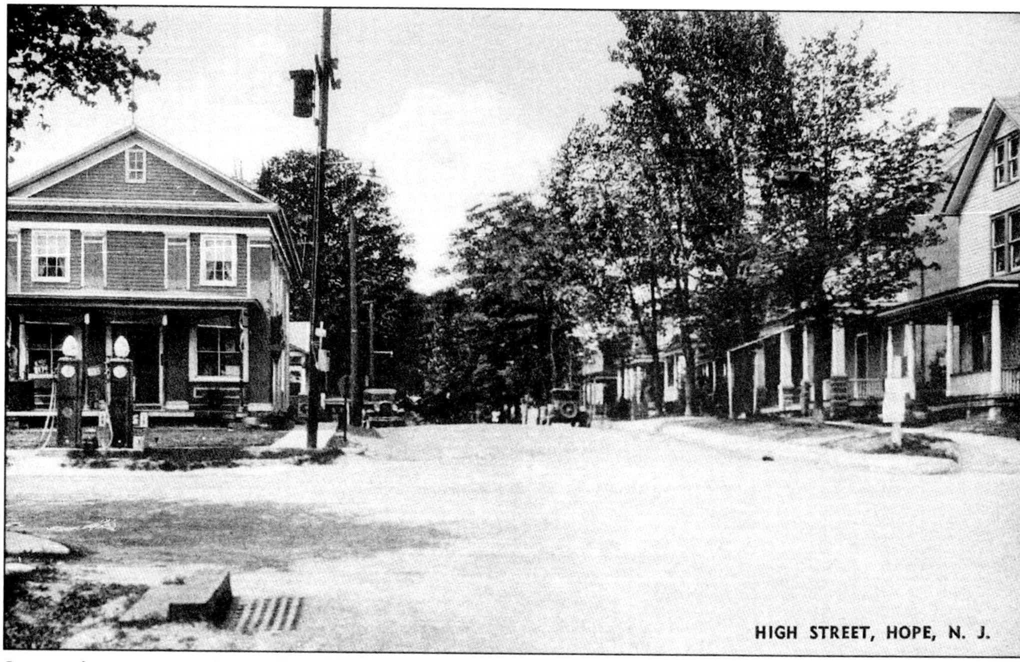

Swayze's store stands at the southwest corner of High Street and Routes 519 and 521. The intersection was created after the 1918 fire, so neither corner building is Moravian, although the stone structure near the right is. The permanent settlement at Hope prospered from 1774 to 1791 and then began a decline. In 1807, a decision was made by church elders to terminate it.

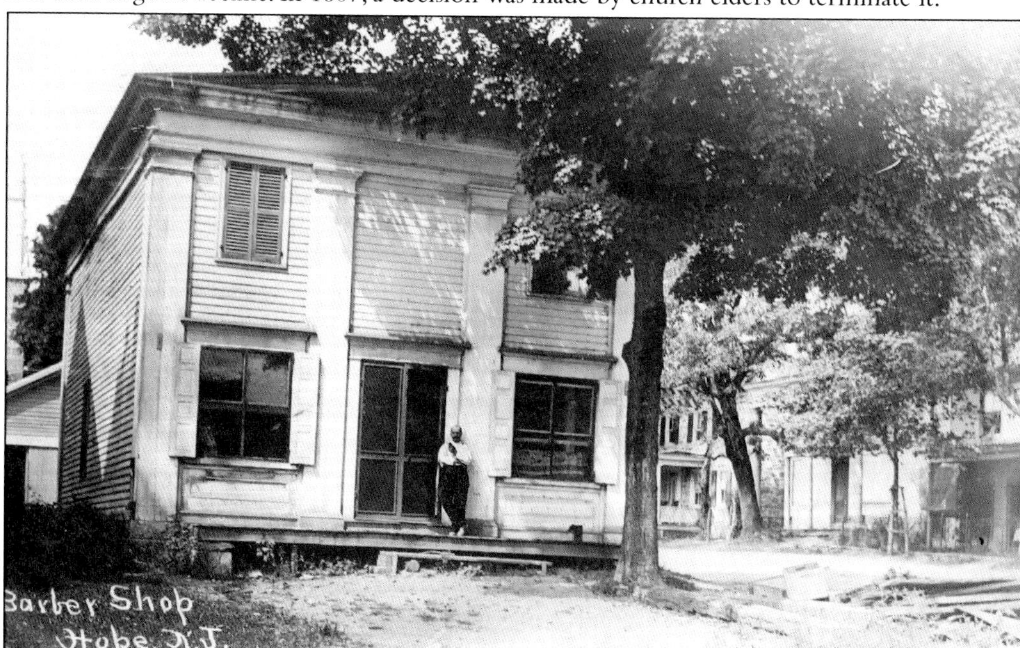

Caleb Swayze was postmaster of Hope from 1889 to 1897, and the post office was housed in his store. By the time this photograph was taken about 1909, it had become the local barbershop. The pile of wood to the right of the building is the remains of a scale that was once used to weigh wagons. The store was torn down around 1963 when the Hope Bank expanded.

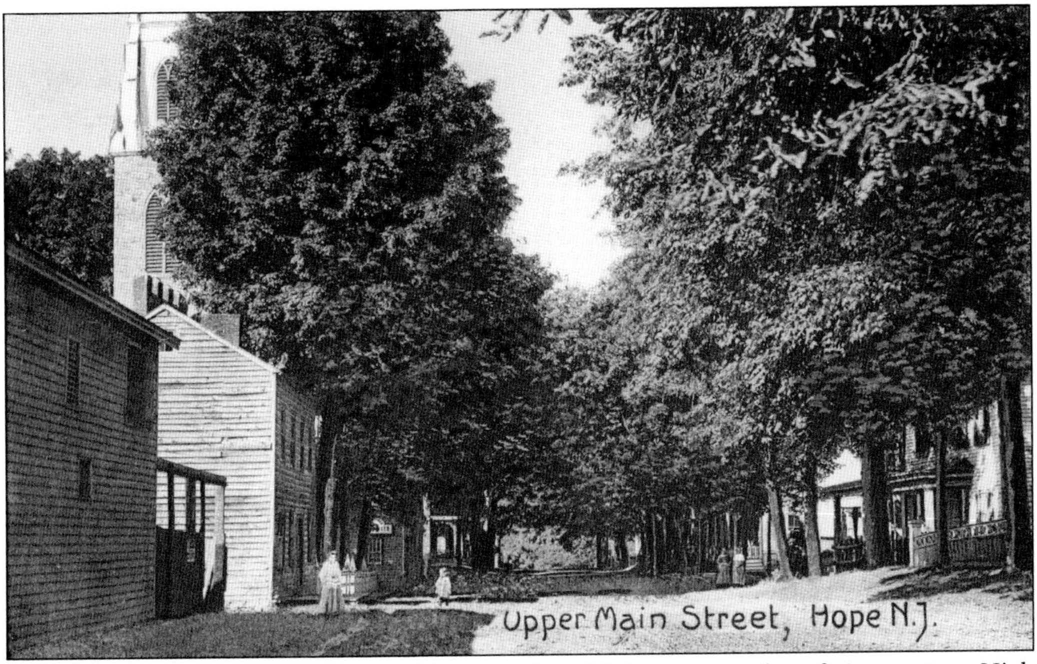

The Moravians had been gone over 100 years when this image was taken, facing west on High Street just past its current intersection with Routes 519 and 521. The steeple of the Episcopal church is at the left, and a mother has no qualms allowing her toddler to wander into the dusty road, which has yet to see a major influx of automobiles.

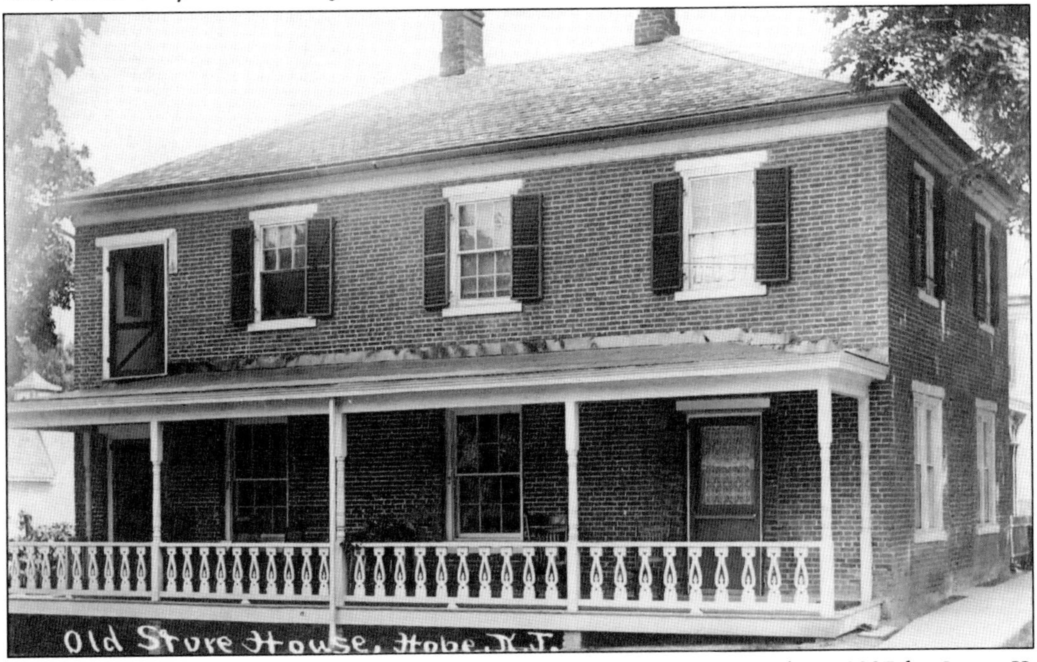

This building at the southeast corner of the same intersection was built in 1827 by James K. Swayze and housed various tenants—butcher shop, hardware store, shoe store, and hat shop. In 1896, Mr. and Mrs. R. M. Van Horn bought it from the Swayze estate; in 1937, Forest C. Van Horn opened his law office here.

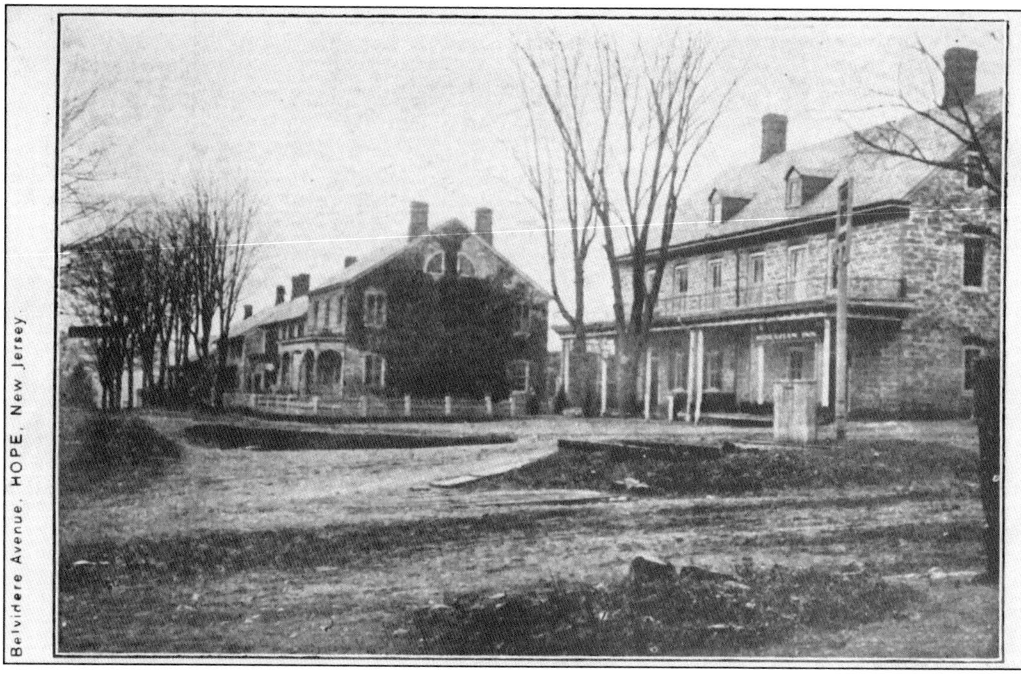

Looking south toward Bridgeville on today's Route 521, the stone building at the right is the Gemeinhaus, which boasted a large hall on the second floor where church services were conducted. The cornerstone was laid on April 2, 1781, by Bishop Reichel. When this photograph was taken, it housed the Moravian Inn, related only by name to the religious order. The two stone buildings beyond are Moravian homes.

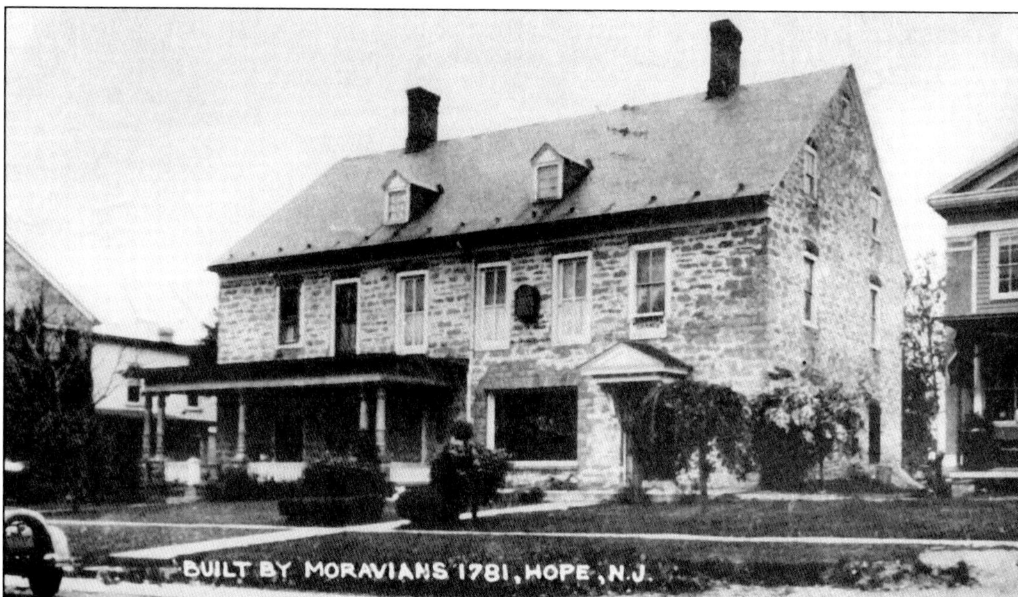

The Gemeinhaus originally had wide stairways at each end, one for women and one for men. The pastor and a boys' school were housed on the first floor. During its years as a hotel, the large second-floor hall was divided into smaller sleeping rooms. In 1824, the first courts of Warren County convened here, and in 1912, the First National Bank of Hope opened in the building.

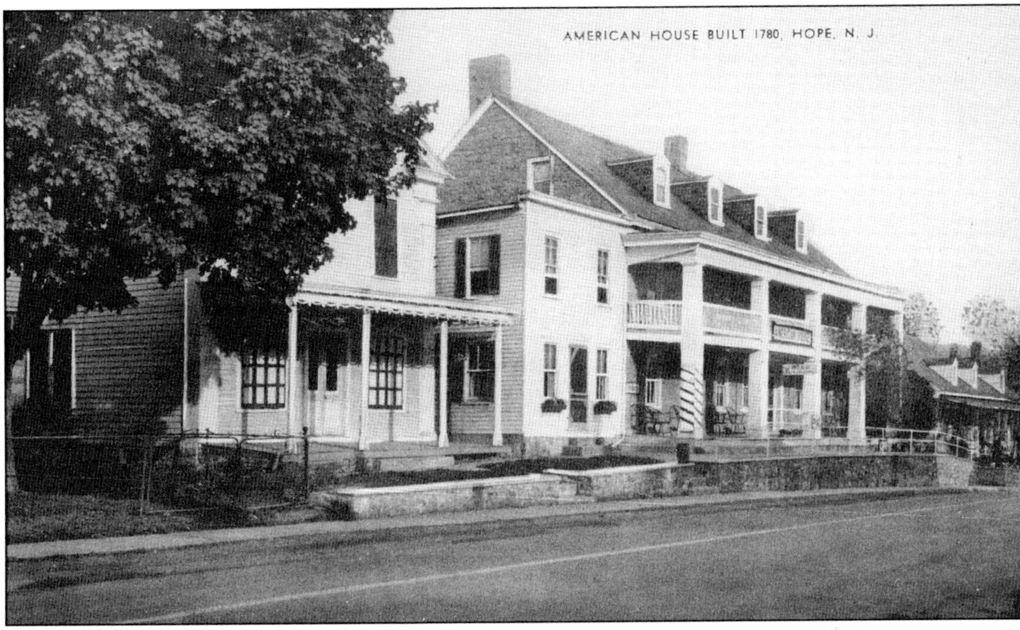

Diagonally south across today's Route 521 from the Gemeinhaus is the Moravian school, the last stone building erected before the settlement was dissolved. Moravian culture was divided into economies, or choirs, based on sex, age, and community position. This building housed the Single Sisters' Economy. It briefly also housed a boys' school, but a failing economy caused that to close within a year. The stone house beyond is also Moravian.

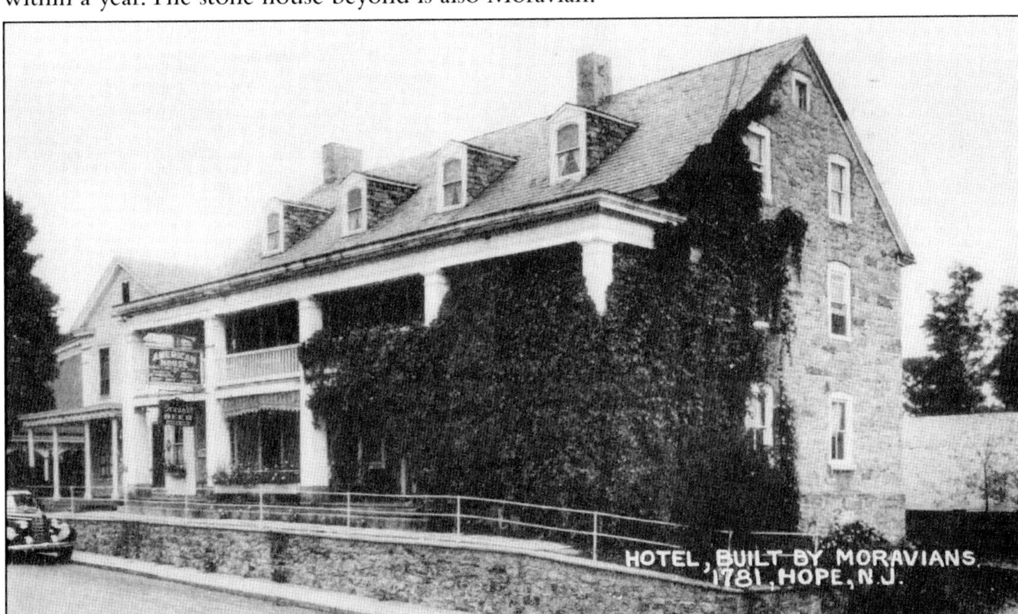

This is another view of the Moravian school, which here houses the American House Hotel. The lower sign proudly advertises "Draught Beer." While the postcard states the structure was built in 1781, the southern section was actually completed around 1797, barely 10 years before the Unity Elder's Conference announced the property would be sold and residents sent to other Moravian towns. It survives today as professional offices.

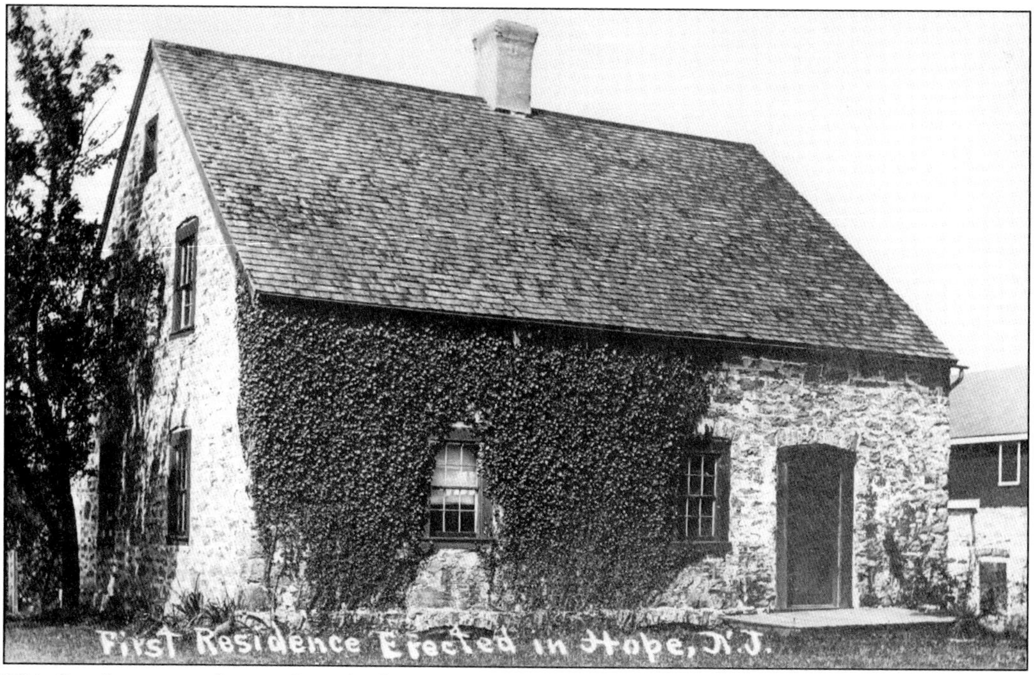

This farmhouse on the north end of Walnut Street is believed to be the community's oldest stone home, built by the Moravians about 1769. It originally served as the residence of the farm manager and has been in continuous use as a farmhouse ever since. Its barn remains as one of two surviving Moravian barns in the village.

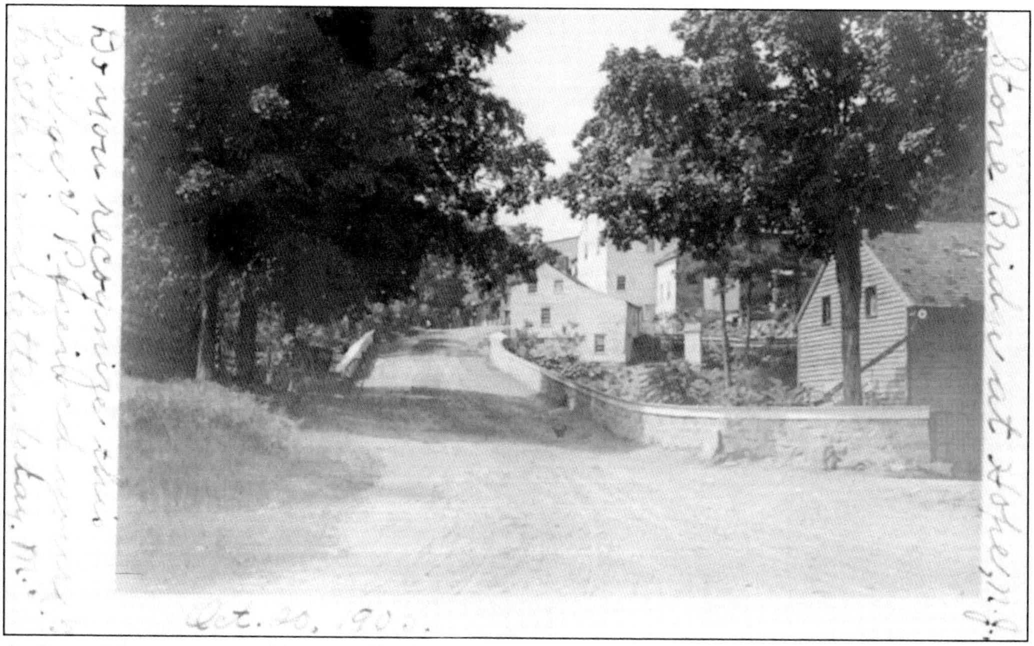

A short drive east over this stone bridge across Beaver Brook brought one to the junction of High Street and the three roads linking Hope with Hackettstown, Johnsonburg, and Blairstown. Although Beaver Brook did not supply the power to turn the wheels of the gristmill built at this corner, usable waterpower was a prime factor in the Moravians' decision to settle in Hope.

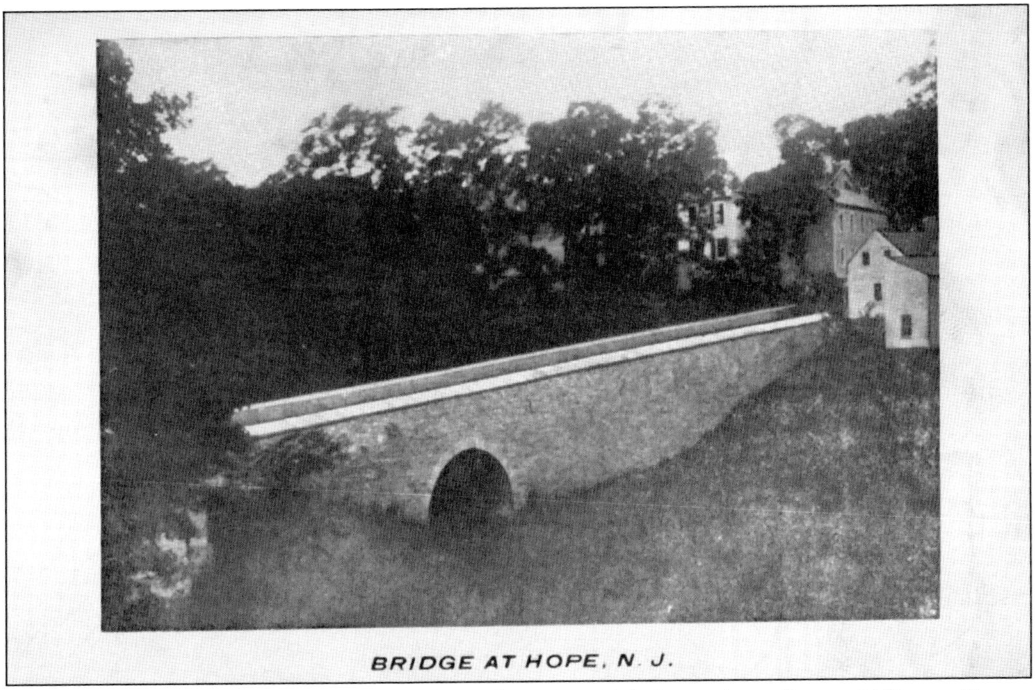

Here are two views of the stone bridge that still carries High Street (now Route 519) over Beaver Brook and down toward the gristmill. Although commonly referred to as the "Moravian" Bridge, unlike most other stone structures in the village, it was not built by them. Taking advantage of abundant local resources, the industrious order artistically created its buildings of random cut limestone and cemented them together with a mortar made of a mixture of clay and lime that was dug nearby and aged for at least a year underground. The strength of this process is evident in the fact that most of their stone structures survive nearly 230 years after they were first assembled.

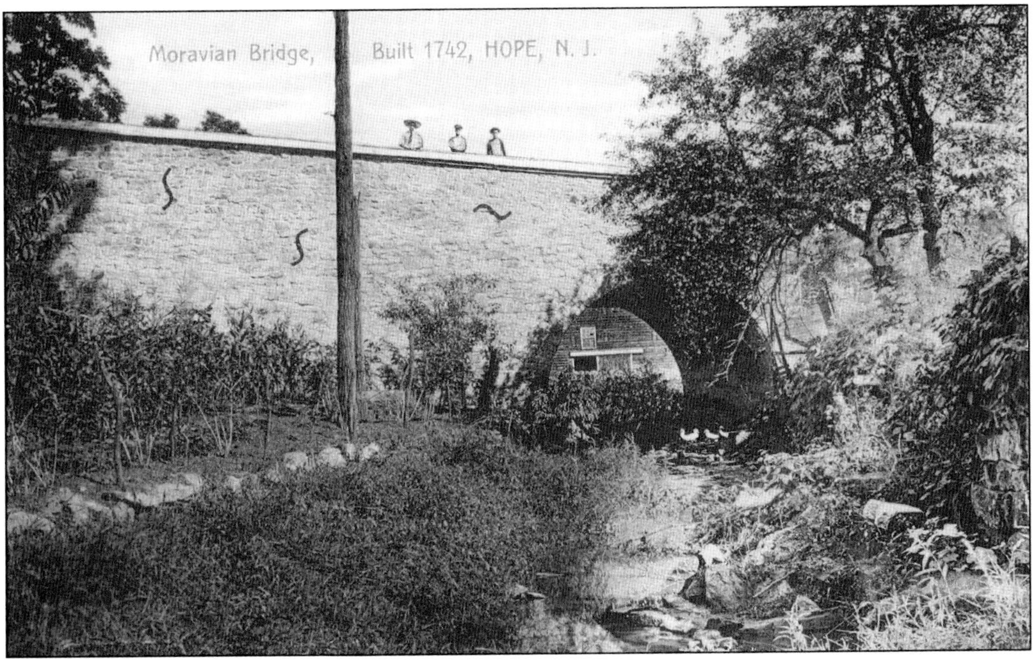

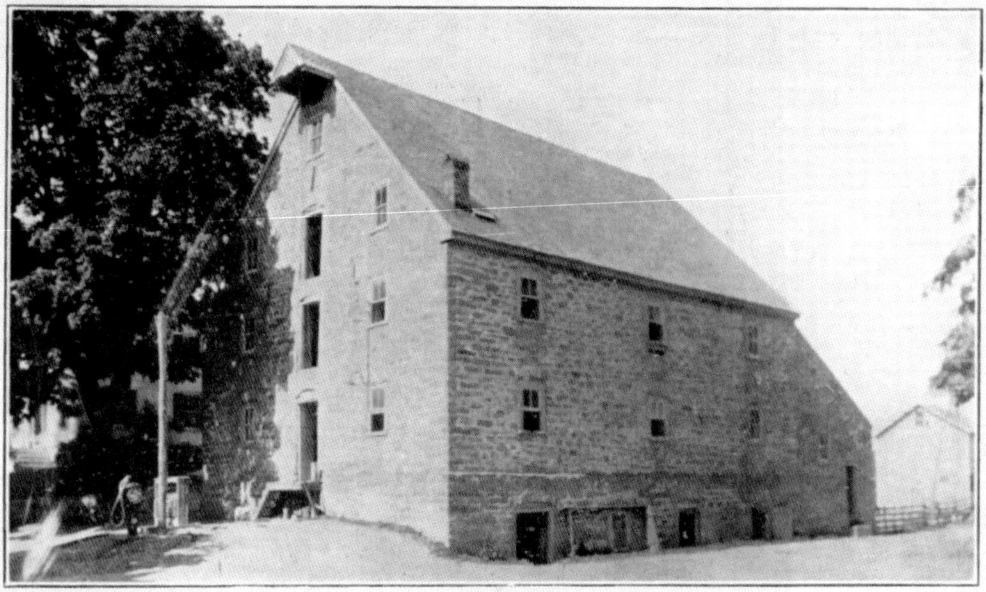

1470 The Old Moravian Mill (1768), Hope, N. J.

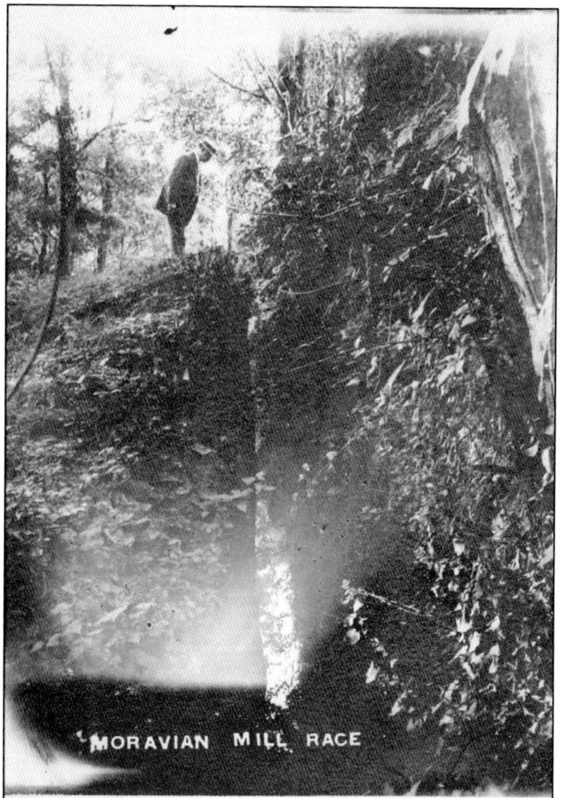

The 3.5-story gristmill, the community's major industry, was the first stone structure completed by the Moravians. It was designed by Christian Christianson of Bethlehem, Pennsylvania, in 1769 and quickly constructed in just one year. The miller, Daniel Hauser, and his family occupied one floor. The thick walls withstood fires in July 1808 (shortly after the Moravians left Hope to return to Pennsylvania) and again in January 1856.

The 1,000-foot millrace was cut by hand through solid slate to a depth of 22 feet. It directed the water of Big and Little Silver Lakes from a millpond north of the building to the mill, where it passed over the large wheel to an outlet on the south side of the building and then under the Johnsonburg road via a tunnel, finally emptying into Beaver Brook.

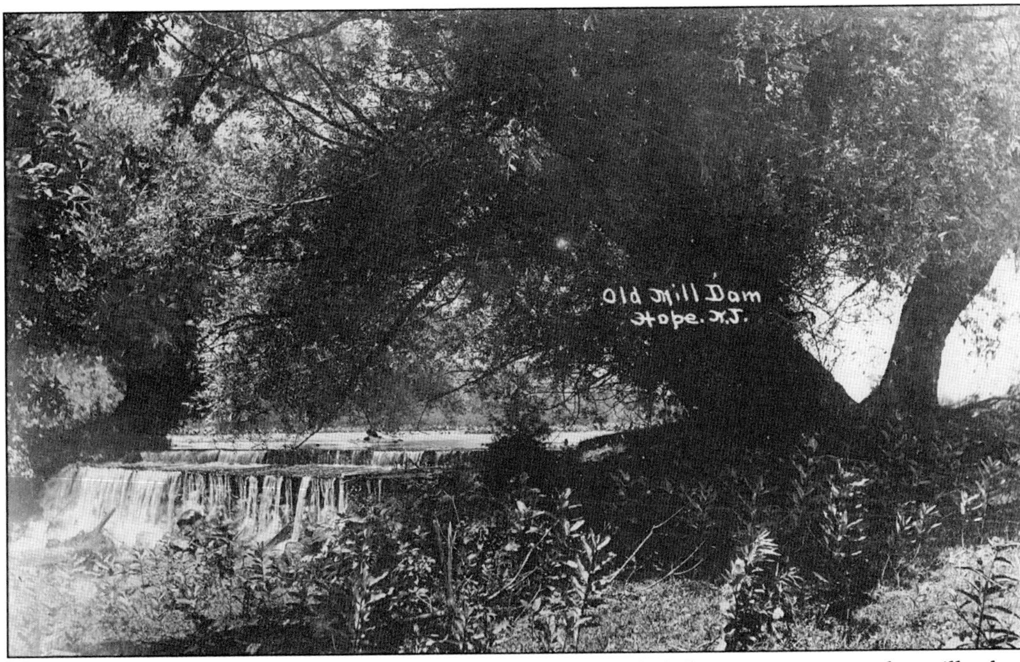

The waters of Big Silver Lake and Little Silver Lake provided the power to turn the mill wheel and grind grain. Although the Moravians were generally apolitical, they did support the American Revolution, and flour produced at the mill in Hope was shipped to supply Washington's troops as they wintered at Jockey Hollow near Morristown, between October 1779 and January 1780.

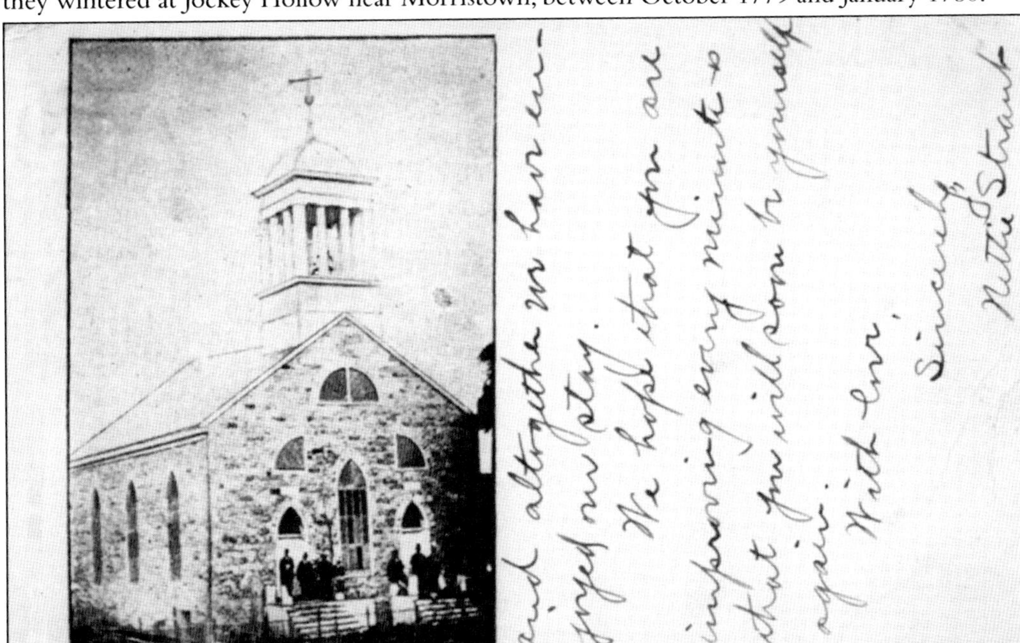

The old Christian church was built in 1841 on the site of a Moravian log tavern that once hosted George Washington and his entourage traveling from the Philadelphia area to Newburgh, New York. It was remodeled in 1896 but suffered damage in the fire of September 28, 1918, when it lost its steeple and much of its interior. The building serves today as Hope's Community Center.

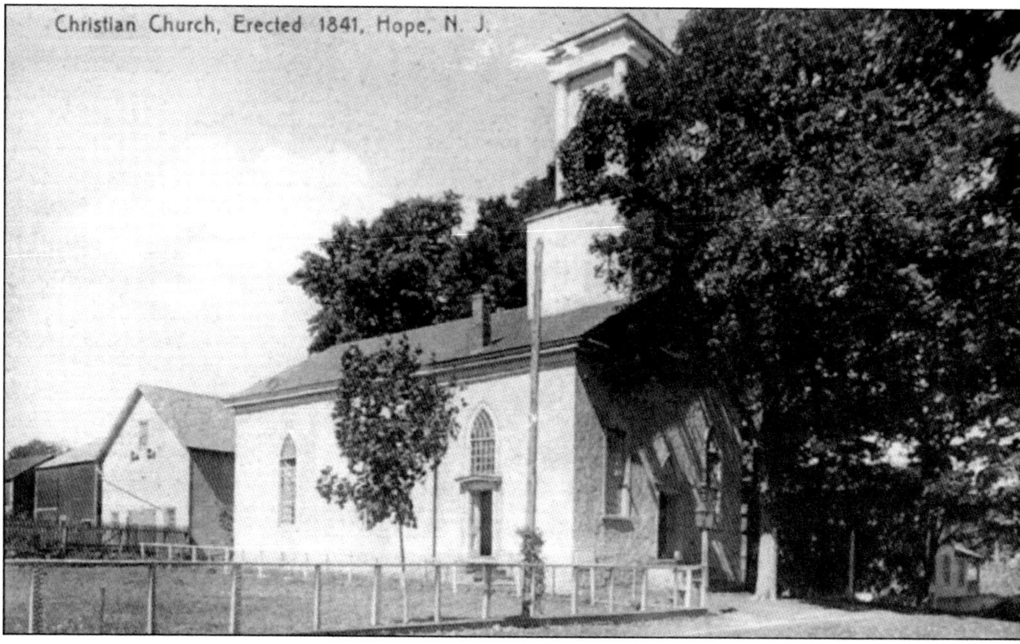

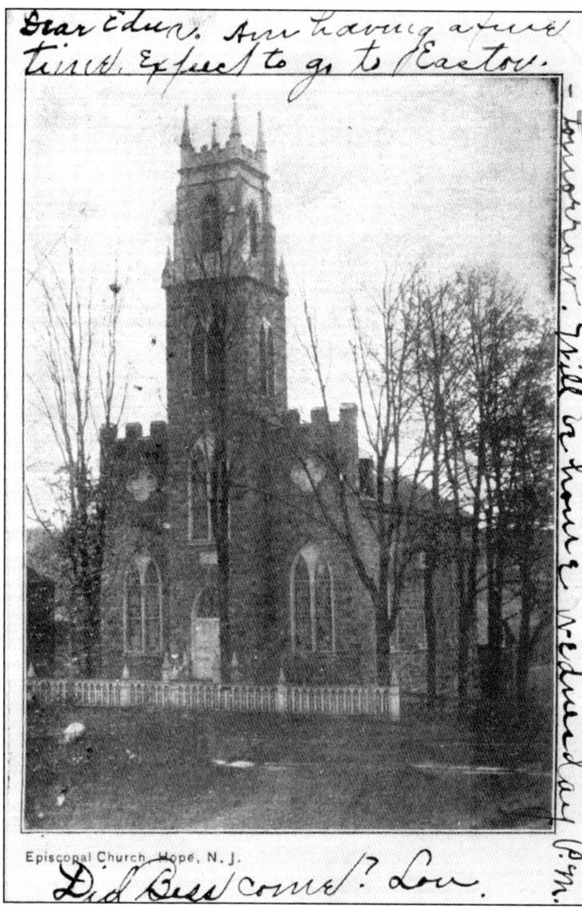

Here is a more recent view of the Christian church. Historically in 1807, the Moravian Unity Elders Conference ended the Hope "experiment" and sold the property for $48,000 to Abraham Horn and Nicolas Kramer, two entrepreneurs from Northampton County, Pennsylvania. On Easter Sunday, April 17, 1808, the surviving congregation held services at the Gemeinhaus and later at the cemetery. They then dispersed to new homes in Bethlehem and Nazareth, Pennsylvania.

The construction of St. Luke's Episcopal Church at the corner of High and Hickory Streets began in 1832. The Gothic-style structure boasted a Christopher Wren–inspired spiral staircase to its choir loft and an organ that, according to local legend, was donated by the queen of England to the Trinity Episcopal Church in New York City and then given to the Hope parish about 1839 when this building was completed.

In 1832, Methodists in Hope purchased property and erected the first St. John's Church on High Street, between Hickory Street and Mount Hermon Road. By 1875, the congregation had outgrown the original building that was badly in need of repair, so the decision was made to tear it down. A new church was completed and dedicated the following year by Pastor J. O. Winner. In the view at right, it still has its stately steeple, while in the view below the steeple is missing and shows some damage at the base, indicating a possible recent accident. In the southwest corner of the cemetery to the right of the church are the graves of the 62 Moravian men, women, and children who died at Hope during the time that the community was settled there.

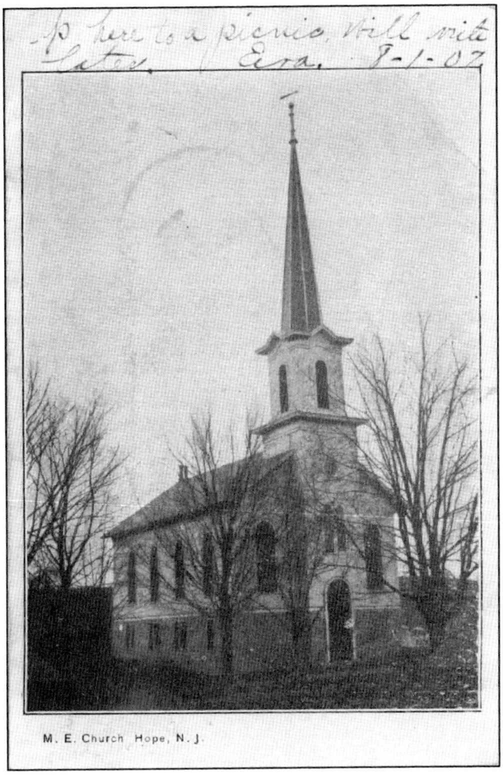

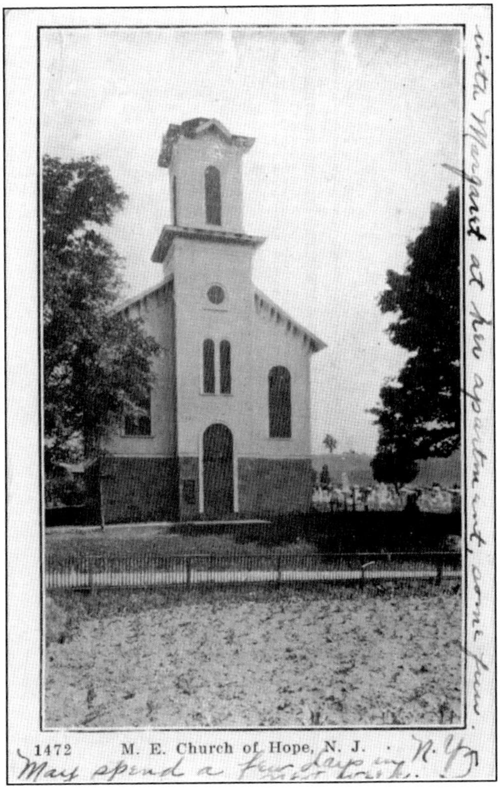

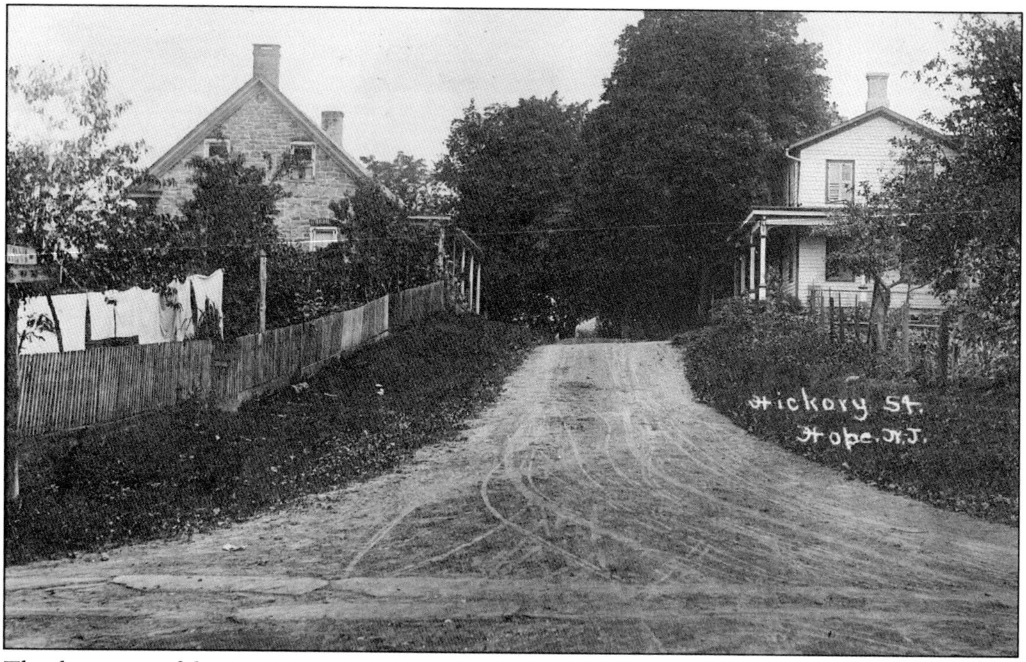

The departure of the Moravians in 1808 and the influx of new farmers preserved Hope's character as a quaint country hamlet. Bypassed by the railroads and the Morris Canal and rejected as the county seat of Warren County in favor of Belvidere in 1825, the village has retained its 19th-century charm. At the corner of High and Hickory Streets, the Stephen Nicolaus house is to the left.

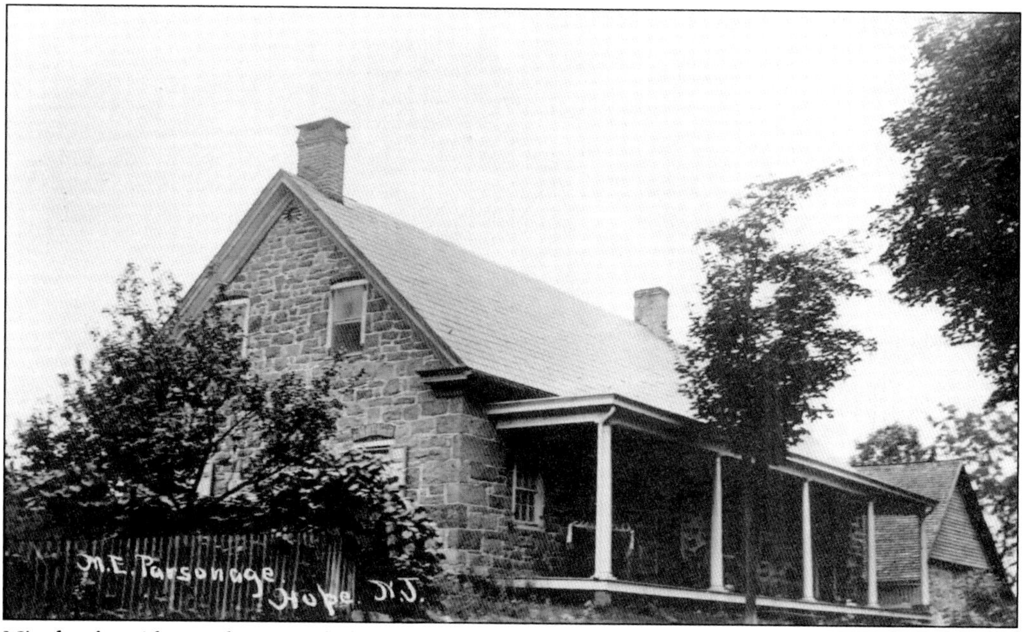

Nicolaus's residence, the second oldest Moravian home in the village, was built in 1775 on Hickory Street. The wooden porch was added around 1900, and its stone barn still stands. Nicolaus operated brick and lime kilns in the area. In 1809, the basement was used as Hope's first public school. The house later became the Methodist parsonage and survives today as a private home.

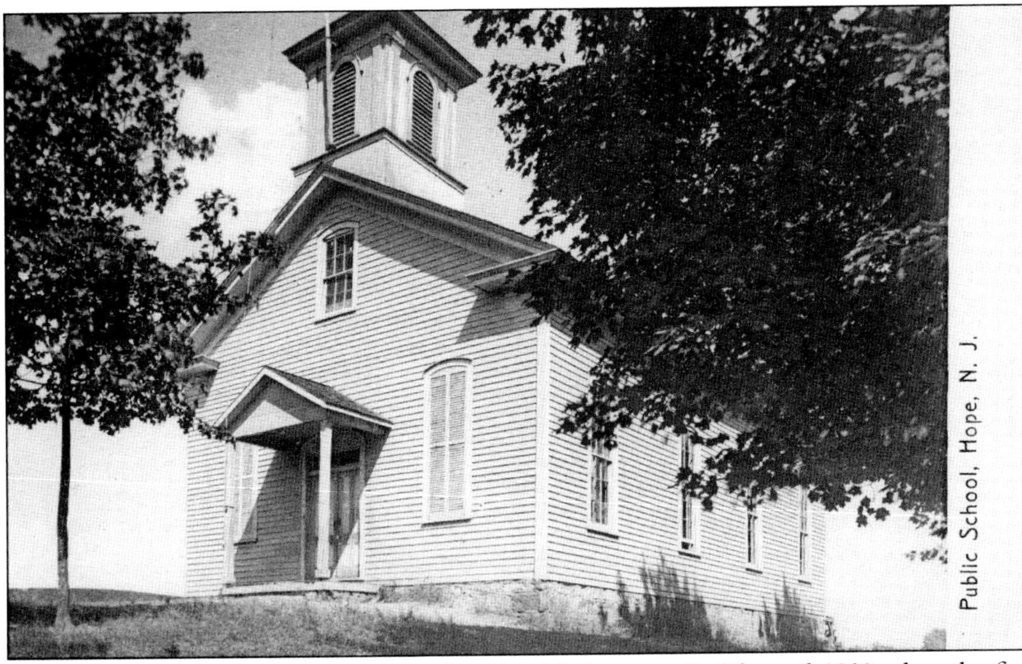

Following a stay at the Nicolaus home, the school led a nomadic life until 1830 when the first permanent structure was constructed of stone just east of the Moravian cemetery. In 1858, property was purchased on the Hope-Johnsonburg Road across from the mill, and this frame building was completed for $6,000. It served until 1925, when it became outmoded, and the central portion of Hope's current school was built.

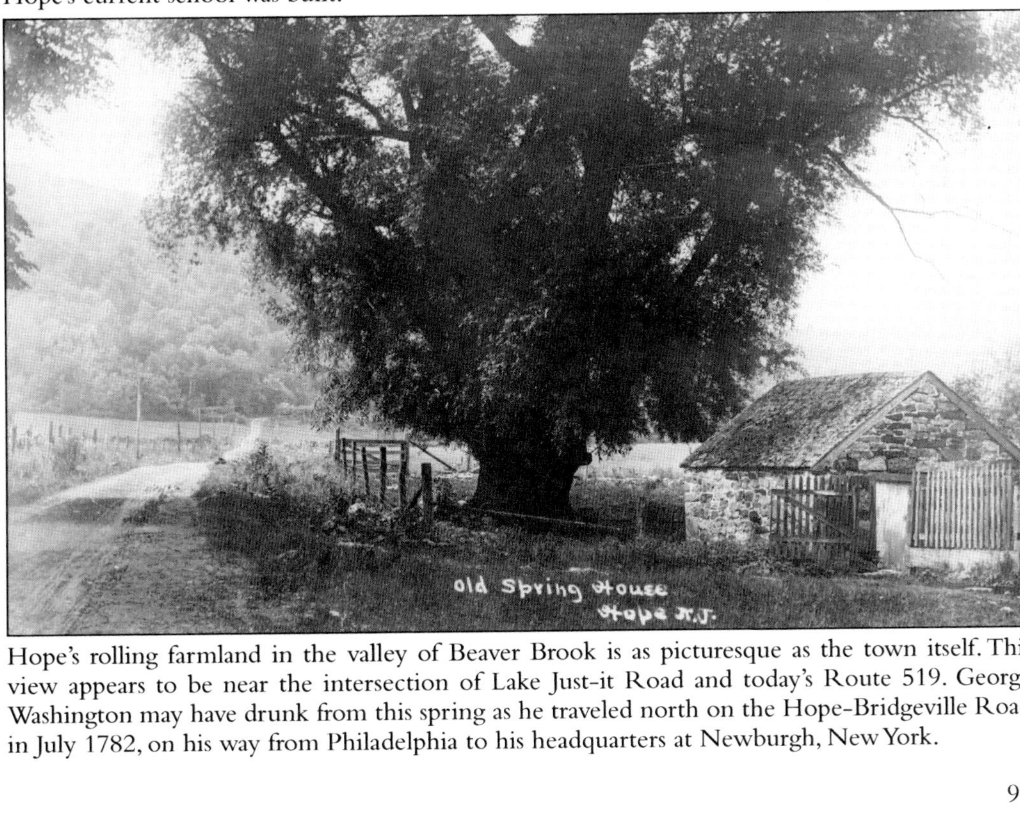

Hope's rolling farmland in the valley of Beaver Brook is as picturesque as the town itself. This view appears to be near the intersection of Lake Just-it Road and today's Route 519. George Washington may have drunk from this spring as he traveled north on the Hope-Bridgeville Road in July 1782, on his way from Philadelphia to his headquarters at Newburgh, New York.

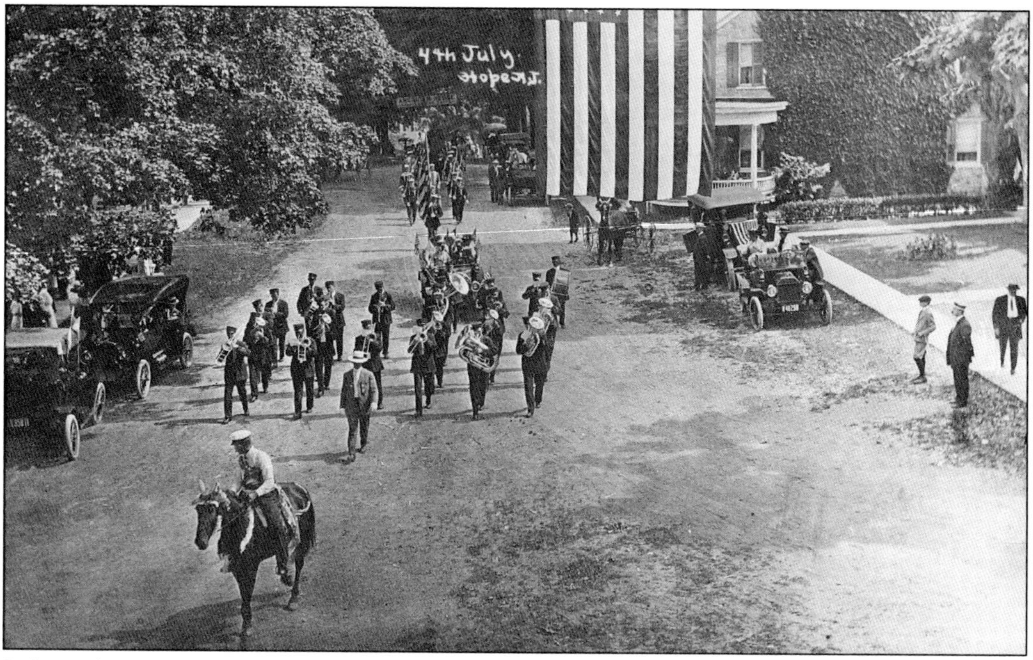

Independence Day was a time for celebrations, and what was a Fourth of July without a parade? The local band passes a group of onlookers as it wends its way through Hope on July 4, 1914. War clouds are gathering over Europe, and it will be barely three years before the United States will join the fray and boys from Hope will be transported to waiting troop trains at Belvidere.

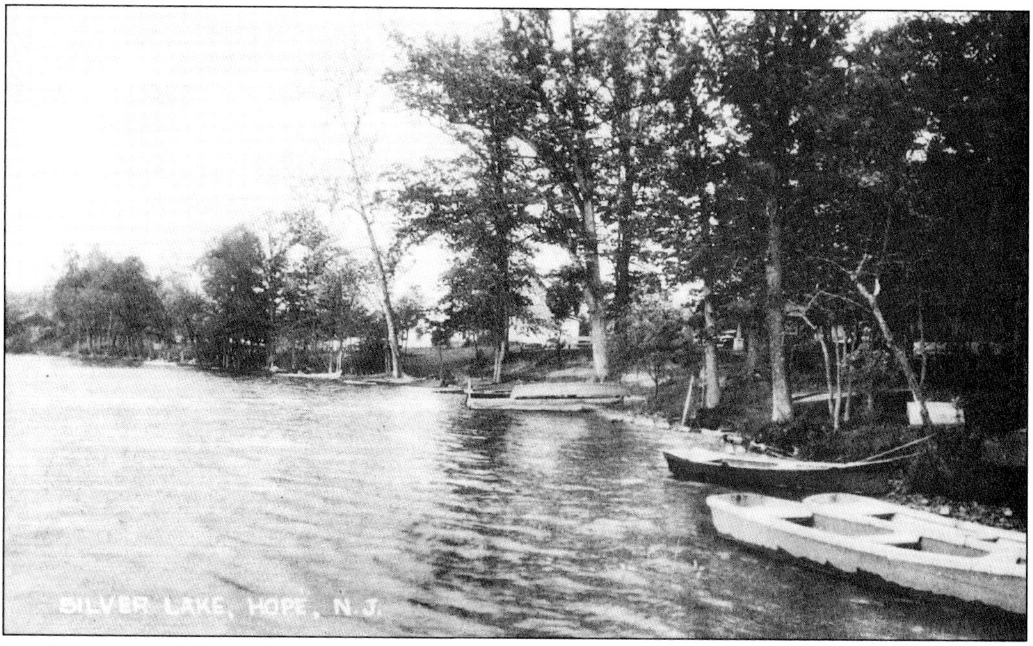

In 1900, spring-fed Big Silver Lake and Little Silver Lake were largely pastoral and frequented only by sportsmen. The lakes, connected by a narrow channel, fed the millpond with their overflow, providing waterpower to turn the giant wheel at the mill in Hope. In 1920, Big Silver Lake was owned by the Albertson family, which divided and sold parcels of land, creating the local resort.

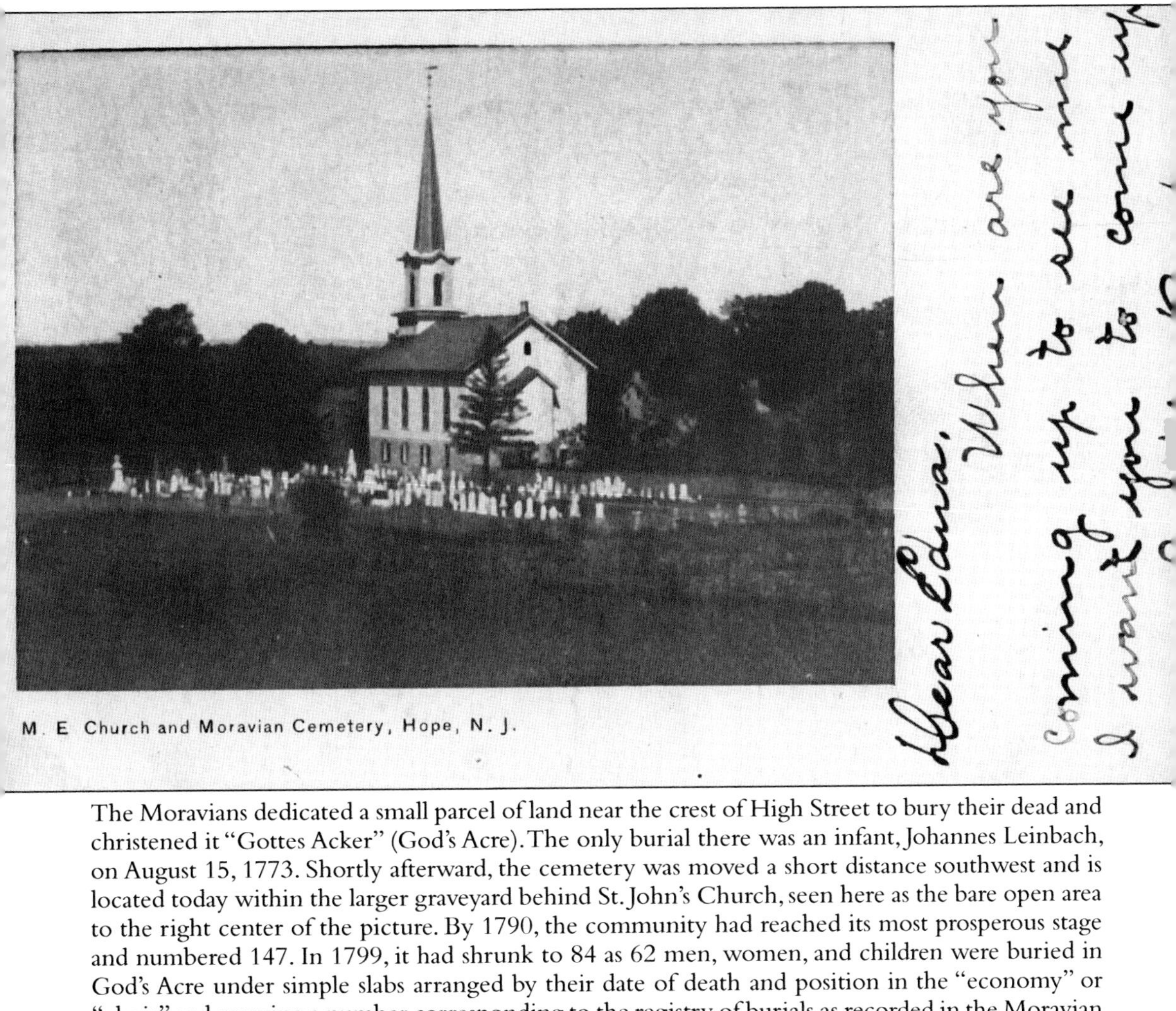

The Moravians dedicated a small parcel of land near the crest of High Street to bury their dead and christened it "Gottes Acker" (God's Acre). The only burial there was an infant, Johannes Leinbach, on August 15, 1773. Shortly afterward, the cemetery was moved a short distance southwest and is located today within the larger graveyard behind St. John's Church, seen here as the bare open area to the right center of the picture. By 1790, the community had reached its most prosperous stage and numbered 147. In 1799, it had shrunk to 84 as 62 men, women, and children were buried in God's Acre under simple slabs arranged by their date of death and position in the "economy" or "choir" and carrying a number corresponding to the registry of burials as recorded in the Moravian Archives at Bethlehem, Pennsylvania. Before leaving Hope forever, the Moravians held their final prayer service at this spot on Easter Sunday, April 17, 1808. They then sadly left their beloved dead behind as they trekked west to new homes in Bethlehem and Nazareth, Pennsylvania.

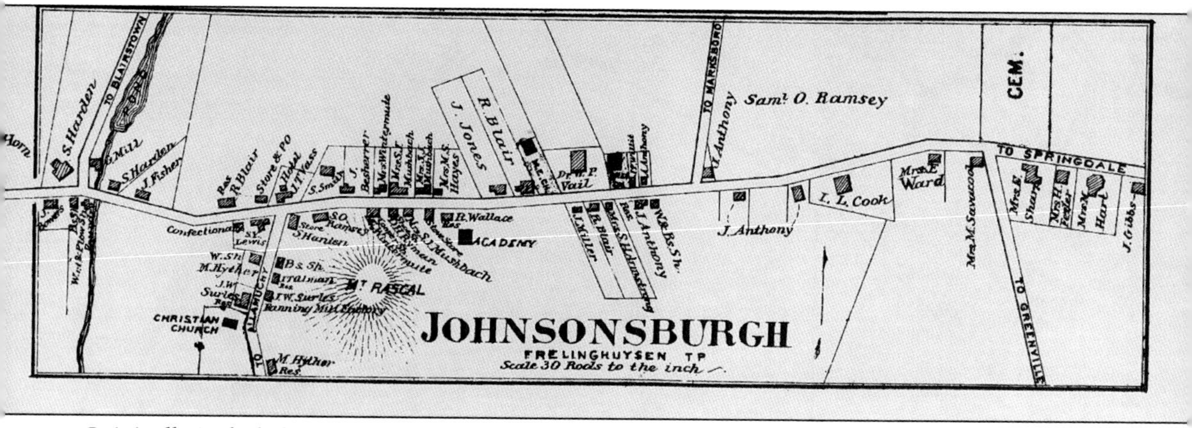

Originally included in Sussex County, Frelinghuysen Township became part of Warren County in 1824 and, like Blairstown, has several distinct hamlets within its borders. Two of the best known of these are Johnsonburg and Marksboro, as their names survive today. Forgotten areas include Kerr's Corners, Southtown, and Shiloh.

Six

Other Neighbors
Johnsonburg, Marksboro, and Hardwick

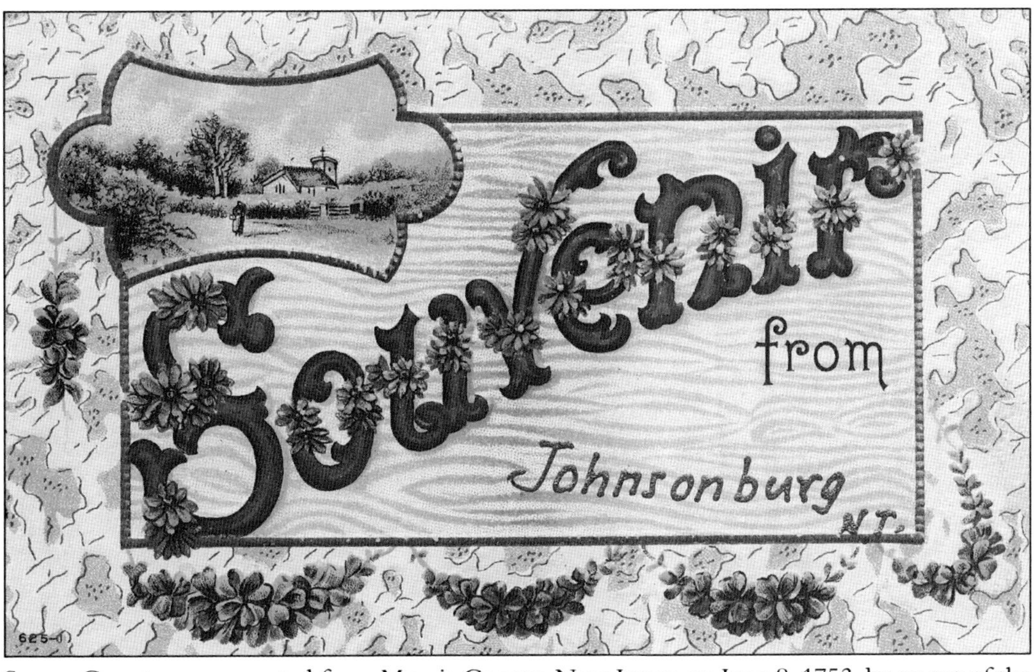

Sussex County was separated from Morris County, New Jersey, on June 8, 1753, by an act of the State Assembly, and the county seat was fixed at the location of today's Johnsonburg. The act also provided for the erection of a courthouse and jail, and the latter was constructed in 1754 of rough timber, giving the village the rather quaint name of Logg Gaol, which it retained for many years.

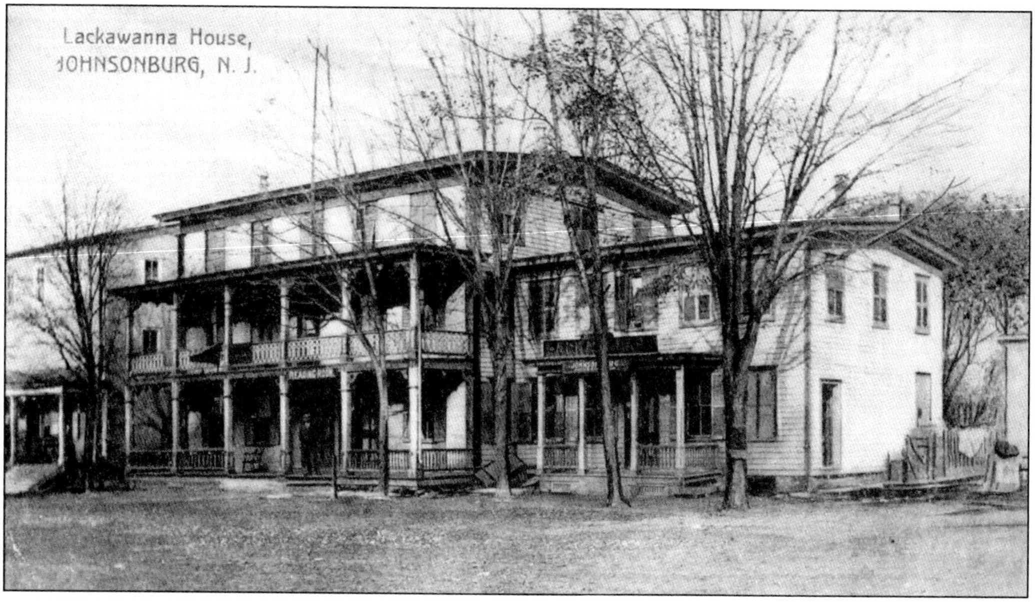

The Johnsonburg Hotel became Lackawanna House after the DL&W Railroad built its New Jersey Cutoff through town in 1911. The log jail remained until 1763, when the county seat was moved to Newton. No courthouse was ever built, that function being handled in the tavern of Jonathan Pettit. Named for a local storekeeper, Johnsonburg became part of Warren County when it was created on November 20, 1824.

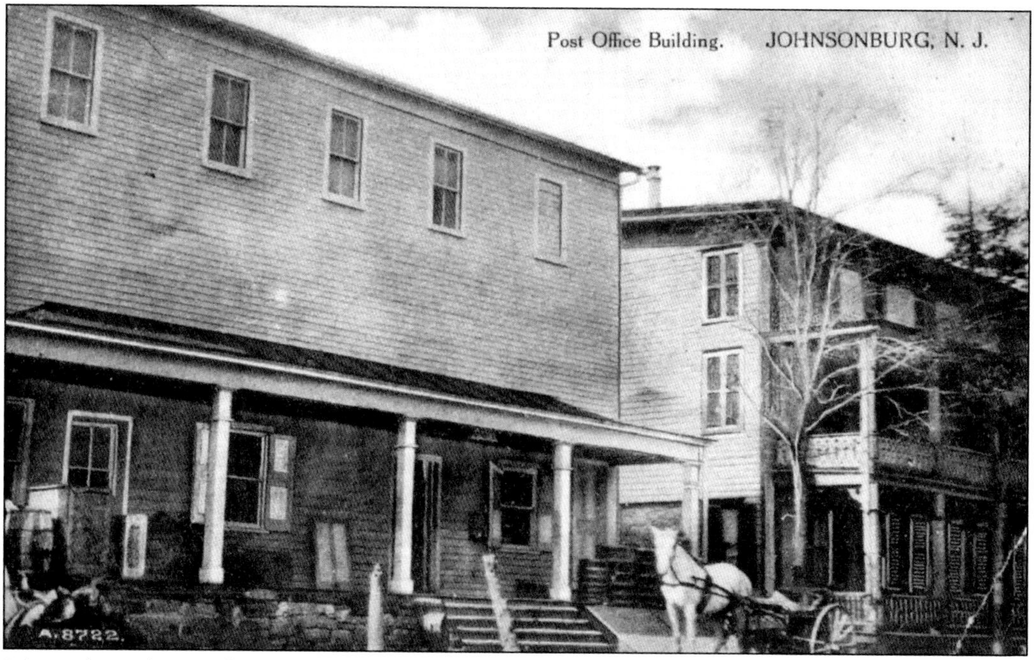

Johnsonburg lies within the township of Frelinghuysen, incorporated in 1848 and named in honor of Theodore Frelinghuysen, attorney general of New Jersey, United States senator, mayor of Newark, New Jersey, Whig Party candidate for vice president with Henry Clay in 1844, and president of Rutgers University. This view shows the post office, with the hotel, operated by a Mr. Kice, at the right. (Courtesy of Ruth Hutchinson Gommoll.)

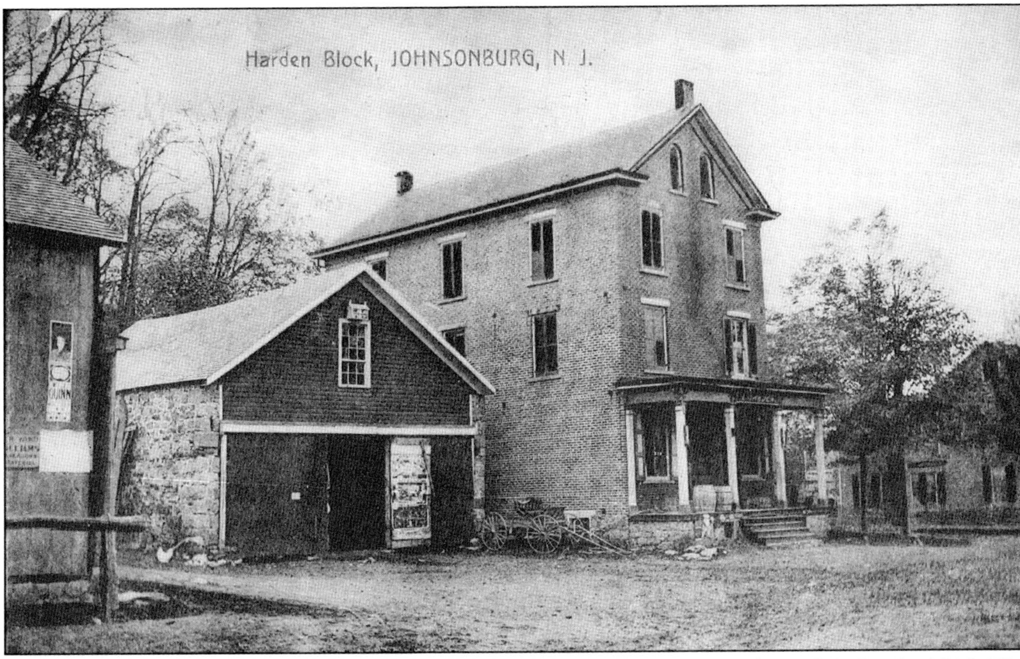

The corner of Main and High Streets in Johnsonburg appears deserted on this day in 1908. The view above looks west on Main Street by the "Harden (sic) Block," named for shopkeeper Elbridge Hardin. The first store in Logg Gaol was in William Armstrong's log cabin. He was succeeded by a Carr, and then by the Johnson for whom the village is named. John I. Blair's brother, Robert, kept a shop here. The view below faces east. In 1911, there were several stores in Johnsonburg, all doing well, partially due to construction activity on the Lackawanna Cutoff. Edward Hardin operated a gristmill on Mill Road, which dated to 1774. Due to the rural nature of the area, there were two blacksmith shops and two wheelwrights. (Both, courtesy of Ruth Hutchinson Gommoll.)

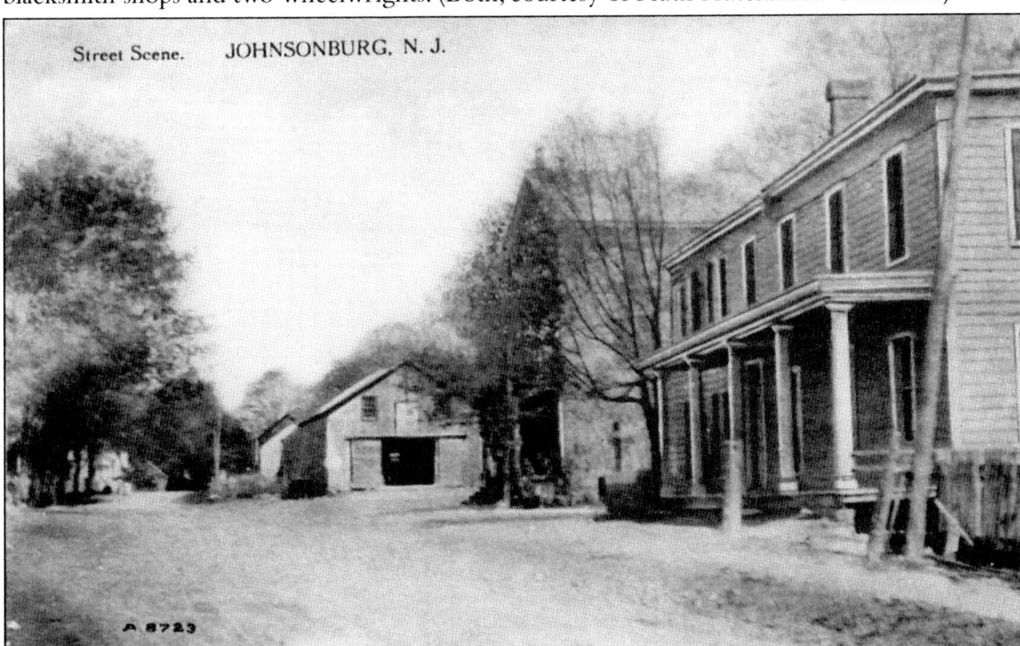

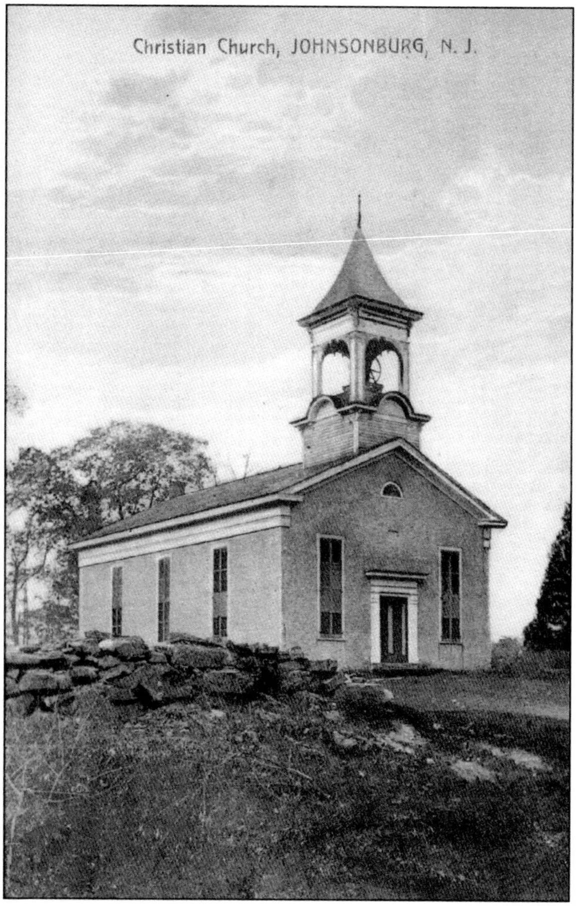

The Christian church was established July 15, 1826, through the efforts of Abigail Roberts, a missionary who had come to the area in 1824. Construction of this building at the top of High Street began in 1838 and was completed 10 years later. It became the mother church of those Christian churches at Vienna and Hope, New Jersey. A Methodist Episcopal church was built on Main Street in 1850.

Looking down High Street from the church, the hotel is visible. Evangelist Joseph Thomas, the famed White Pilgrim (so called because he dressed in white and rode a white horse), preached a sermon in Johnsonburg in April 1835 and died shortly after, presumably of smallpox. He was buried at the Dark Moon Cemetery outside of town but later exhumed and reburied in the Christian Cemetery on High Street. (Courtesy of Ruth Hutchinson Gommoll.)

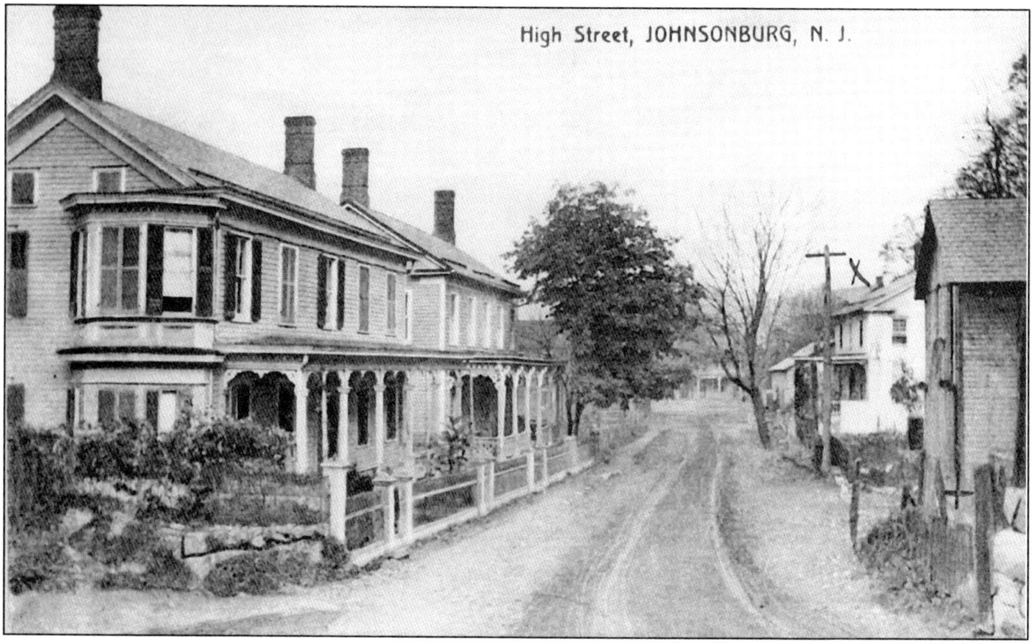

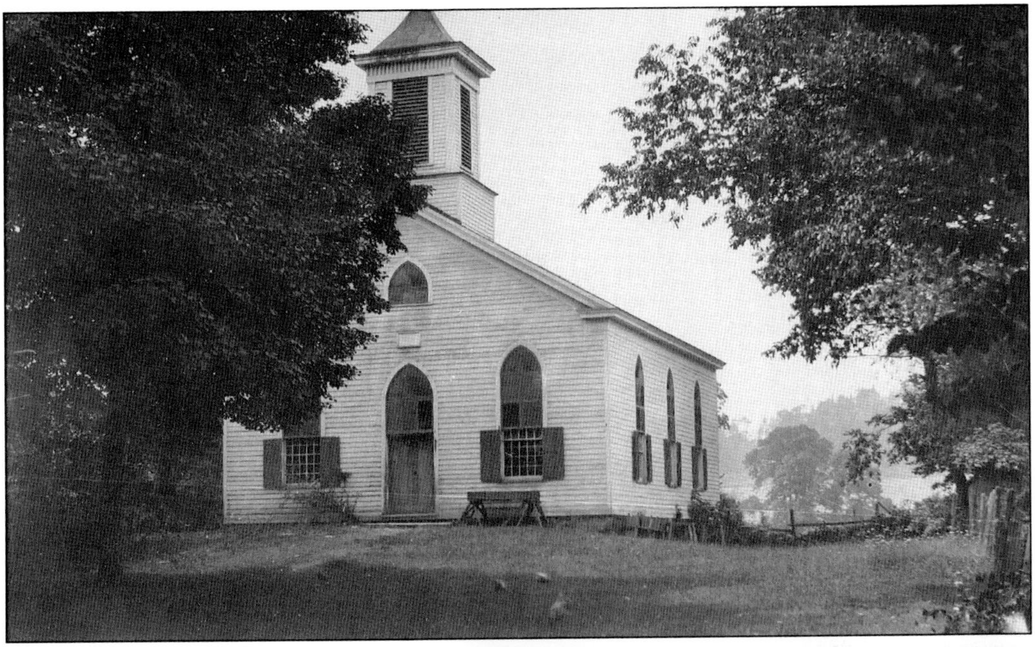

Rev. George Banghart and other Methodist circuit preachers visited Johnsonburg frequently and held services in the shaded groves in the summer and in farmers' barns during the winter. In 1850, Isaac Dennis donated a plot of land on Main Street for the construction of an Episcopal church, at which the Methodists were permitted to hold services. (Courtesy of Ruth Hutchinson Gommoll.)

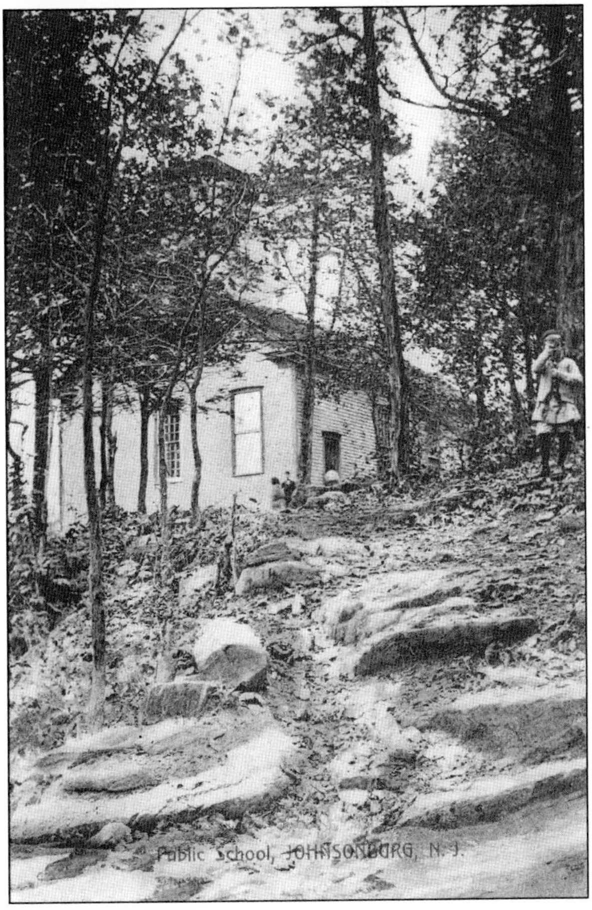

In 1881, the Johnsonburg School District owned this building, which was valued at $1,000. It had been constructed in 1868 at a cost of $3,000 and could hold 80 students comfortably. There were 76 pupils on the register, but the average daily attendance was only 34, clearly demonstrating that farm work was more important to parents than education in the 19th century. (Courtesy of Ruth Hutchinson Gommoll.)

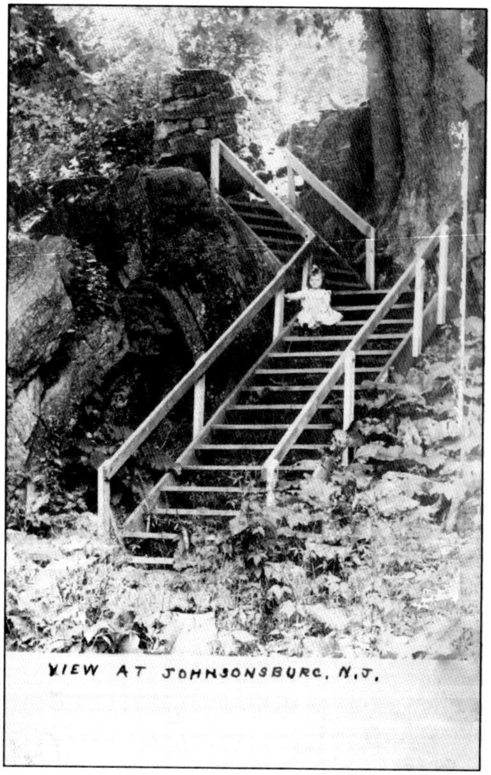

Much of Frelinghuysen Township was hilly with lots of small valleys and rocky knobs. One of these knobs is located just across High Street from the Christian church and its cemetery. Since card playing and other sports were forbidden on the Sabbath, miscreants who practiced these "evils" would congregate at the top of this knob to imbibe in their "immoral" activities. Hence, this area became locally known as "Mount Rascal."

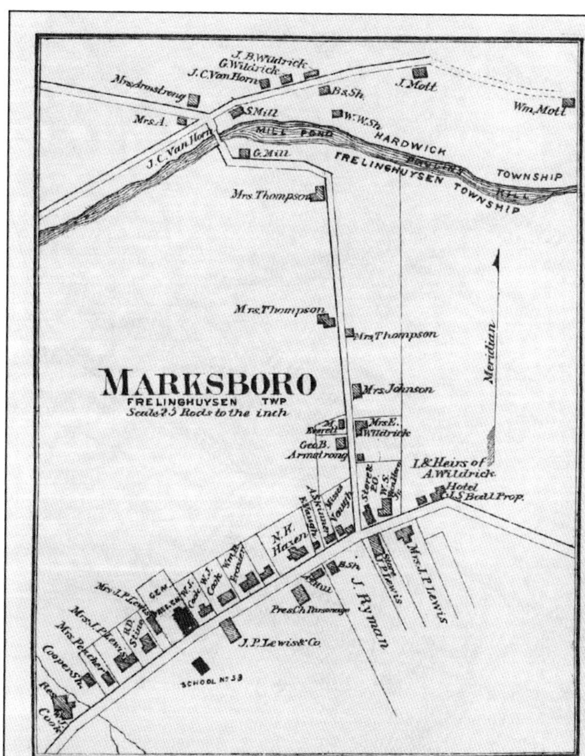

The New York, Susquehanna and Western Railroad had not yet been built when this plot map of Marksboro was drawn in 1874. Though namesake Mark Thomson had already been dead for over 70 years, his family still had extensive holdings, including the gristmill that was the largest industry in the village. Although not a major waterway the Paulinskill provided ample power for light industrial undertakings.

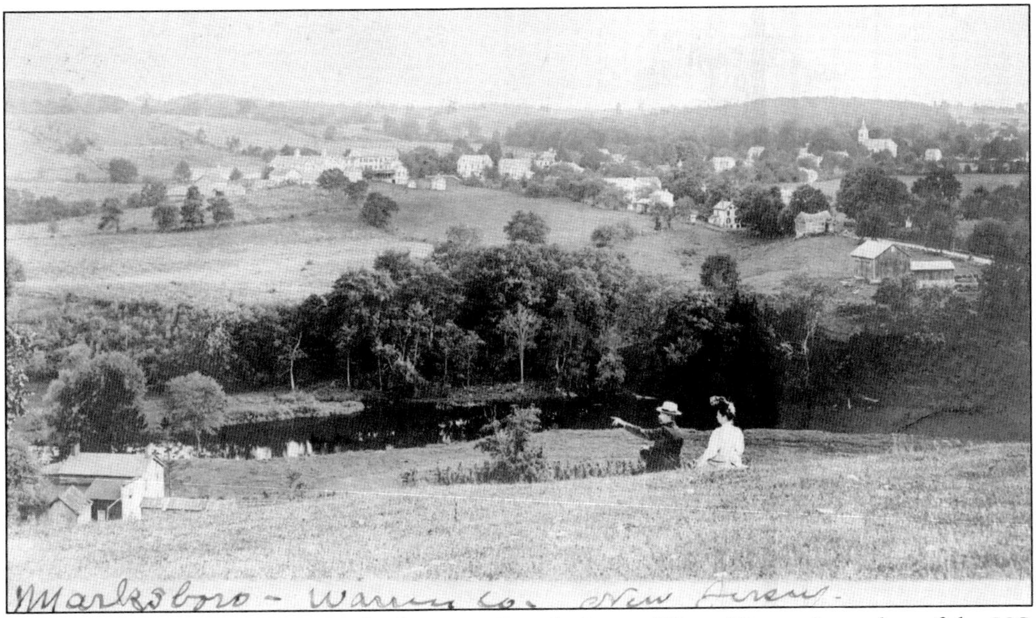

Marksboro is named for Col. Mark Thomson, Revolutionary War soldier and member of the U.S. House of Representatives from New Jersey. Thomson was born in Pennsylvania in 1739. He moved to New Jersey and eventually purchased 3,000 acres in Frelinghuysen Township where he built his home and gristmill along the banks of the Paulinskill River. Thomson died December 14, 1803, and is buried in the Marksboro Presbyterian Church cemetery.

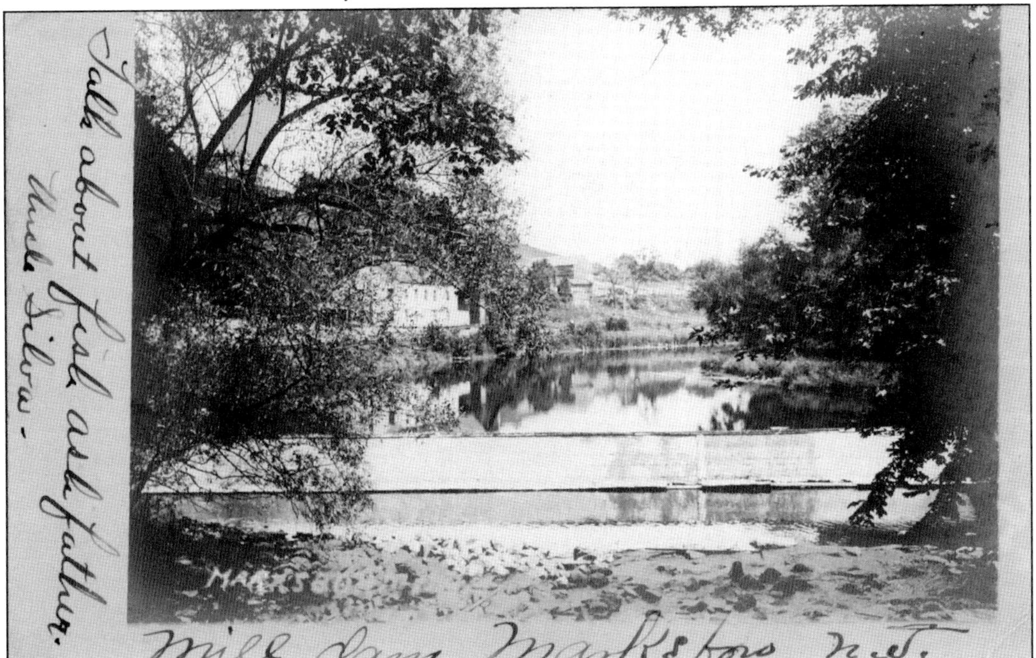

The Paulinskill River was dammed at Marksboro to create Thomson's millpond. Thomson's grand home still stands on the hill above his mill and boasts a small stone rear outbuilding constructed with musket slits in the walls to serve as a fort in the event of attacks by Native Americans. Thomson was elected to Congress on the Federalist ticket and served from March 4, 1795, to March 3, 1799.

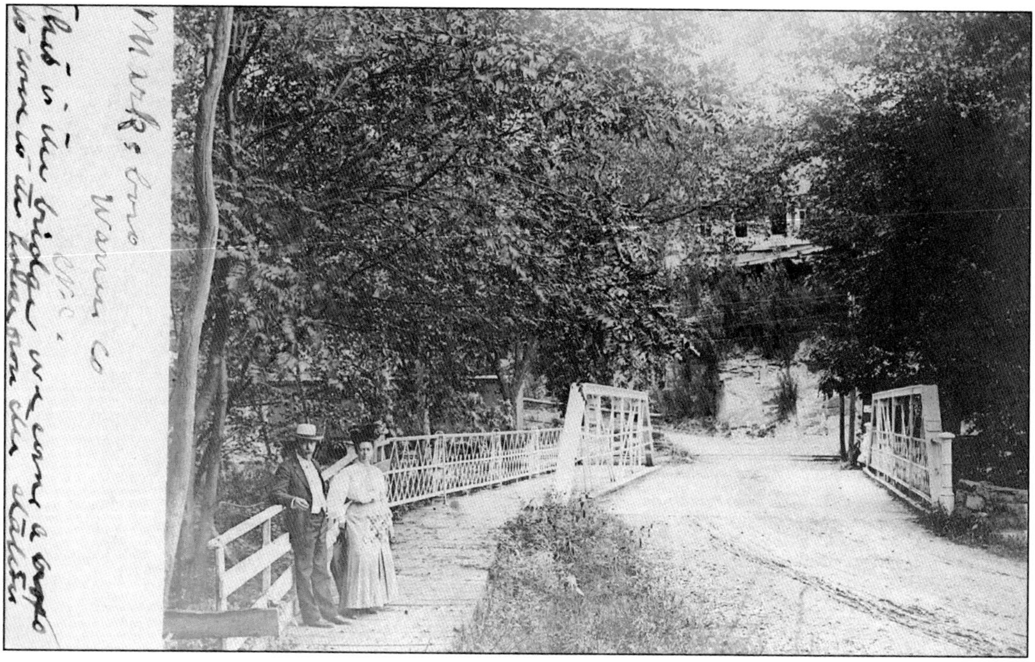

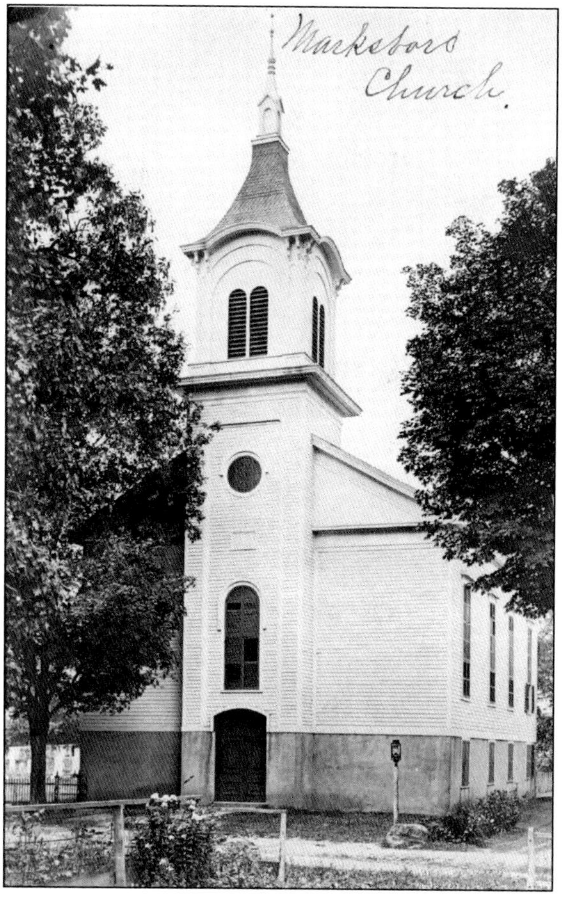

The road from Marksboro to Hardwick crossed the Paulinskill on this iron bridge located adjacent to Thomson's mill, which can barely be discerned through the trees at the left. The photographer is standing on the crossing of the New York, Susquehanna and Western Railroad, which paralleled the river and passed through Marksboro on its way from Jersey City to Blairstown and points west. A quaint depot stood here until 1938.

The Marksboro Presbyterian Church was organized November 1, 1814, with Rev. Robert Finley as pastor. Services were held in Frederick Snover's barn until a building could be completed. This structure, the second of the congregation's three churches, was dedicated in 1859. It was struck by lightning and burned on June 26, 1943. With insufficient insurance, the congregation could only settle for a smaller replacement that was opened September 17, 1950.

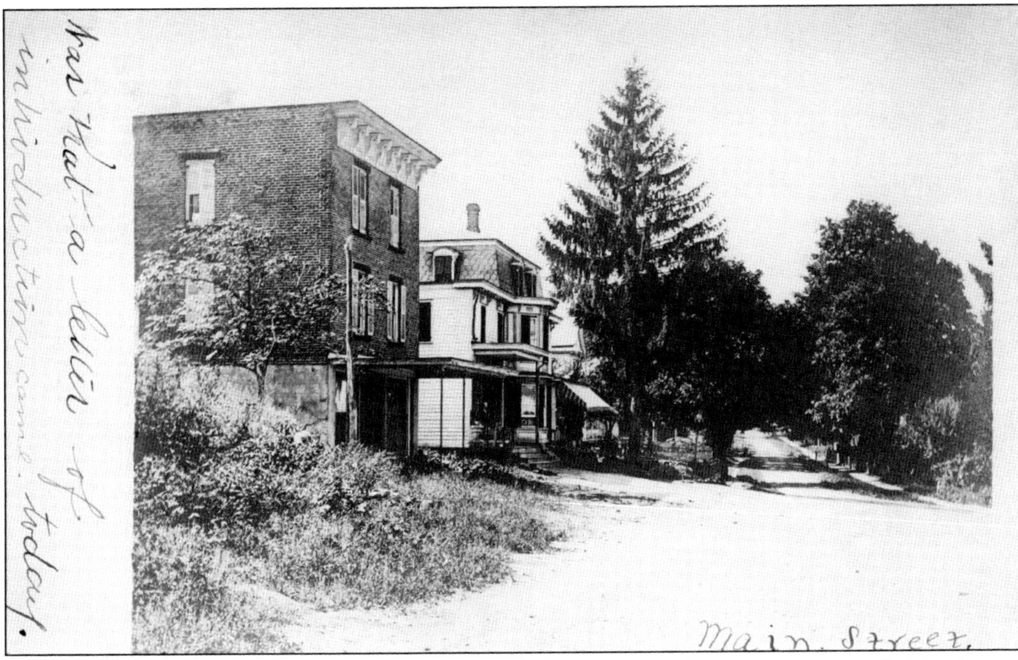

Travelers rolling southwest through pastoral Marksboro over 100 years ago enjoyed this view on the predecessor to today's Route 94. Little has changed in this quiet hamlet since the photographer snapped his shutter and recorded the scene. William Shafer was the first storekeeper here, having immigrated to the region in 1742.

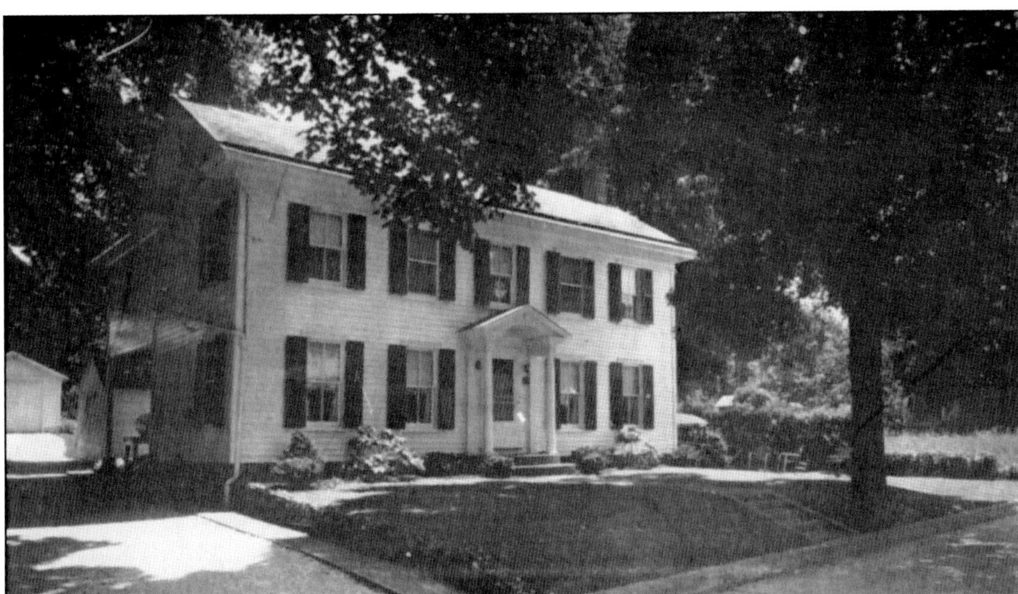

Mr. and Mrs. Harry Vough operated the Maple Lodge on Route 94, advertising "Room and Breakfast for Overnight Guests." With automobile travel becoming popular and roads improving, the need for accommodations in obscure hamlets like Marksboro increased as city dwellers came west to sample the bucolic features of rural New Jersey. Those who shunned larger hotels and boardinghouses found the ancestors of today's bed and breakfasts delightful.

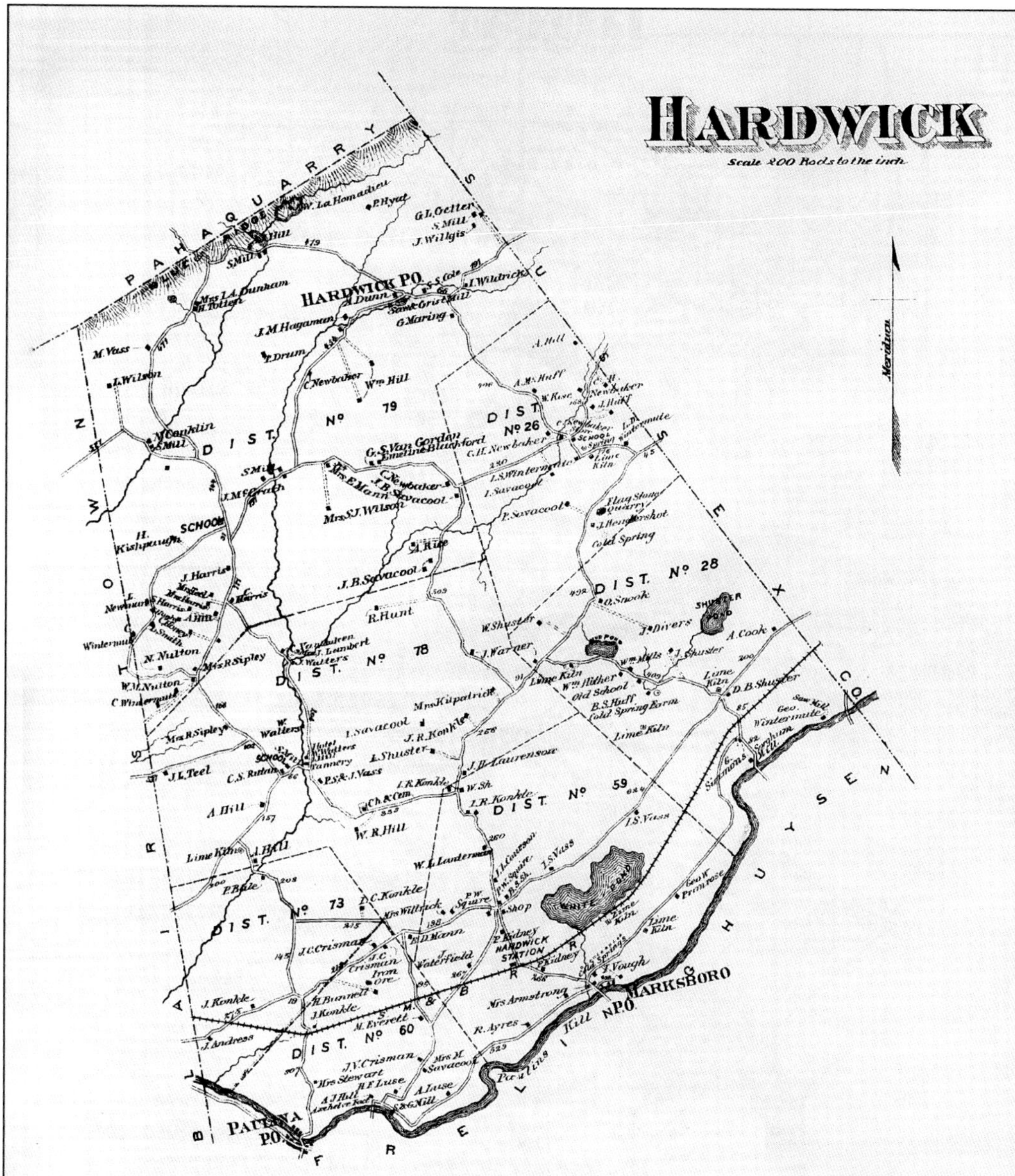

Hardwick was created by royal charter on January 22, 1749, while part of Morris County. On June 8, 1753, it was transferred to the newly created Sussex County. The township was incorporated by an act of the New Jersey Legislature on February 21, 1798, and added to Warren County on November 20, 1824. Hardwick had but one postal district and only 639 residents in 1874 when this map was drawn. The overzealous draftsman included the tracks of the South Mountain and Boston Railroad that was planned but never built through this region. Portions of the SM&B eventually became the Lehigh and New England Railway, a subsidiary of the Lehigh Coal and Navigation Company, which found it more economical to use trackage rights over the New York, Susquehanna and Western Railroad from Swartswood to Hainesburg rather than build its own right-of-way.

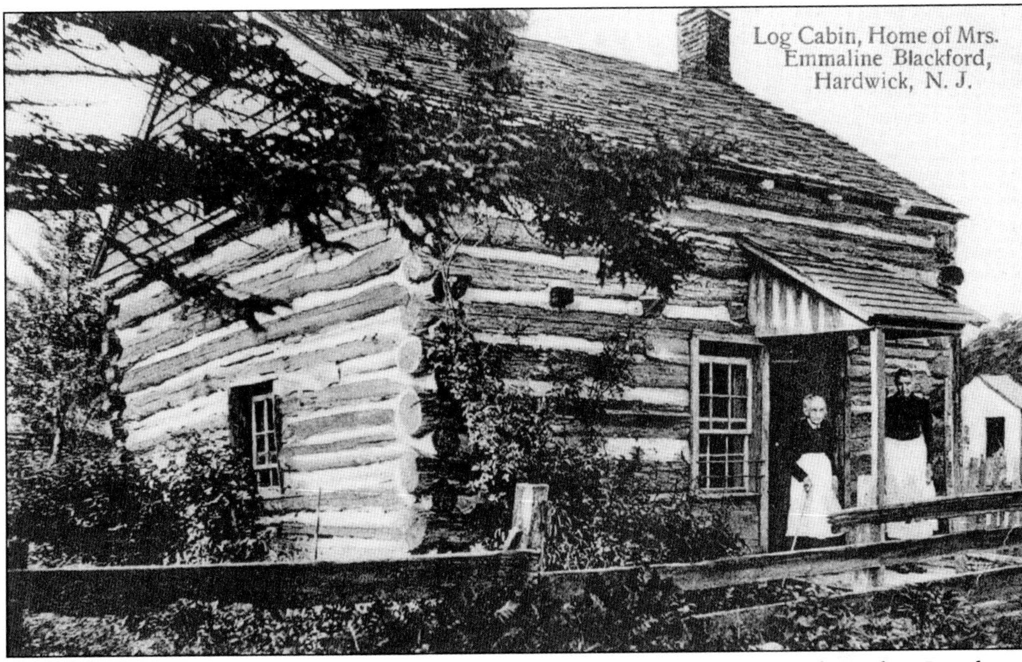

Emmaline Blackford and her daughter pose at their log cabin near Birch Ridge Road and Newbaker's Corner.

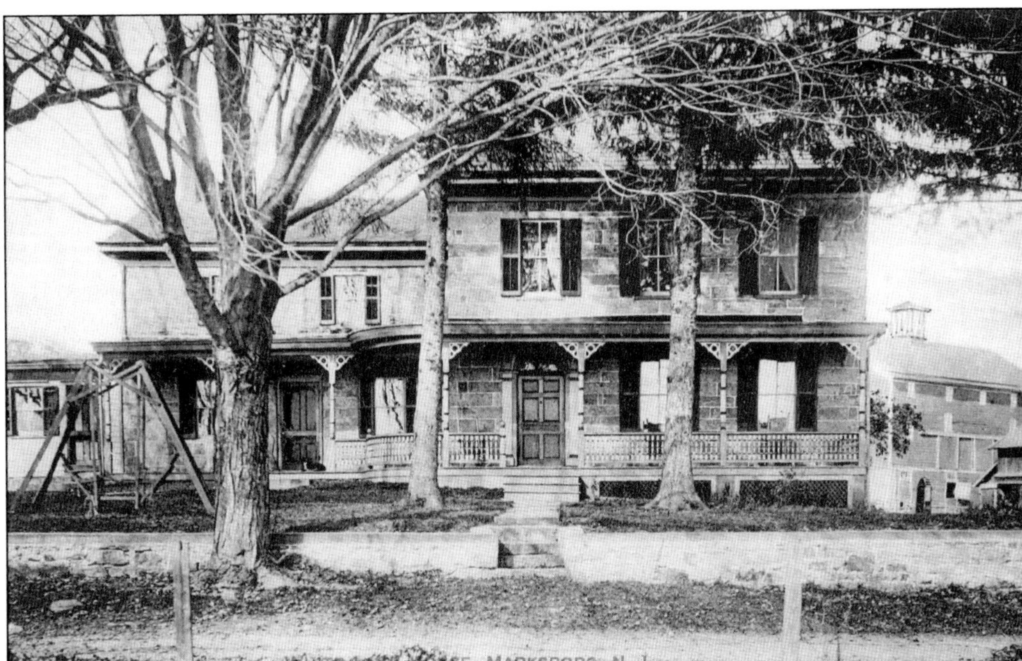

In 1802, German immigrant Johann Vass (originally Wass) acquired 550 acres opposite White Lake. By 1812, Vass had built this stone house and the Germanic barn visible in the background. Vass raised apples, rye, oats, corn, alfalfa, flax, buckwheat, and even sheep, pigs, and poultry. White Lake Farm remained in the Vass family until 1921, when it was sold to George Van Riper, who converted it into a dairy operation.

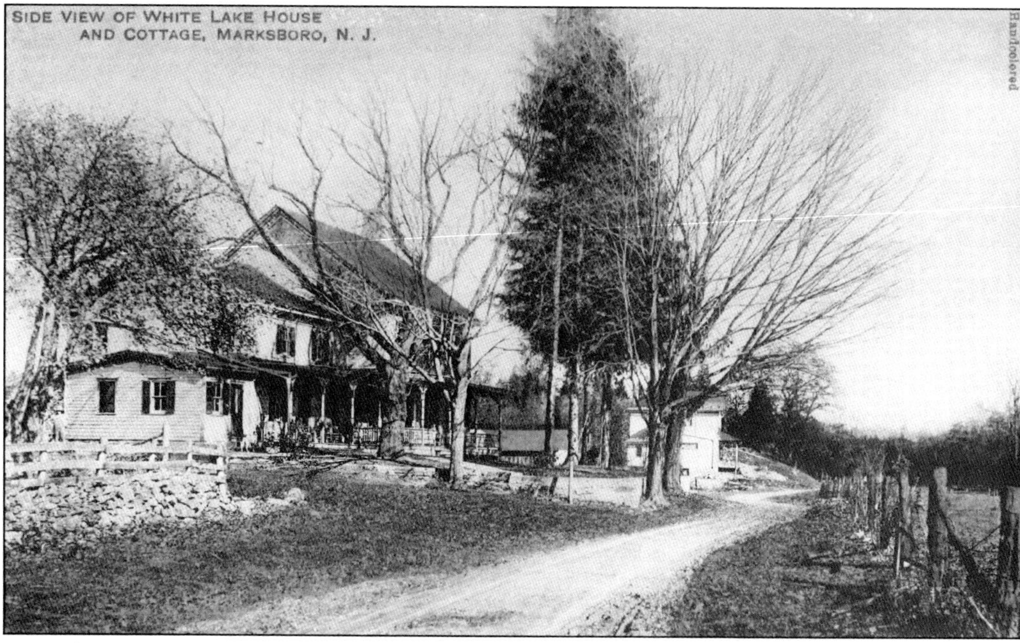

An early-20th-century view of White Lake Farm shows the "guest cottage" (in the background) built by Frank Vass, third generation of the family, for use by a tenant farmer. The main house was enlarged with several wooden additions shortly after it was built. Johann Vass's son Isaac inherited the property upon his father's death in 1852 and was involved in local politics, serving as tax collector, constable, and township committeeman.

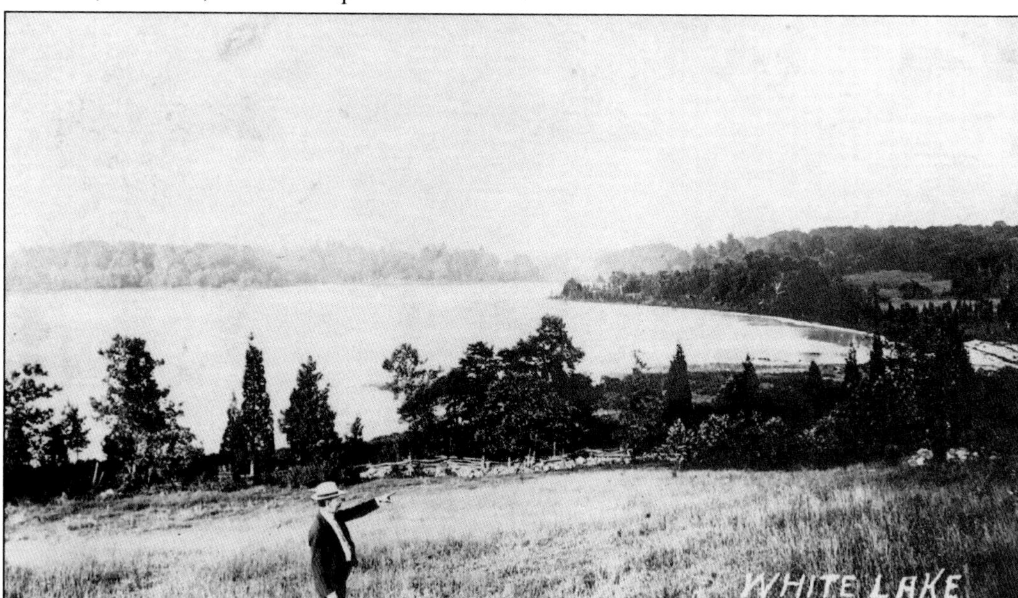

White Lake was named for its clear water and bed of marl, the white shells of deceased aquatic organisms. In the 1800s, an attempt was made to harvest lake ice by the Knickerbocker Ice Company, which built an icehouse on the south shore. Before commercial refrigeration, ice cut from local ponds and stored in these huge structures provided the means to keep food from spoiling in the warmer months.

Cutting ice was seasonal and, since marl had value as fertilizer and as an ingredient in cement, Knickerbocker began mining it. The Newark Sanitary and Manufacturing Company also got into the marl business at White Lake and processed it in a plant constructed of stone on the south shore. To facilitate shipment, the New York, Susquehanna and Western Railroad ran a spur into the plant from its main line at Marksboro.

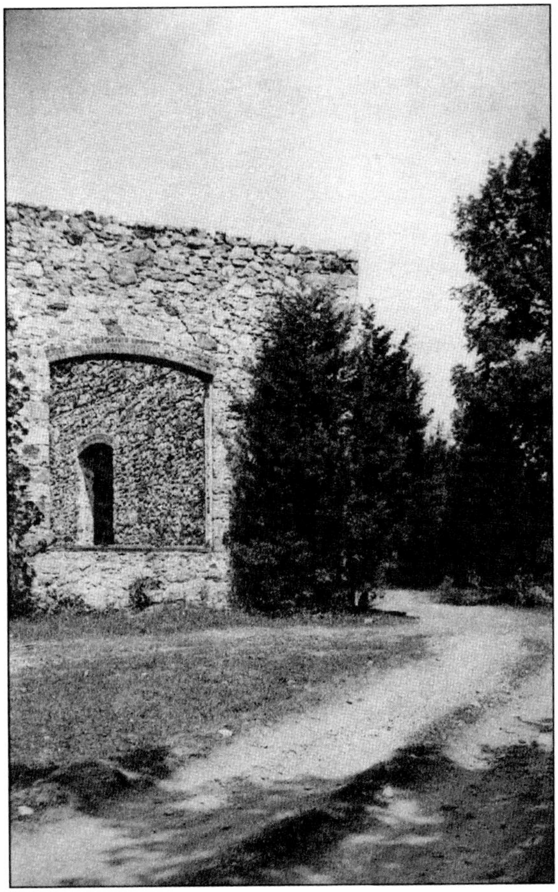

Ferla's Cedarmere Inn on Spring Valley Road in Hardwick (Blairstown postal area) traced its roots back to Quakers who settled in the area in the mid-1700s and constructed buildings on the site, the foundations of which still exist. The location was a stagecoach stop and became a popular summer resort in the 20th century. Local legend holds that during Prohibition its isolated location made it an ideal spot for a still.

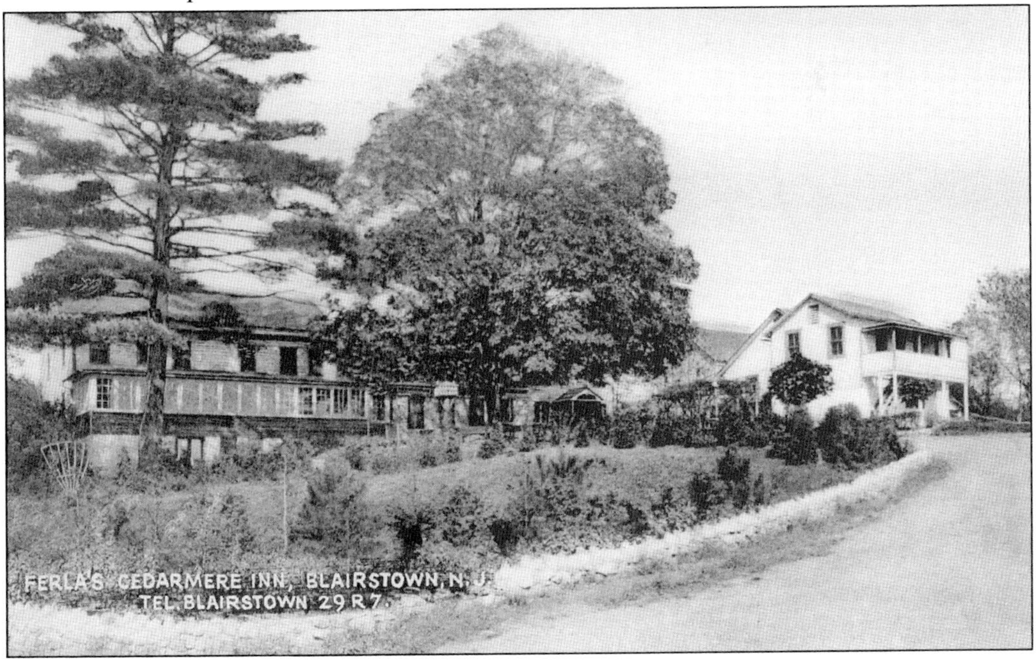

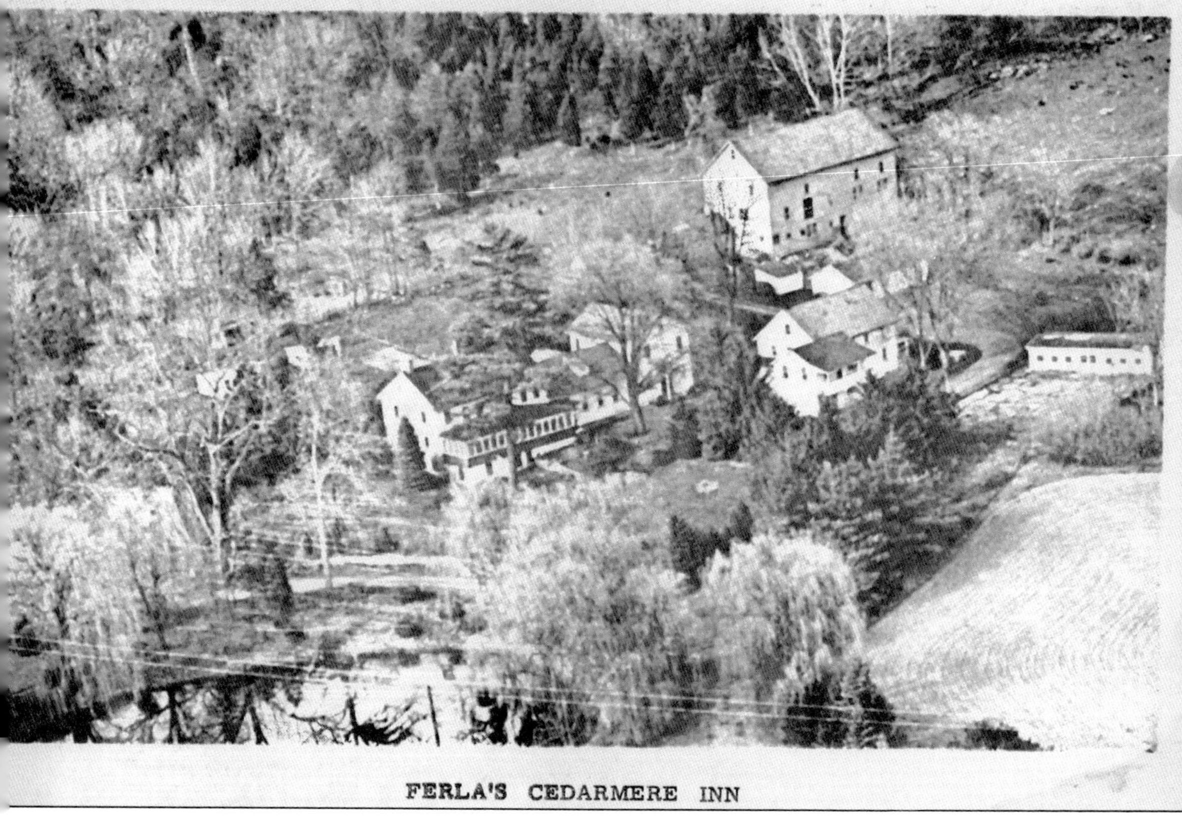

This aerial view of the Ferla's resort complex was probably taken sometime shortly after the end of World War II. Ferla's underwent several renovations, additions, and ownership changes throughout the 20th century, ultimately surviving as a fine restaurant until, during its final reincarnation as the Hardwick House, it was totally destroyed by a fire on November 15, 2009. Only the large barn survives today.

Seven

CAMPING
KING OF THE SUMMER

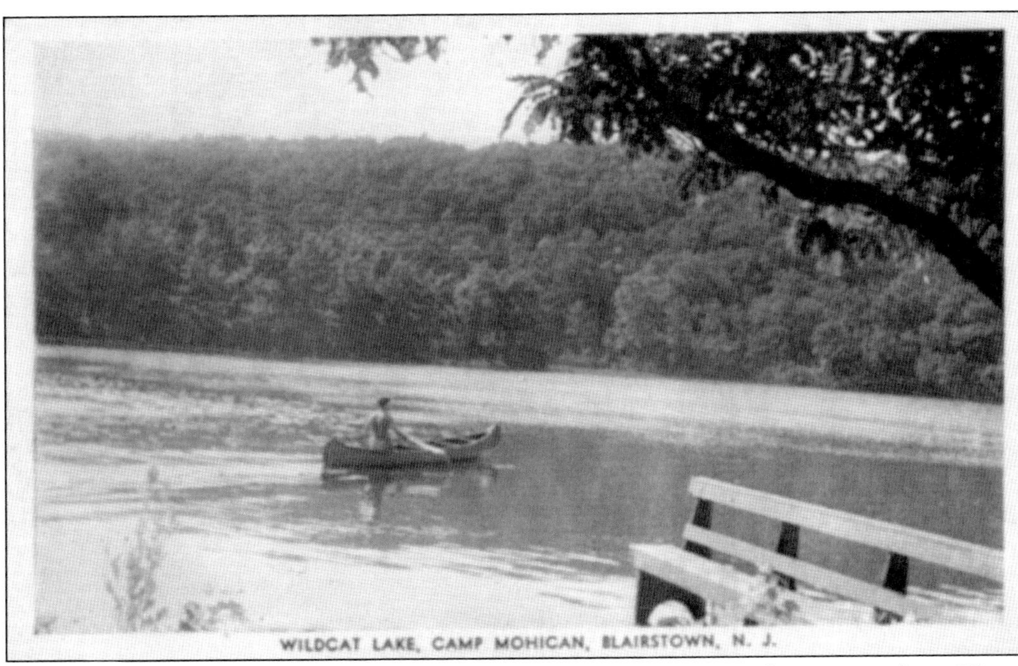

With its rolling woodlands, myriad of small lakes, and inexpensive real estate, northern Warren County became a mecca for youth camping in the 1920s. Several Boy Scout councils in New Jersey took the opportunity to snap up low-priced property in the Blairstown area to establish summer adventure camps for their troops. One of the best known was Camp Mohican on Wildcat Lake, which was purchased by the Newark Council in 1925.

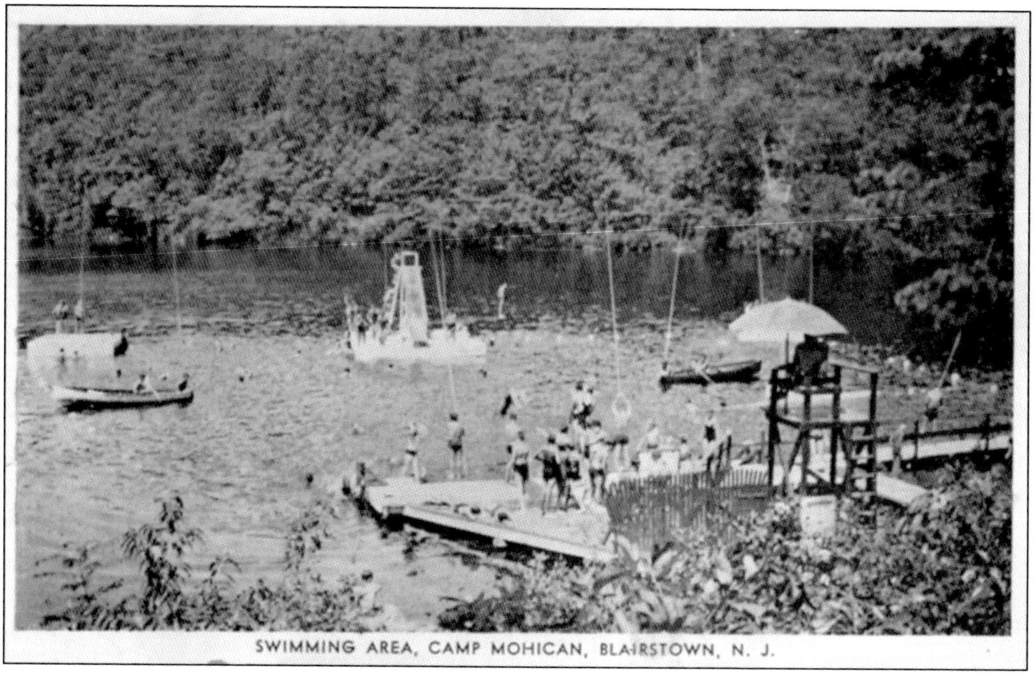

The lake is crowded with eager Scouts on a hot summer afternoon in the 1930s. Learning to swim was an absolute requirement during a boy's stay, and beginners started their lessons in the wooden "crib" at the lower right corner of the view. After the council closed the camp in 1976, the manly Wildcat Lake was rechristened as the far more visitor-friendly Catfish Pond.

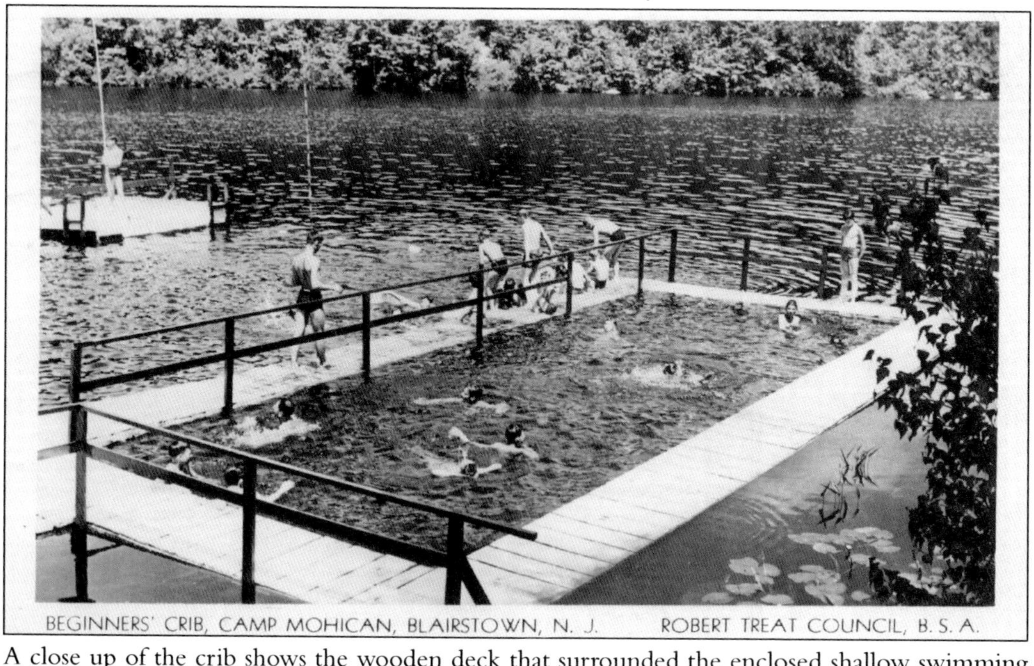

A close up of the crib shows the wooden deck that surrounded the enclosed shallow swimming area. Scouts honed their natatorial skills in the crib and graduated to the lake when they could swim a few laps unassisted. It has been reported that some scoutmasters would "brand" a nonswimmer by painting his nose with Mercurochrome to identify him with a red badge of disgrace.

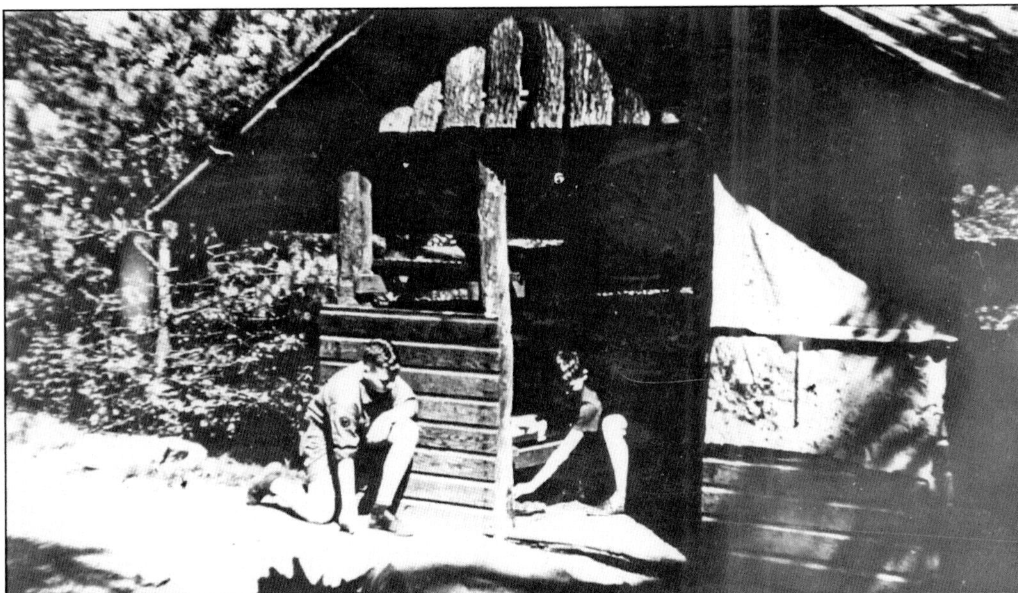

A TROOP SITE AT CAMP MOHICAN, BLAIRSTOWN, N. J.

Scouts either tented or slept in open-air cabins like this. No doubt the photographer told these two to "look busy." The potpourri of daily activities included swimming, boating, fishing, archery, rifle, handicrafts, hiking, and nature education. Many proud city dads and moms displayed the tooled leather belt or carved napkin rings brought home by a smiling son after a few weeks at Camp Mohican.

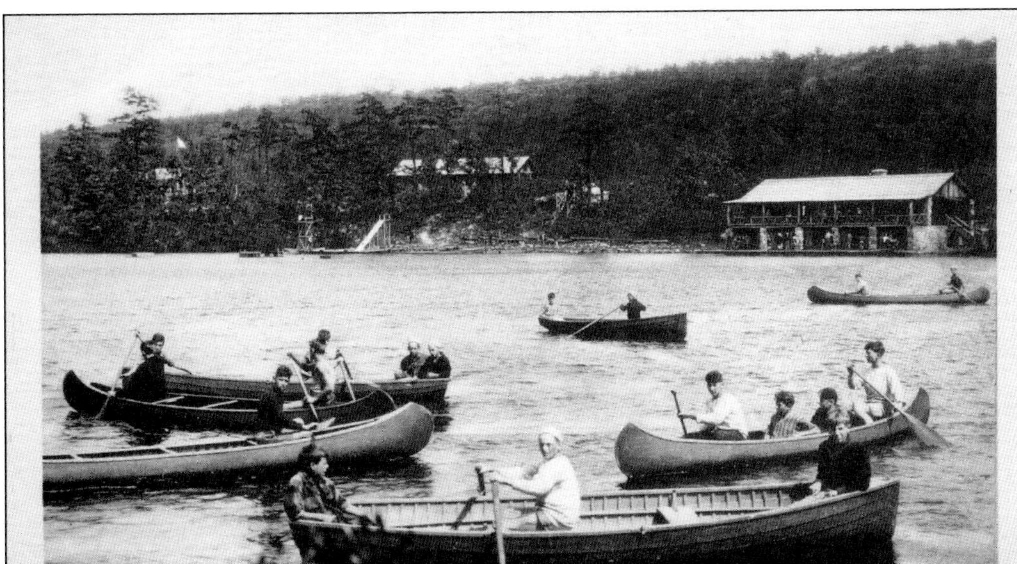

BOATING AND CANOEING, WILD-CAT LAKE, CAMP MOHICAN, BLAIRSTOWN, N. J.

Rowboats and canoes were always in ample supply at Camp Mohican. In an era unaware of life jackets and safety appliances, Scouts had to be able to swim before they were permitted the privilege of boarding a watercraft on the lake. The lodge building is visible on the far shore.

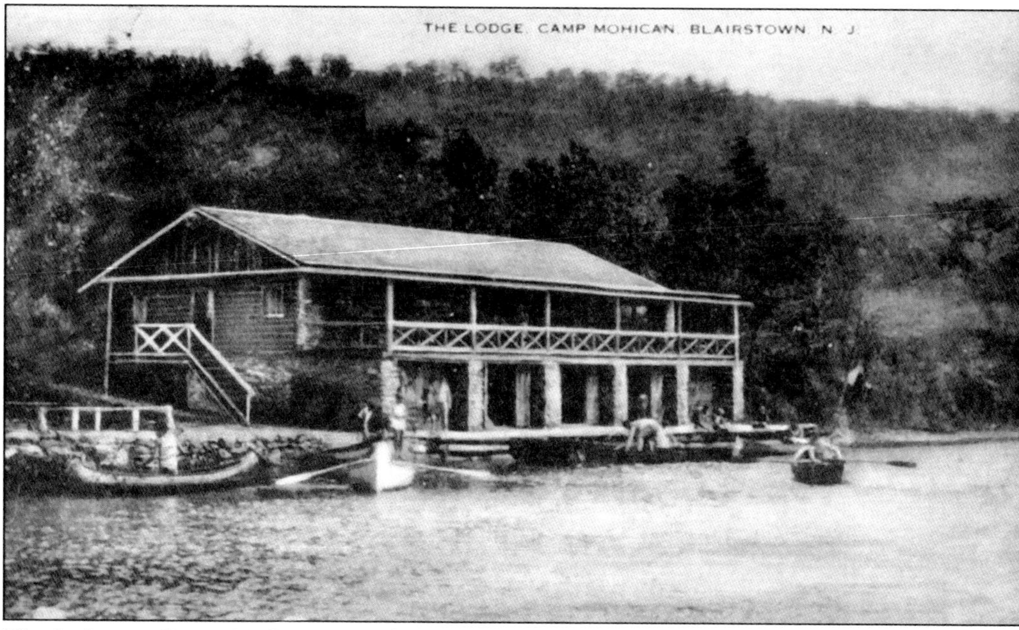

The lodge at Camp Mohican was located at the water's edge and similar in design to those constructed at other camps in the Blairstown area. Camp Mohican was closed in 1976 and the property purchased by the federal government. It is now part of the Delaware Water Gap National Recreation Area,. The lodge survives as part of the Mohican Outdoor Center, a facility of the Appalachian Mountain Club.

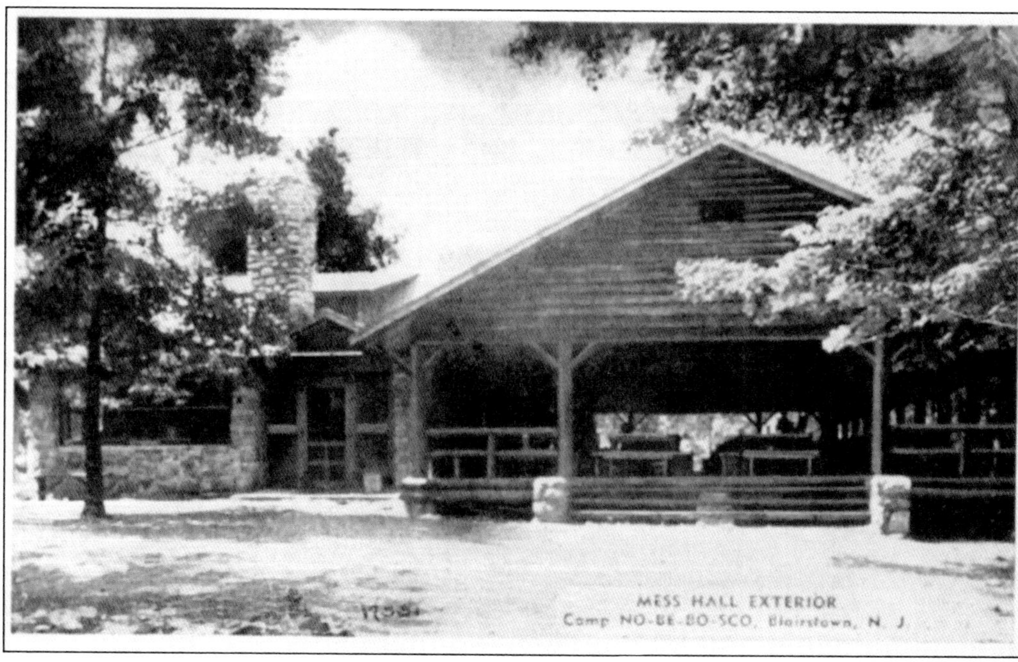

No-Be-Bo-Sco sounds like a Native American name, but it is short for "North Bergen Boy Scouts." Formed in 1921, the council purchased 807 acres of land at Sand Pond in Hardwick and Stillwater Townships in 1925. The first camp was held in 1927, and over the course of the next four years cabins were added. The dining hall burned in 1934 and was replaced by this structure.

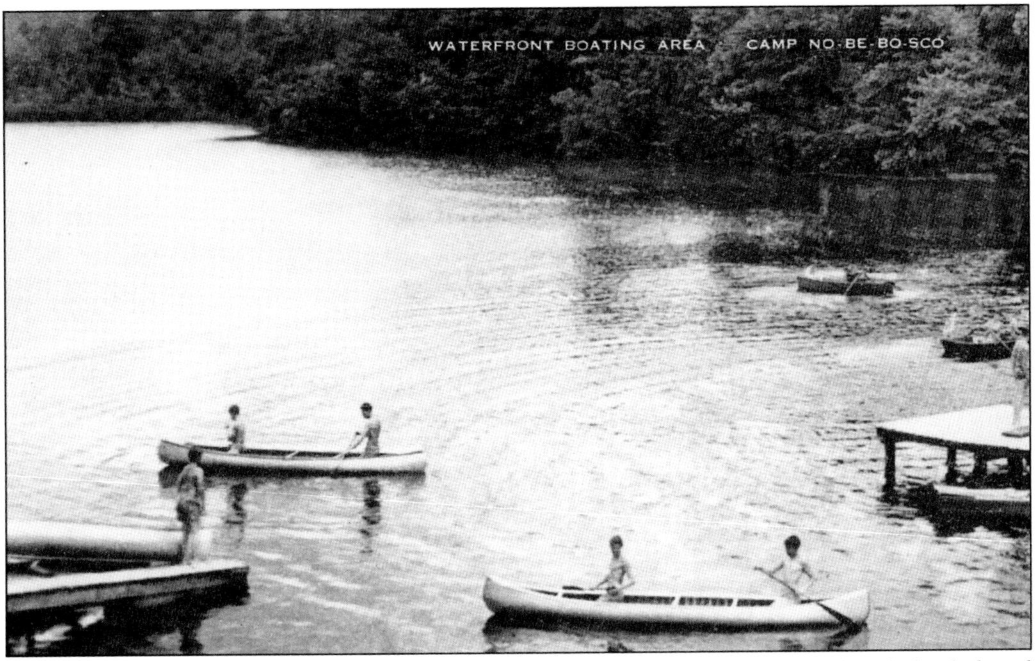

Further development of the camp occurred after 1942 when the council hired the beloved Woodruff Newton as camp ranger. Unlike many facilities, No-Be-Bo-Sco stayed open during the war, although it was touched briefly on February 22, 1944, when a B-17F Flying Fortress crashed in a dense fog into the east face of the Kittatinny Mountains nearby, killing all 12 crewmen.

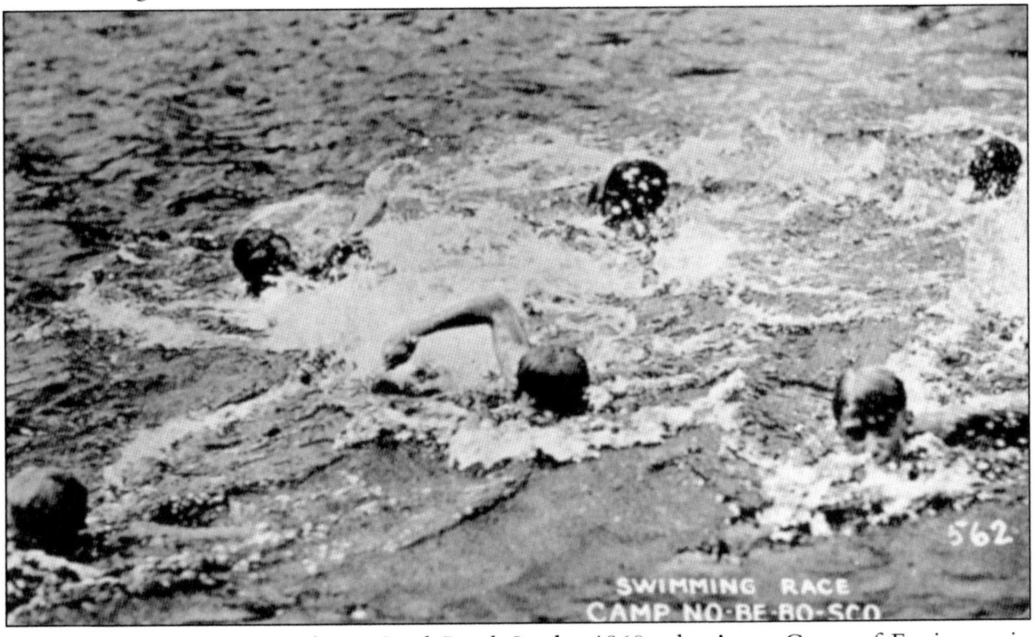

Swimming races were popular at Sand Pond. In the 1960s, the Army Corps of Engineers, in conjunction with the National Park Service, bought tens of thousands of acres of land along the Delaware River in preparation for building an enormous dam at Tocks Island. Although the ill-advised project was ultimately shelved, No-Be-Bo-Sco lost over 430 acres from the face of the mountain, and many other camps were forced to close.

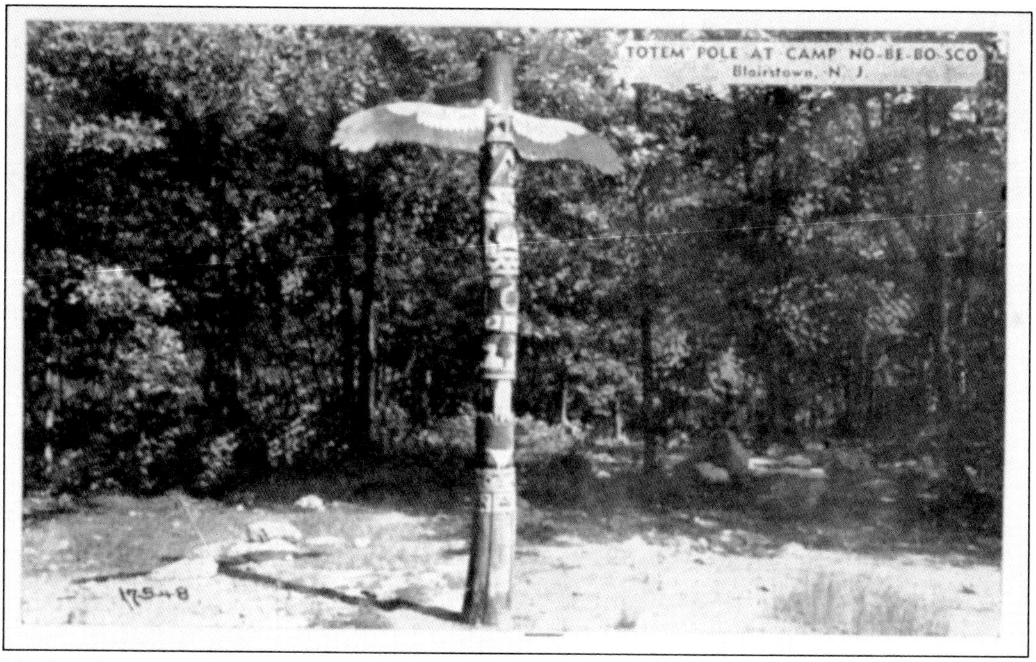

No Boy Scout camp was complete without a totem pole where Scouts could congregate at dusk and tell hair-raising ghost stories or Native American tales. Sand Pond received its name because of the fine white sand that lined its bottom and shores. In 1812, the sand was processed and shipped by wagon to Francis Meyerhoff's works in Columbia, New Jersey, where it was used in the manufacture of glass.

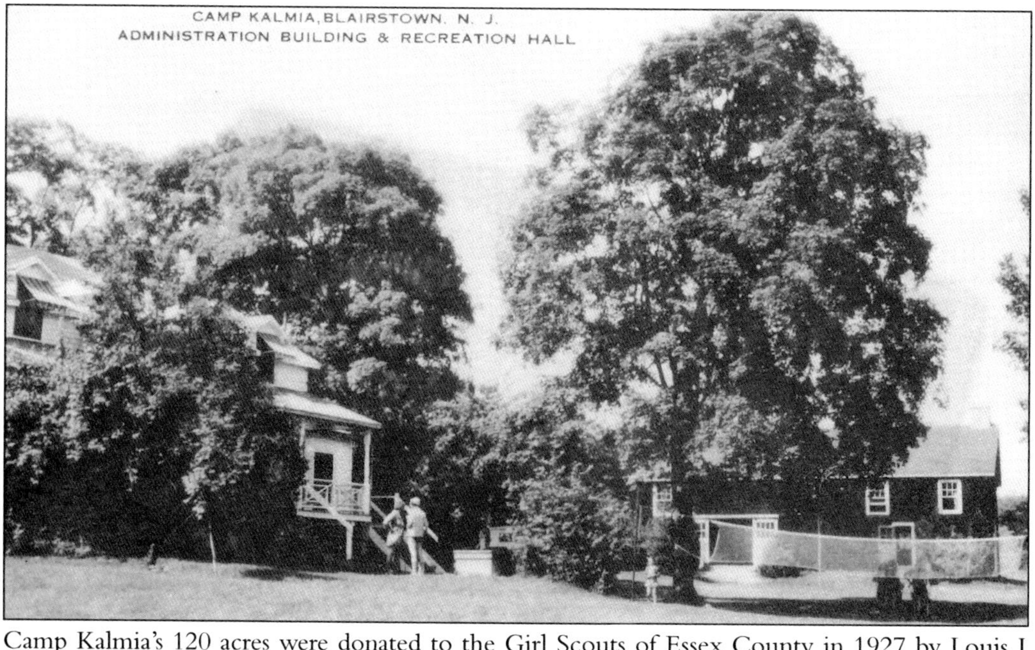

Camp Kalmia's 120 acres were donated to the Girl Scouts of Essex County in 1927 by Louis J. Bamberger. A German American Jew, he was born in Baltimore, Maryland, in 1855 and came to Newark, New Jersey, in 1892 where he turned one dry goods store into a retail empire. In 1928, L. Bamberger and Sons' sales of $28 million made it the fourth highest-grossing store in the nation.

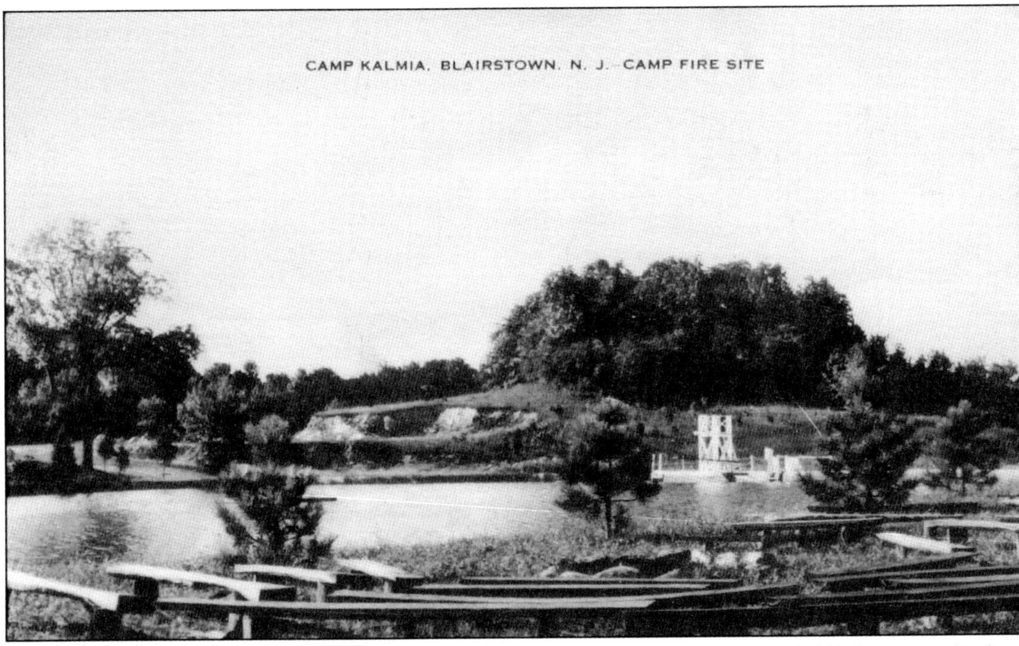

Although Louis Bamberger was a busy entrepreneur, his first love was philanthropy and, along with his sister Caroline Bamberger Fuld, he donated to many charities, museums, societies, and funds. After Fuld's husband died in 1929, Bamberger sold his retail chain to R. H. Macy so that he and Caroline could concentrate on furthering their humanitarian activities. During World War II, Bamberger assisted many European Jews to escape persecution and death under the Nazi regime.

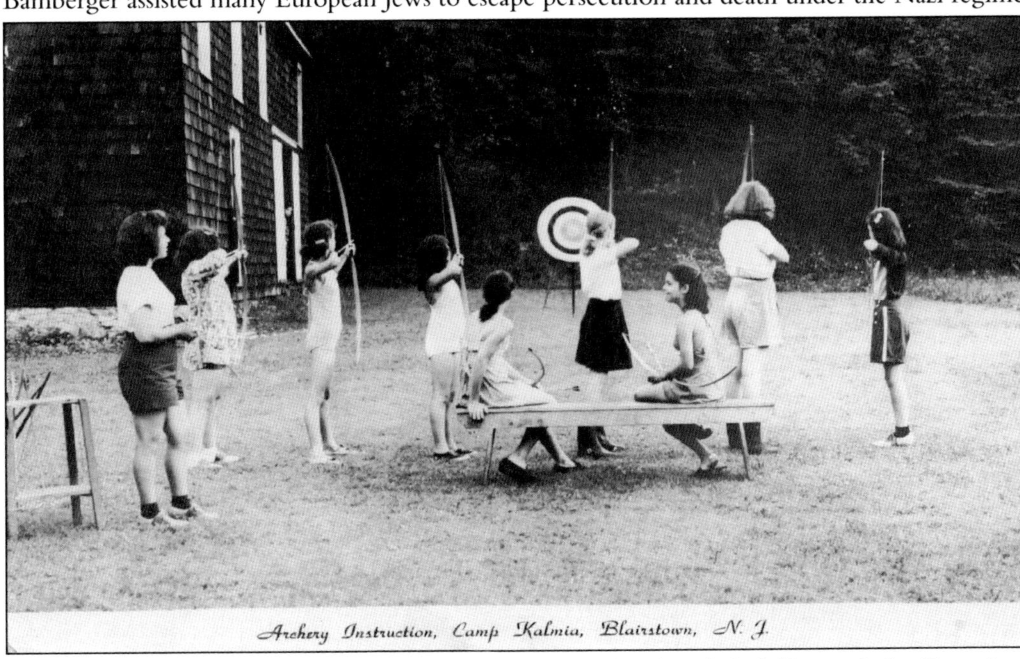

The Bamberger property was located off Mohican Road and included 30-acre Lake Genevieve. Bamberger's intent was to give the Girl Scouts an outdoor educational nature experience. Within a few years, additional buildings had been erected, and girls from the greater Newark area were camping there each summer. Here a group of Scouts hone their skills on the archery range.

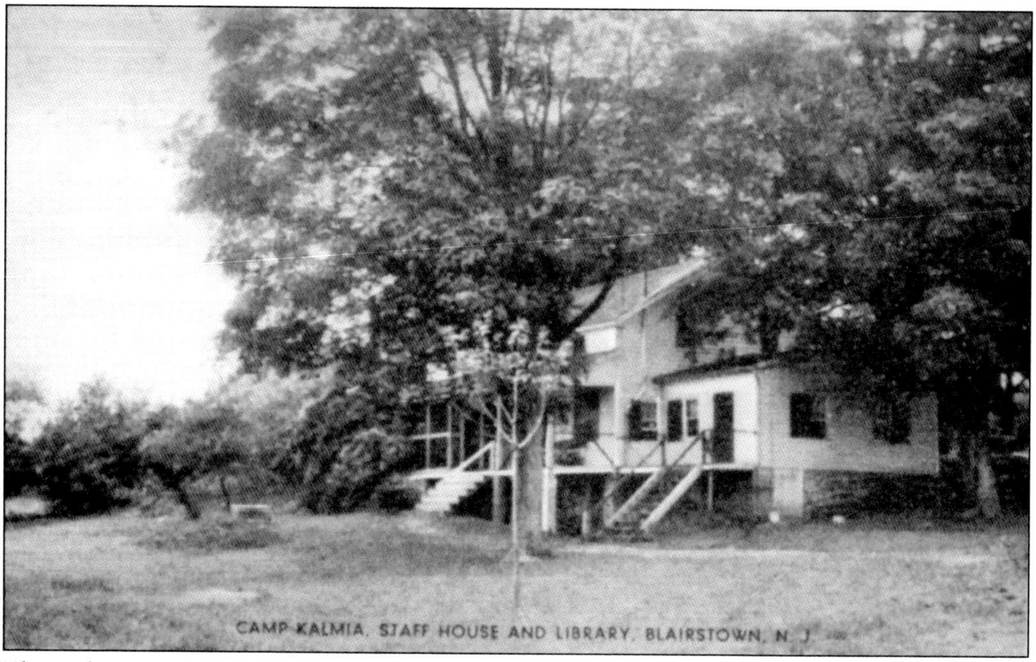

The Kalmia counselors and administrative staff were housed in the "White House," a former farmhouse that also contained a library that allowed the girls to keep up with their reading during the summer. A spacious lawn surrounded the building. Louis Bamberger died in 1944 and was so beloved that the City of Newark declared three days of mourning.

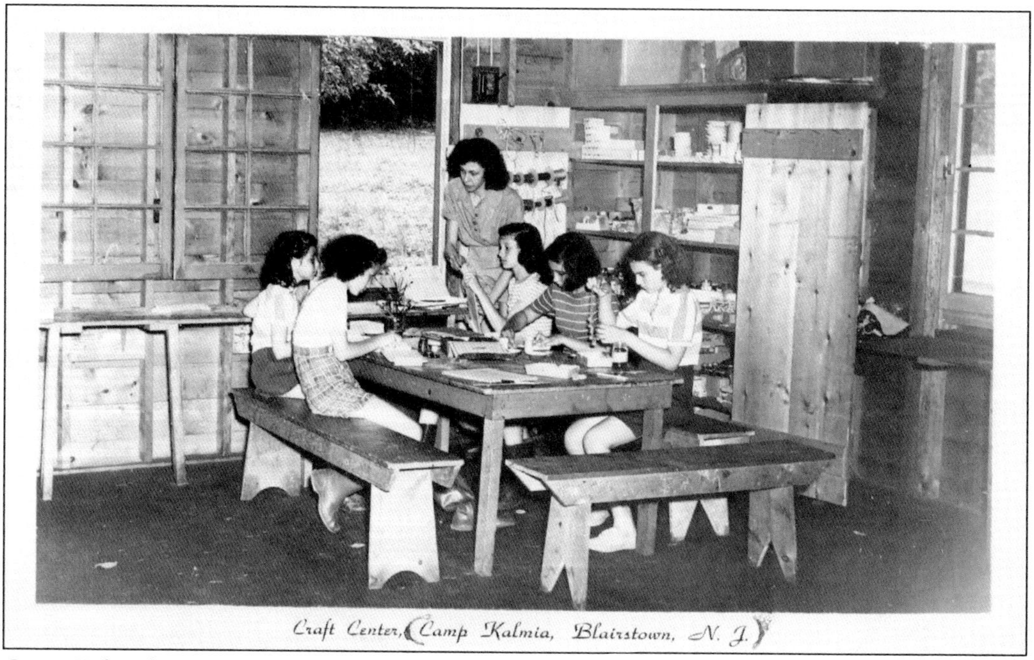

Camp Kalmia's recreation hall was a former barn and was spacious enough to allow for a variety of activities, including arts and crafts. Here an enthusiastic group works on their projects under the watchful eye of their counselor. Perhaps some lucky mother or father was getting a handmade Christmas present in 1948.

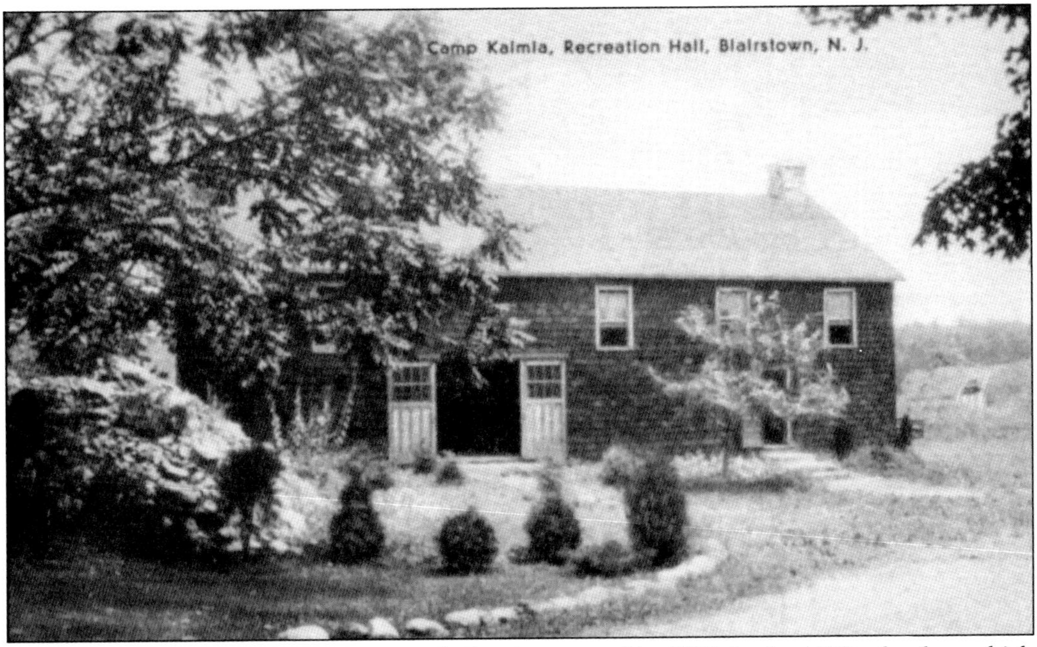

This photograph captures the recreation hall as it appeared in 1937. In the 1970s, the dam which created Lake Genevieve was deemed to be in need of major repair. Because of the enormous cost of that restoration and maintenance, potential safety concerns for the young campers, and a decision to discontinue outdoor camping, Camp Kalmia was permanently closed around 1980.

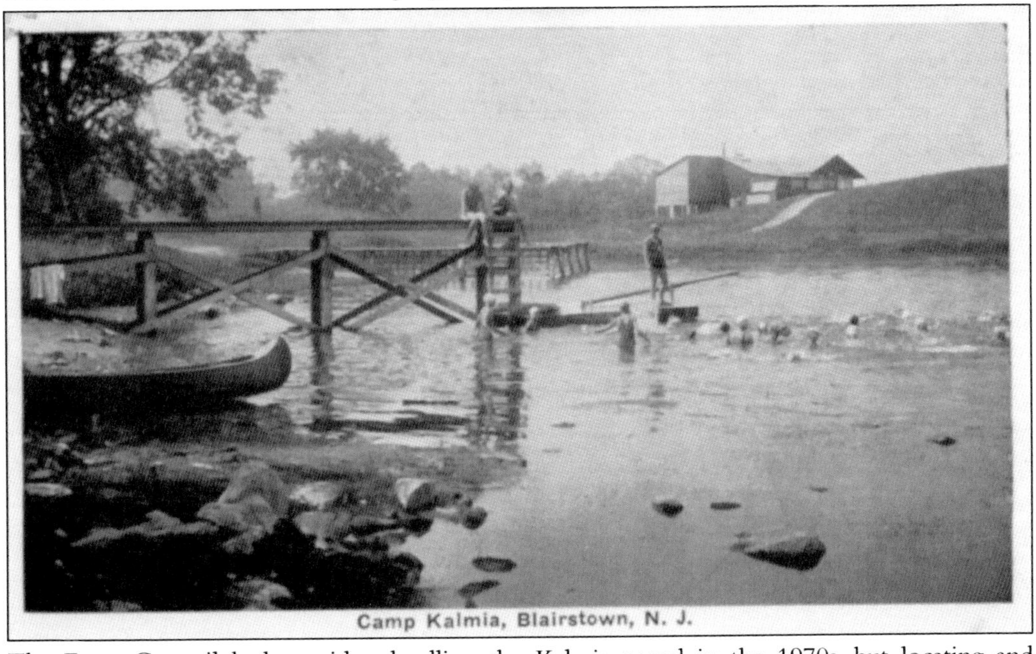

The Essex Council had considered selling the Kalmia parcel in the 1970s, but locating and obtaining permission from all of Bamberger's heirs seemed impossible. Faced with either fixing the dam or being fined by the New Jersey Department of Environmental Protection, the council finally received permission from remaining family members and sold the land to Blair Academy in 2006.

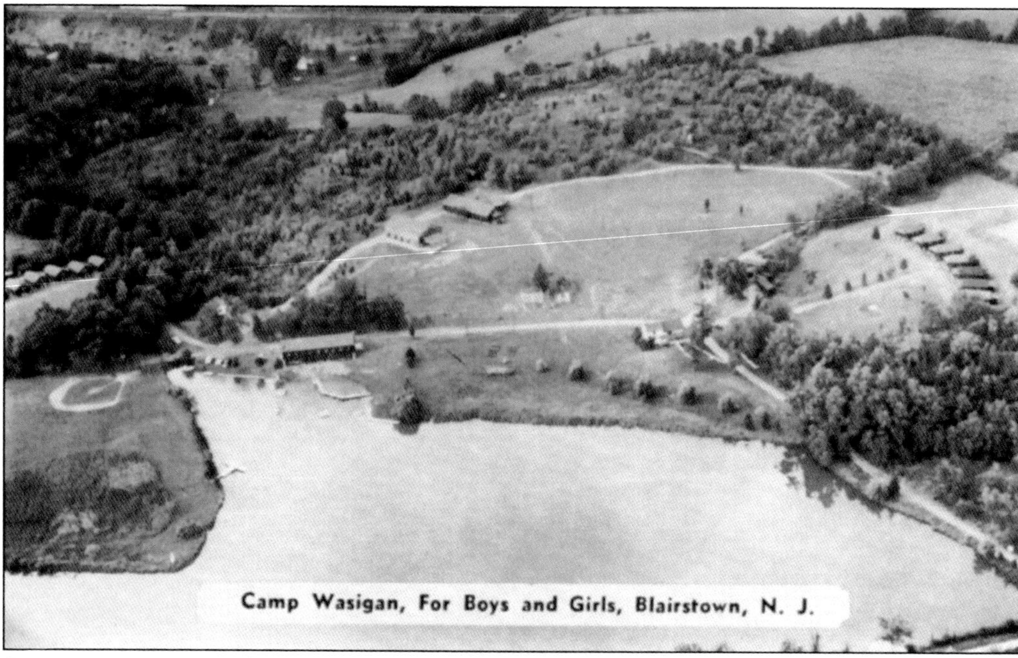

Camp Wasigan, a coed sleepaway camp in Frelinghuysen Township, operated from 1936 until 1966. This aerial view from the 1940s gives a good perspective on the lodge and camper housing. Both boys and girls were accommodated and enjoyed a variety of activities, including drama and music, in addition to the typical camp pursuits. Color wars were a particular favorite.

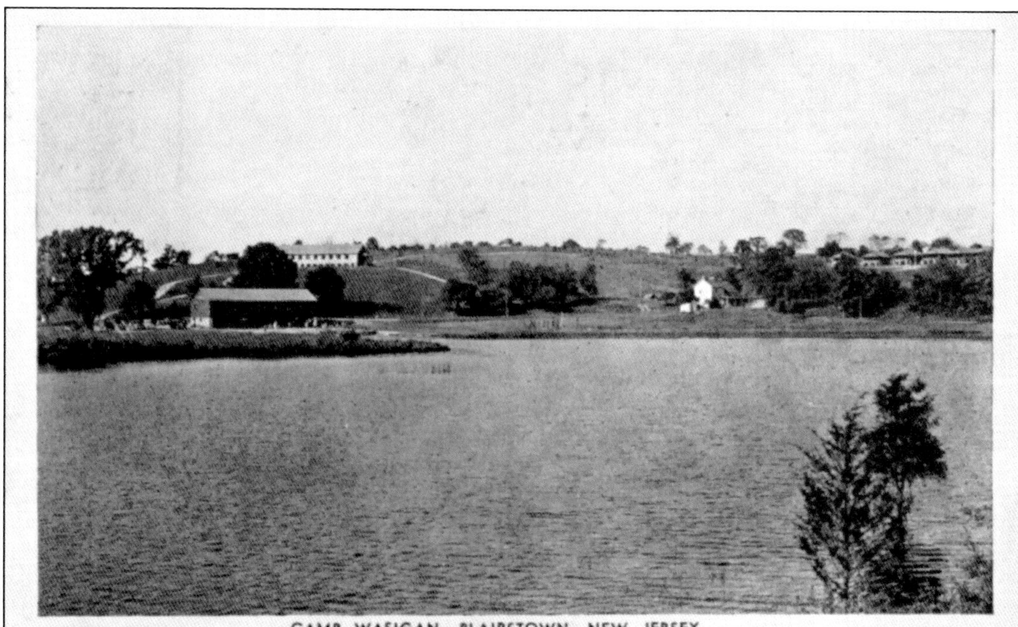

Participants came to Wasigan primarily from the New Jersey area, so owner Anne Lieberman and her daughter Charla personally visited and interviewed each one before accepting them. Counselors were mostly college students, and camp alumni remember those who were not on duty going into town after hours and coming back with pizza or hamburgers for hungry campers.

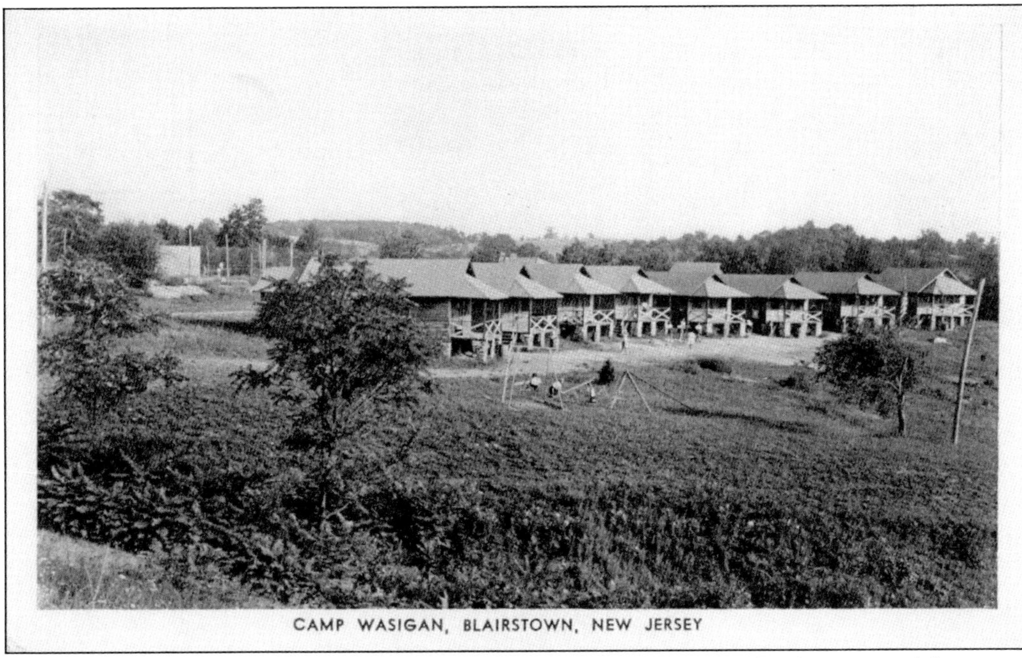

Campers were awakened from their bunks in these cabins each morning by the not-so-dulcet tones of Anne Lieberman over the public address system: "Good Morning Boys and Girls! Everybody up, up, up. . . . It's a beautiful Camp Wasigan morning!" In the postwar era, it most certainly was.

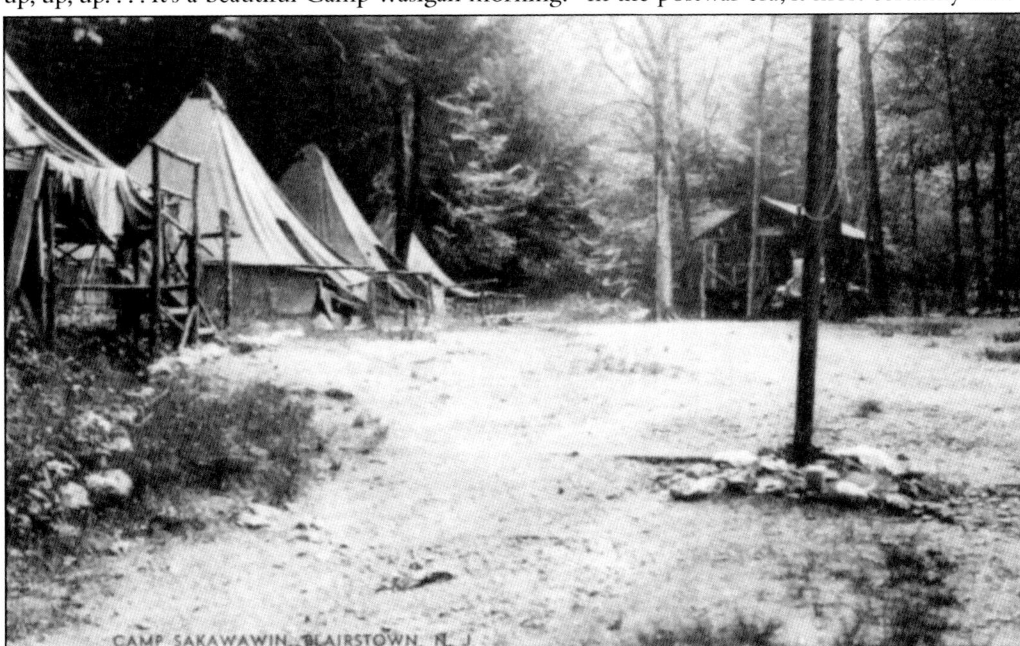

The Middlesex Council of the Boy Scouts of America established Camp Sakawawin, the first permanent summer camp at Cedar Lake, in 1929. "Permanent" is a misnomer as the Scouts still tented at the west end of the lake; only an administrative building and mess hall were substantial structures. Scouts were occasionally transported to camps in Sussex and Warren Counties by special trains operated by the New York, Susquehanna and Western Railroad.

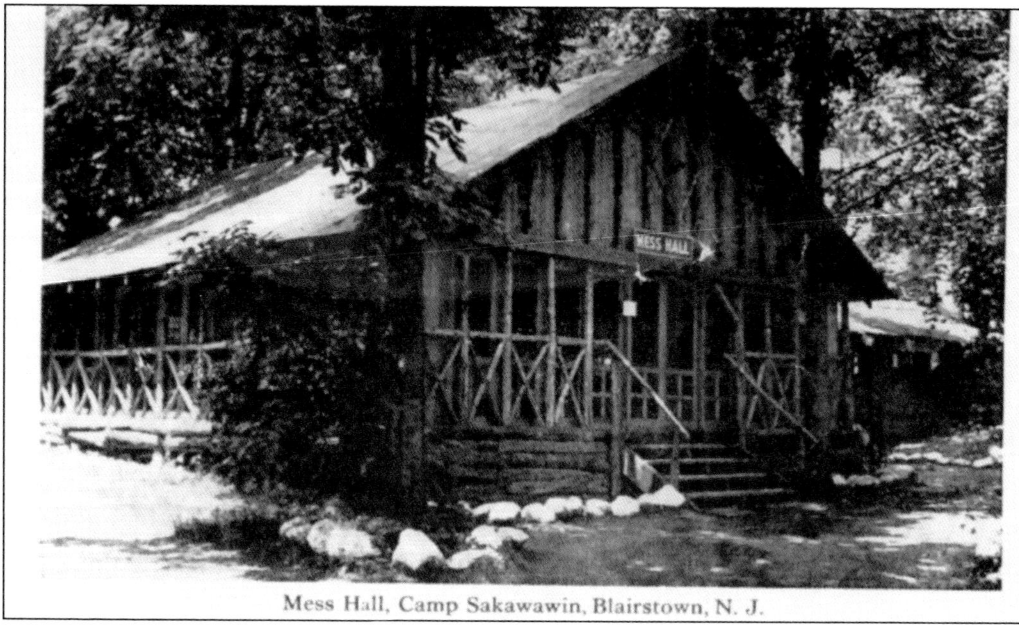

The mess hall at Sakawawin was a typical open-sided camp structure used to efficiently feed large numbers of Scouts simultaneously. As in the case of seasonal resorts, the quality of food was important in getting campers to return year after year. Camp Sakawawin closed about 1947, and Scouts were relocated to other facilities.

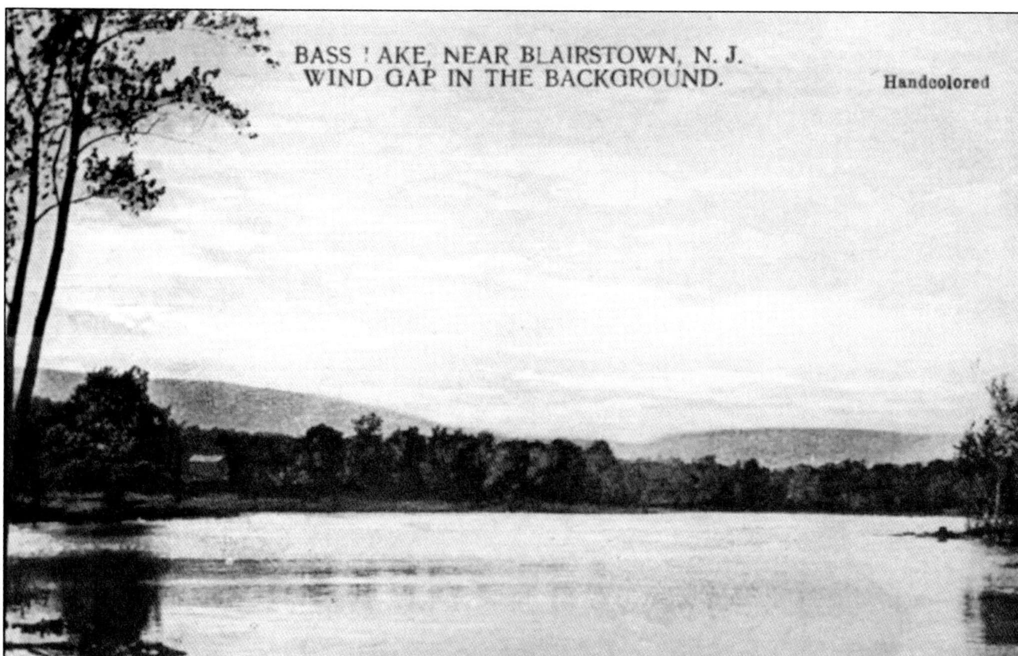

The Princeton Summer Camp, founded at Bay Head, New Jersey, in 1909, moved to a 170-acre site on Bass Lake in Blairstown in 1930. Its original purpose was to serve young men of New York and Philadelphia and the African American and Italian American communities in the Princeton area. Coeducational since 1970, the camp now operates as the Princeton Education Center.

BIBLIOGRAPHY

Beers, F. W. *County Atlas of Warren, New Jersey*. New York: F. W. Beers and Company, 1874.

Cummings, George Wyckoff. *History of Warren County, NJ*. New York: Lewis Historical Publishing, 1911.

Dale, Frank T. *Smoking Engines! Flaming Villages! Warren County Chronicles #13*, Self-published May 2001.

Delaware, Lackawanna and Western Railroad. *Mountain and Lake Resorts on the Lackawanna Railroad*. New York: Passenger Traffic Department, 1903 and 1915.

Hamlin, Arthur T. *Blair Academy: A Sesquicentennial History*. Blairstown, New Jersey: Blair Academy, 1991.

Harpster, Richard, et al. *Historical Sites of Warren County*. Belvidere, New Jersey: Warren County Board of Chosen Freeholders, 1965.

Hartung, Hester Harris, compiler. *200 Years of Hope, NJ 1769-1969*. Blairstown, New Jersey: The Blairstown Press, 1969.

Heilich, Frederick W. III. *The History of the Blairstown Railway*. Livingston, New Jersey; Railroadians of America, 1981.

Hope Historical Society. *The Moravian Contribution to the Town of Hope, NJ*. Hope, New Jersey: Hope Historical Society, 1955.

Krause, John, and Ed Crist. *Susquehanna: New York, Susquehanna and Western Railroad*. Newton, New Jersey: Carstens Publications, 1980.

Lucas, Walter Arndt. *The History of the New York, Susquehanna & Western Railroad*. Livingston, New Jersey: Railroadians of America, 1980.

Murray, Leo P., ed. *A Bicentennial Picture Book of Hope*. Hope, New Jersey: Hope Bicentennial Committee, May 21, 1976.

Snell, James P. *History of Sussex and Warren Counties, New Jersey*. Philadelphia: Everts and Peck, 1881.